Hiding Places

Hiding Places
A Mother, a Daughter, an Uncovered Life

DIANE WYSHOGROD

excelsior editions

State University of New York Press
Albany, New York

Cover art paper sculpture by Morris Wyszogrod.

Published by State University of New York Press, Albany

For information, contact State University of New York Press, Albany, NY
www.sunypress.edu

Excelsior Editions is an imprint of State University of New York Press

Production by Ryan Morris
Marketing by Fran Keneston

Library of Congress Cataloging-in-Publication Data

Wyshogrod, Diane.
  Hiding Places : a mother, a daughter, an uncovered life / Diane Wyshogrod.
    p. cm.
  "Excelsior Editions"
  ISBN 978-1-4384-4243-3 (hardcover : alk. paper)
  1. Wyshogrod, Diane. 2. Jews, American—Israel—Biography. 3. Clinical
psychologist—Biography. 4. Holocaust survivors—United
States—Biography. 5. Mothers and daughters—Biography. I. Title.

  DS113.8.A4W97 2012
  940.53'18092—dc23   2011028315
  [B]

10 9 8 7 6 5 4 3 2 1

To Chaim
and
Yonatan, David, and Yehoshua
The loves of my life

and

With everlasting gratitude to
Emil and Maria Łoziński

Prologue

"I don't want you to write this book."

My mother is emphatic.

"I mean, writing it is okay, as long as it's for the family," she continues. "But you never said anything about publishing this. Oh, no."

She's shaking her head now. Each shake has its punctuation:

"No."

"No."

Each "no" raps like a judge's gavel. Sentencing complete.

"I don't want strangers to read about my life. And all those stories about my childhood? You and your brother, the kids, okay. But others? Oh, no."

"I don't see why not." My mind is racing. I force myself to talk slowly, to keep my voice level. "There's nothing there that could embarrass you. You didn't do anything wrong—"

"Of course not," she interrupts, indignant. She doesn't yield. "But I'm a very private person. Besides, I never liked to talk about it. Unlike your father. I mean, I never hid it either. You knew what happened to me, but it's finished and I don't like to think about it."

Our voices are braiding in and out of each other.

"I *know* that." I'm not giving in either. I'm not her daughter for nothing. "But your story's important. It should be recorded. People should know. Besides, it's not just about you. It's about us, you and me."

"Well, then, keep it in the family. For the family, okay?"

Here it was, the reaction I had dreaded for years. But I thought I'd worked all that out, that she and I had an understanding. That she knew what I was doing and approved of it. I'd hoped to be spared exactly this.

I was wrong.

It may sound like just another one of those mother-daughter differences of opinion, a clash of wills neither likes losing. But it's more than that. Otherwise, my guts wouldn't be whirling like a food processor while I struggle to keep my cool. What we are really talking about is something that goes so deep, that's been so buried, I'm not sure I've fully excavated it yet. I'm being challenged to mount my defense, and I can barely utter a word. Not to her. Especially not to her.

This is a story I have spent fifteen years of my life writing. And all the years of my life living.

I wasn't looking for this story. In fact, for most of my life, I was perfectly happy to leave it where it was, curled up quietly in the background, not hidden, but not being paraded about either. Like my mother. She didn't hide what had happened to her, she just didn't dwell on it. She'd shrug.

"Nothing happened to me."

Her "nothing" consisted of being hidden, together with her parents, in the cellar of a Polish Christian couple during World War II. They were in hiding for sixteen months. Maybe it seems like "nothing" to her, compared with what my father went through. He survived the Warsaw Ghetto and ten concentration camps. His entire family was wiped out by the Germans. Now *that's* a story, my mother says. What's her story, *anyone's* story, compared with his?

This is my mother's way, to treat her experiences matter-of-factly, to put it all behind her and move on. And, I must admit, I was more than happy to move on with her. My father's frequent references to Those Days more than made up for her reticence. Against the roar of my father's pain and rage, hers was but a still small voice, barely a murmur.

For a long time.

For the longest time.

Until something changed.

I didn't see it coming. I didn't plan on it. I wasn't out hunting war stories, certainly not this one. I was catapulted against my will into *this* one. This story came and got *me*. It grabbed me by the neck and wouldn't let go. It dared me to take it on, or shake it off—if I could. I couldn't. It's been years now, the story clawing me, me clutching back, trying to tame it. Years of writing and self-analysis and talking it over with friends, and tears, lots of tears, trying to live with this thing living inside me. Years of struggling to attain some more or less equal footing, so that this story wouldn't wring me out like a *shmatte*, a used-up rag.

Keep it in the family? I wish I could. It would certainly make my life easier. But keeping it private, in the family, is not doing it justice. Because if I do that, I'm pushing my mother back down into that cellar. I won't be an accomplice to her staying in hiding. I want to rescue her. To take her out of there. I want this—and her—out in the light, even if that light is bright and glaring and hurts the eyes.

I want to be my mother's champion, riding into the jousts, her token on my sleeve, fighting for her. I can't do anything else, now, sixty-five years too late. I can't save her anymore from Then, from what happened, much as I would like to turn back the clock and do so. Give me this chance, Mom, to tell the world what you mean to me. To say, out loud, for everyone to hear, that you were there, that you survived, that you overcame. That they couldn't put you into a silent hole in the ground and keep you there. That it did not become your grave. It became your womb, and ultimately, it birthed me.

That's why I have to write this book. And publish it. To celebrate that life. Yours. Mine. Ours.

That's what I would like to say to my mother. As is most typical for me, who learned this style from her, I don't. I keep my mouth shut and all this inside. I'll bring it up again, another time. Maybe. Maybe time will work its magic, and this will work itself out. In the meantime, this project and I stagger forward, dance backward, lumber onward, clutched in an embrace of life and death.

Chapter One

It's almost eleven o'clock on a weekday morning in November 1994. Back in New York, I would already be shivering in the bone-chill of late autumn, winter already breathing frostily down my neck. But on this day in Jerusalem, where I now live, the weather is still summer-like. A beam of yellow sunlight slants like a leaning tower through the tall windows of my kitchen, bouncing off motes of dust dancing in the air. I am grateful for the cool cocoon created by the two-foot-thick stone walls of the house we are renting in Jerusalem's Greek Colony.

I love this time of day. Chaim's at work, the boys are at school. The atmosphere around me is tranquil, the frantic eddies of the early morning rush having subsided. I'm relatively rested and focused. I have deliberately not scheduled any patients today, a luxury born of the flexibility of running my own private psychotherapy practice. Today, I have a date with my mother, due to knock at my door any moment.

She and my father are back for another visit to their beloved, traitorous daughter who left the Upper West Side of Manhattan—and them—three years earlier to pursue a lifelong dream of living in Israel. The move wasn't unexpected. That didn't make breaking the news any easier.

"*What?* You're doing *what?*"

"Moving to Israel. This summer."

1

"*This* is how you tell me? Don't you think you should have sat down and discussed it with me, with Daddy, before you made a decision like this?"

"Discussed it? Are you kidding? We've been talking about this forever. You knew we've wanted to do this for years. Ever since Chaim and I met. That's almost—what—eighteen years ago! This isn't a surprise."

"That's true, you've been talking about it for years. That's why I thought you weren't going to do it. But now, with the kids, and the situation? Do you realize how dangerous it is there?"

"No, I hadn't thought about that at all."

"Don't take that tone with me. That's not fair."

"Sorry. I know this is hard—"

"Of course it is. I know you've always talked about moving there. But I thought—I hoped you'd given up the idea. And anyway, when you talked about it, it was years ago. We were younger then. Maybe if you'd moved when we were younger, Daddy and I. But we're not that young anymore."

"Oh, c'mon, Mom. Stop that. You're young. You have more energy than almost anyone I know. You've got more energy than I do, sometimes. What does that have to do with it, anyway?"

"It would have been easier for us to get used to it. We would have had more time to get used to it. But now . . ."

"Well, you can always move too. Why don't you? That way you can be with the kids, watch them grow."

"You should have thought of that before you decided to move. *We're* not moving."

"Well, then you'll have to come visit."

And so in August 1991, Chaim and I, with our three sons—Yonatan, age seven, David, four, and Yehoshua, two—boarded an El Al plane en route to making Jerusalem our home.

Chaim and I *had* planned this for years. In our very first conversation, we had been delighted to discover that we each planned to live in Israel someday. Okay, so it took us a while: eighteen years. But now we were finally doing it.

My parents love and cherish Israel. It is the glowing counterweight to the darkness of the Holocaust, the pillar of fire to

2

the Shoah's pillar of smoke and ash. Israel is the realization of a redemptive, protective dream: had the Jewish state existed during The War, the Holocaust would not have happened, and all the grandparents, all the aunts, all the uncles, all of the six million, would still be alive. My parents believe wholeheartedly in the importance of building the Jewish state, of being part of the miracle, and they had educated me toward this ideal all my life. But losing one's daughter, son-in-law, and grandchildren—three grand*sons*, no less—to that far-off country, still at war, still at risk? *That* was another story altogether. My mother dripped pain whenever she talked to me about it.

This was not new to me. Growing up, I had certainly felt the bonds holding me to my family. I knew that for survivors, separation from family members, even for events as casual as vacations, is never easy. In fact, it verges on the traumatic. For many, the last time they'd been separated from their loved ones, it had been final: they never saw them again. I also knew about the deep sense of responsibility many children of survivors feel toward their parents, the compelling need to take care of them, becoming, in effect, their parents' parents.

In graduate school, training to become a clinical psychologist, I read the relevant literature that gravely discussed "survivor syndrome" and "survivor guilt" and reflected on survivors' particular form of separation and death anxiety. To me, this was no abstraction. I carried it within me, deep in my cells.

Sometimes these syndromes had an upside, one my mother-in-law counted on quite explicitly. When I married her younger son, she confidently declared that at least she didn't have to worry about *this* son moving far away, and to Israel, no less, as her older son had done several years earlier. My in-laws lived only a few blocks away from my parents and she was sure I would never leave my mother.

But now, against all odds, I *was* leaving my mother and my father and moving to Israel. I knew all about the connection between separation and death. I knew all about being responsible for parents. I had watched my mother devotedly taking care of her aging father and mother until their respective deaths in 1973 and 1980. I admired and loved that about her. But I was adamant:

I would live my own life. I was sticking to my plan. Besides, I argued—with her, and with myself—she was nowhere near as old, as infirm, as my grandparents had been. On the contrary, she and my father are two of the healthiest, most energetic people I know. I should have their stamina, their zest for life when I'm their age. Hell, when I'm *my* age.

So I ordered the obligatory 220-volt appliances, the dependable Maytag washer and the twenty-two-cubic foot Amana refrigerator, packed all our stuff, marshaled all my arguments, and steeled myself against the final good-byes. Anyway, I told myself, these were not final good-byes. It's only a ten-hour flight from JFK to Ben Gurion Airport. We're a long way since the days when covered wagons bore relatives away from each other forever. We have faxes and international dialing. Sure, the separation would hurt. I convinced myself that my mother would handle it.

What I didn't take into account was whether *I* could.

Israel. Chaim eventually found work, getting happily involved in a start-up software company brimming with hope and energy. I began to develop my private practice as a clinical psychologist. We enrolled the kids in their respective schools and preschool programs. Two were happy, one was not. But over the next few months, they, and we, began to adjust to our new environment. On a macrolevel, the transition was going smoothly.

On a microlevel, the transition was exhausting. I was hell-bent on making this Zionist Experiment work. I was flushed with Zionist fervor. Everyone I met—on the street, at the grocery, at the filling station—was a long-lost Brother or Sister, every experience a Zionist Miracle. No wonder I was wiped at the end of every day's hunt for Meaningful Moments and Portentous Signs.

Much of the time, I felt as though I'd entered a house of mirrors: everything was recognizable, but just distorted enough so that when I reached out to touch the image, it wasn't quite where I expected it to be. This applied to so many things: the supermarket, lined with cans and jars and containers of products I recognized—almost. The school system, which didn't provide us with a regular schedule of dismissal times and vacations because "everyone just knows it." The plus signs in my kids' math workbooks, which were written like an upside-down T, missing the lower "leg" of the little cross I was used to. I took the disappearance of that "lower leg" personally. The first few times my kids drew this new, amputated symbol, I corrected them. They corrected me right back. "*This* is right, Mommy," they told me patiently, then not so patiently, until I gave up. And I remembered my mother helping me in math back in elementary school. Her division sign was strange to me: a colon, with no horizontal line separating the two dots. I corrected her too, back then. She, too, was amused at first—then irritated. What had been good enough for the hen was no longer good enough for the chick. Now I knew how she felt.

Living in a new language posed endless challenges. A whole new life needed to be deciphered, decoded. Banking statements—in Hebrew. Recipes—in Hebrew, and in grams and kilos. Converting the weather report—or a child's temperature—from Celsius to Fahrenheit or back.

Our kids slid into fluent Hebrew—its cadences, nuances, and accent—within several months. Their growing proficiency soon outpaced our knowledge of the language. They started making a point of identifying their English-speaking friends as such, to save us the trouble (and themselves the embarrassment) of our butchering the grammar or the accent. They served as my grammar- and spell-checkers every time I had to send off a note to school. It made me appreciate what my parents had gone through, learning to function in English after they came to America. They speak with relatively light accents, but there are words my mother will never quite get her tongue around. She still pronounces *colonel* just as it's spelled, in three syllables, "co-lo-nel," despite years of coaching her to think: kernel. She cannot hear the difference between *color* and *collar*. And *drawer*: I learned the hard way—the snickering of my second-grade classmates ringing in my ears—that it's not two-syllabled, as my mother says it, but that you draaaaw it out in one long "draaaawr." Now it was my turn to be the greenhorn. My kids laughed at how Hebrew gutturals got stuck in my throat. In stores, cashiers often switched into English when handing me my change—broken English at that—and who asked them, anyway?

All these small, daily adjustments scraped against my skin like fine-grained sandpaper: the clumsiness of mangling a foreign language, the inability to escape my accent, the feeling of marginality, even among an immigrant population that turned out to have its own insidious pecking order. No mortal wounds, these, but enough to hurt, to chafe, to keep me tottering and unsteady.

My insides fluttered in a brittle dance of exhilaration and angst. Had I been in a laughing mood (and sometimes, in my better moments, I was), the irony (poetic justice?) of this might have been funny: in my private practice, I specialize in anxiety and stress reduction. I daresay none of my clients needed my skills as much as I did. All my training, all my techniques got a power workout. And when being breathless with excitement turned into simply being unable to breathe at the thought of the day's looming challenges, there was one particular godsend: the massive jasmine bush outside the kitchen window. I am eternally grateful to that bush for its hands-on lesson in stress reduction: sucking in its perfumed exhale forced me to breathe deeply, to calm down whenever the strain of adjustment became overwhelming.

I began to appreciate what my parents had gone through, arriving on strange American shores after the war. But *I* had made the choice to immigrate freely. They hadn't. They had been ripped from their moorings, flung from their land and culture, weighed down—in a world where such concepts were still unknown—by the long-term effects of trauma. How *had* they coped?

And one more Something lurked, just below the surface, just below the daily struggle to adjust. Some faint shadow-feeling prowled and skulked, refusing to be identified, remaining maddeningly elusive.

I felt off-balance. Irritated. Damn it, I'm a psychologist, I'm supposed to be able to figure this out. Well, at least I knew enough to accept that I'd just have to wait for the cloud of swirling mess inside to settle—like coffee grounds settling in a cup—for the outlines to become clear.

In the meantime, my intrepid parents visited us, flying back and forth between New York and Israel, their suitcases loaded with treats: the latest best-selling books for adults and children, culled from the *New York Times Book Review* and plucked from the shelves at the majestic Barnes and Noble at 82nd Street and

Broadway. Decaffeinated English Breakfast Tea from Zabar's. From the discount dry goods stores on the Lower East Side, Eckstein's and Kreinen's, came thick fluffy sweatsuits for us all, and Superman and Batman pajamas for the boys. All those touches of "home," those "essential," more grown-up incarnations of the teddy bears and "blankies" intended to ease the transition from one developmental stage to another.

Their visits were like their suitcases: cram-packed full of goodies, multilayered as an archeological dig. And very, very heavy. Sure, it was wonderful seeing them radiate with joy at being with their grandchildren and watching the kids bask in that love. All the while, however, I had to steel myself against the undercurrent of sadness, the knowledge that, all too soon, once again, this would end. In the space of weeks, we tried to compensate for the separation of months. The joyous lightness of reunion balanced precariously with the dead weight of good-byes already looming. We stoked for the coming period of starvation by gorging on shared experiences: attending the children's class parties, cheering them on at judo exhibitions, sharing Shabbat and holiday dinners. Moving through the visit, I'd feel nourished, then sated, and finally stuffed and cranky. The partings were difficult. The kids wailed and sobbed every time my parents left us. I didn't handle it much better; I was just quieter about it. During the last days before their departure, I'd slide into a funk that didn't dissipate until several days after they'd gone and I'd settled back into my routine. Relief was always accompanied by the hollow pain of loss.

Sometime in the early autumn of 1994, I found myself at a writing class in Talpiot, a nearby Jerusalem neighborhood. I put it that way because going there was a spur-of-the-moment thing.

Not that writing was a foreign idea. As a child, I dreamed of becoming a writer, like Betsy of the Betsy-Tacy series, Jo March, and Anne Frank. I scribbled reams of stories and poems.

In my first semester at Barnard College, a Freshman English instructor callously skewered my writing—and my confidence. After that, I confined myself to term papers, long letters to friends, and lots of journals. Instead of a writer, I became a psychologist, sublimating the desire to analyze subtle literary themes into help-ing flesh-and-blood creations explore their motivations and find the poetry hidden in their lives. I thought I had laid to rest the urge to write. But here I was.

The assignment was straightforward: "Go back in time and write about an incident that happened to someone you know. Get inside their skin. Tell their story from your perspective."

Five women, strangers to one another, perched their note-books on their knees and scratched away in the dark light of the living room. The story of my mother's stomach-wrenching journey to America by storm-tossed Liberty Ship in 1949 flowed onto a page of yellow lined paper.

Diane Greenberg, the teacher, asked us to read out what we'd written.

My turn: I began to read, feeling nervous about being scru-tinized, about giving my silent thoughts voice. Halfway through, a huge sob heaved itself out of me. Past my astonished Censor. Out into the open. In full view of five perfect strangers.

They sat silently, watching, while tears poured down my face. I was mortified. Aghast at the loss of control; I hadn't seen it com-ing. A few ragged breaths later, I could push enough of it back down to resume reading, my voice shaking and tight. I finished and stared at the page.

"Is it a true story?" Diane asked, quietly. "Whose voice is it?"

"Yes, it's true," I answered. "It's my mother." Barely meeting her eyes, I explained that my mother was a Holocaust survivor. I had heard this particular story many times, growing up. But I had no idea why it had produced such a strong reaction now.

As I talked, taking refuge in intellectual explanations, the waves of turbulence within me began to subside. I could pretend to ignore, for a moment, the upheaval and my horrified disbelief at how I had let down my guard, or rather, how something much more powerful than I ever imagined had cracked through the walls of my defenses.

In her gentle, elegantly British tones, Diane suggested that perhaps something was begging for expression. Perhaps I should even consider writing about it—and not just about my mother's experiences, but about my own reactions to them as well.

"That's a story, too," she said.

The other women—when I dared to glance at them—were nodding vigorously.

Maybe. At the moment, I was focused on getting my guts to stop quaking, and on convincing myself that I would survive even if the women present still secretly thought I was a fruitcake.

There was no denying, however, that something *was* trying to get through to me.

I gradually began to understand what it was.

This "Separation = Death" thing was working all right, but in reverse. What if this was the last time I saw my parents? It was unthinkable, yet I was thinking it: How did one survive the loss of one's parents? How did you make your way from one day to the next to the next, knowing you'd never see them again, never be able to talk to them again? Never be able to call them up and hear that explosion of sunlight as they recognize your voice on the phone. "Come *quick*," my father always yells to my mother when he's the one to answer first, "your daughter is on the phone!"

But it was more than that. If "Something Happened to Them"— that's as close as I could bring myself to give voice to the fear— would I have known them? *Really* known them, as people, not simply as my parents. Who they were, before me, aside from me. The details of their lives.

My father had recently spent over one hundred hours being interviewed about his life and wartime experiences by Professor Michael Wyschogrod, a close family friend. I had the transcripts of those conversations. Although they didn't contain all that I wanted to know, at least there was some record of his life.

There was no such record of my mother's. If "Something Happened," how would I ever get to know her?

That thought was becoming unbearable. But my growing desperation was met with resistance that was just as desperate: I did not want to get into "Holocaust stuff." I had been very, very grateful when it didn't have to be me interviewing my father, when Michael had stepped into the breach. But there was no one else to do this with my mother.

Maybe it wouldn't be so hard. As my mother herself said on those rare occasions when she discussed this at all: hers weren't horror stories like my father's. She had never made a big deal about her experiences, so maybe there was nothing to worry about. Besides, I would only be chronicling her childhood, slaking my thirst for anecdotes that could be passed on to my kids, about zany aunts, maybe, or daredevil uncles, or mischievous childhood pranks, the kind of scrapes my childhood heroes—the March sisters in *Little Women*, the Bobbsey Twins, the Hardy boys—always got into.

So, later that fall, when my parents arrived on yet another visit to the Holy Land, I had a Plan for this oral history project that I hoped would help me avoid the pitfalls.

I knew just how to do it.

Back in 1984, just after our first son, Yonatan, was born, I had been browsing in a local stationary store on Upper Broadway when I spied it: a grandmother's memory book. Similar to a baby book, it was designed to help a grandmother create an heirloom of her life for her grandchildren. It laid out everything simply, coherently, and chronologically, and walked you through your life with questions to be answered, a family tree to be completed, and blank squares to be filled with photographs. I thought: Great! This is pretty straightforward, almost easy, even for someone who doesn't like to write. Perfect for my mother. What a great gift for both the new grandmother and the new baby.

I presented it to my mother. She thanked me, rewrapped it, and put it carefully in a drawer. And left it there. From time to time, as the years passed, and two more sons were born, I'd ask her about the memory book. She hadn't done a thing with it. Someday, she said, she would sit down with me and we'd fill it in together. We never got around to it.

Once, during one of those parental visits to Israel, my mother reached inside her suitcase, pulled out the memory book, still carefully wrapped, and handed it to me.

"You keep it," she said.

I did.

"We'll get to it," she said.

We didn't.

Somehow, it was never the right time.

Now it was time.

Chapter Two

I hear the squeak of the sagging white metal garden gate, the quick footsteps on the uneven flagstones, three decisive raps on the broad wooden door.

"Di-*yen?*" As always, she sings my name in two distinct syllables, the second one soaring.

I throw open the door and she bursts through it, a broad smile on her face. We hug. Over the years, as she herself jokes, she seems to have gotten smaller, shorter. I laugh when she says she's shrinking, but uneasily—it *does* feel easier to encircle her in my long-armed embrace, so similar to her own. Still, her movements are as energetic as always. I usher her into the welcoming spaciousness of the large, square kitchen as she asks about each of the kids, about Chaim, about me.

Around us, the counters are filled with the debris of my everyday life. Boxes of Cheerios vie for space with arrays of spice bottles. Children's audio cassettes, everything from Raffi to Uncle Moishy and the Mitzvah Men to *Peter and the Wolf*, crowd up against the large black "ghetto-blaster" tape deck the shelf beside the window. In the far corner, neatly folded piles of laundry squat atop the clothes dryer. But in the center of the room, the atmosphere is open and uncluttered, like the airiness of the kitchen under the fourteen-foot ceiling. I have cleared the round butcher-block table of all but two mugs of warm tea and some ballpoint pens. Medium point. Blue ink. And the memory book, in its brown-paper wrapping.

My mother and I settle into chairs on opposite sides of the table. She was with me when I bought it at some butcher-block store in Manhattan. Just as she was with me at Macy's, during one of their one-day sales, when I purchased the square tablecloth that now bedecks the tabletop in a riot of fruit in shades of yellow, purple, and green. Despite her misgivings about my plans to move to Israel, she was always ready to help me with the preparations and kept me company on many of these shopping trips.

I unwrap the memory book and open it. It's still as fresh and uncracked as the day I gave it to her.

I sit up straight, perched over the table, pen in hand, ready for the downstroke.

"Okay, Mom, tell me about when you were little."

She smiles slightly, her eyebrows and shoulders rising a little. I recognize this in her, the readiness to cooperate shrugging up against the wonder as to what the fuss is all about.

"What do you want to know?" she asks.

What do I want to know? Everything, actually.

"Okay, first tell me about Żółkiew."

I make her spell it for me, with all the accents, and say it again, slowly and clearly. I echo it back carefully, sculpting the word with my ears, my lips, my tongue. The first syllable, "Żół," rhymes more or less with *rule*, and the opening ż sounds like the soft French *j*. "Kiew" sounds like *keff*. In the middle is that special *ł*, which I struggle with. It's not an *l* really, and not a *w* either. Something in between. We laugh at my efforts to say it correctly, as we have every time I've tried to pronounce Polish since I was little. There weren't all that many attempts; my father hated the thought of my speaking "that cursed language."

I run to bring in a map of prewar Poland and unfold it carefully on the tabletop. My mother's long bony fingers skim over its rumpled surface, pointing out highlights: Galicia, then southeastern Poland, today part of the Ukraine. Her town, Żółkiew, so close to Lwów, the nearest city.

"How many people lived in Żółkiew?"

"It was small, maybe about fifteen thousand people before the war. Poles, Ukrainians, and Jews. A nice little town."

Having looked up Żółkiew in a history of the town and its Jews compiled by one of the survivors, I already know that, despite its small size, Żółkiew was quite a bustling and cosmopolitan town, and that its Jews played a leading role in all aspects of its civic, cultural, and business life. Many were doctors, lawyers, teachers, and pharmacists—one of whom was my grandfather, Josef Rosenberg. They developed the town's fur and grain industries, and the public transportation system between Żółkiew and Lwów, about an hour away. This proximity allowed the inhabitants of Żółkiew access to Lwów's cultural opportunities, which even included a university. This was important to my grandparents, for whom opera, symphonies, art, literature, and education were as essential to life as breathing.

"How did everyone get along?" I wonder.

"Maybe they didn't love each other, but they treated each other with respect," says my mother. There were darker undercurrents. She tells me, for example, that although my grandfather owned his pharmacy, he could not be listed as the owner because there already were a number of Jewish owners of similar businesses. He paid the previous Christian owner, Pyszynski, a fee to keep *his* name officially listed on the deed. However, my grandparents had both Jewish and non-Jewish friends. The Ukrainian doctor Sapruka and his wife were regular partners at my grandparents' weekly card games.

Relations between the town's Jews were also cordial, despite their many differences. The Jewish community was comprised of the entire spectrum of religious and political expression, from freethinkers to socialists to Hassidim. Zionism was represented by the *Chalutz* (pioneer) movement; as a preschooler, my mother learned her first Hebrew words from a young woman who was a member of this movement. Miss Cohen, or simply *G'veret*, Miss, as my mother called her, was part tutor, part big sister, and my mother adored her. Hebrew was also taught at the Tarbut (culture) school; my mother attended afterschool classes there, stopping only when attending Jewish schools was later considered "subversive."

My mother's family belonged to the more "assimilated" minority of Żółkiew's Jews. Her family was not kosher, and her mother lit candles only on the High Holy Days of Rosh Hashanah and Yom Kippur, although she was scrupulous about lighting *yahrzeit* candles in memory of the dead. When I ask my mother how her family's assimilated ways were received among the more religious Jews of the town, she looks surprised.

"It was never a problem," she says. "Everyone knew, and that was it. And," she adds, "on the big holidays, everybody prayed together in the big synagogue."

She is referring to the town's huge fortified synagogue, built in 1687 under the patronage of King Jan Sobieski III. With its dramatic architecture and the ornate wood- and brass-work gracing its interior, the "Sobieski shul," the pride of Żółkiew's Jews, was considered a Polish national treasure.

I lug in the heavy red-bound photo album I received from my grandparents as a gift back in September 1964. The inscription on the first page, in my grandfather's elegant spidery script, exhorts me to "Enjoy this and remember always the grandparents who loved you from the bottom of their hearts." In it, I keep my precious collection of the few photographs which survived the war, and which my grandparents entrusted to me, way back then, along with the album. There are two photographs of the imposing synagogue, one from the front, the other from the rear. There's a snapshot of the town square, the *rynek*, and of the *Glinska Brama*, *brama* meaning gate, one of several large stone gates marking the entrances into the town. Some of the photos are tinted in shades of rose, aqua, and teal. I remember my grandmother telling me that at one time my grandfather had been interested in photography; he had taken and developed the photos, and also had experimented with tinting them.

My mother and I turn to the photographs of my grandmother, Agatha (whom everyone called Tusia) Schenker, and grandfather, Josef Rosenberg, both of whom came from Brzeżany, a town in southeastern Poland. Every time I look at these photos, I'm always surprised by the hair. When I knew my grandmother, her brown thinning hair was short, styled carefully into a neat coiffure by regular visits to the Polish hairdresser she found in Washington Heights in Upper Manhattan. (I remember those occasions well: she often brought home a delicious *babka* from the European bakery she'd pass on the way back to the subway.) But when she was young, her hair was luxuriantly long and glossy. In a snapshot of her at about age thirteen, her hair, gathered demurely at the top of her head, spills over one shoulder and cascades down her arm, almost reaching her wrist. By World War I, she was already keeping it short.

The bigger surprise is my grandfather's head of wavy dark-brown hair and his mustache, captured forever in the few photographs dating from around World War I, in his medical adjutant's uniform. He apparently went bald soon after that, in his early twenties, and that's how I remember him, the few remaining soft strands of white hair neatly combed behind his ears. And no mustache.

My grandparents married in 1921. Shortly before the wedding, my mother tells me, Agatha's father, Mozes Schenker, died. A year earlier, during a period marked by violent confrontations between Ukrainian and Polish nationalists, he had been attacked and savagely beaten by a mob of Ukrainians angered by his pro-Polish sentiments. The injuries he suffered never healed properly due to his diabetes and he died several days before the wedding. Agatha was in shock and wanted to postpone the ceremony. The rabbi intervened. "A wedding takes precedence over everything," he told the young couple gently. Agatha and Josef got married as scheduled.

My mother talks and I write rapidly, keeping my handwriting small and neat, trying to fit the information into the allotted spaces on the creamy white pages. I record the fact that one year later, in 1922, the young couple moved to Żółkiew, where my grandfather had bought a drugstore.

This was a hard move for Agatha; she'd never gotten over the death of her father, and here she was leaving her mother, Laura (née Majblum) Schenker. Three years later, in 1925, when my mother was born, Laura came to Żółkiew to help her daughter with the new baby. Her son-in-law invited her to stay on with them and she did, living with the family until her death in 1941, sleeping in the same room as her new granddaughter.

Smiling wistfully, my mother points to the picture of her grandmother in my album. It dates from before World War I, according to the inscription in *my* grandmother Agatha's up-and-down wave-like handwriting. I've seen this photo before, but I am still awed by my great-grandmother's tiny waist.

"Look," I say, making a circle with my hands, the fingertips almost touching. "That small!"

My mother laughs.

"You know," she says. "I used to try on her dresses when I was little. But I could never fit into them."

"Just like Scarlett O'Hara!" I say, thinking of that famous scene at the beginning of *Gone with the Wind*, in which Mammy laces Scarlett into an eighteen-inch corset in order to attract "beaus" at the barbecue at Twelve Oaks. My mother took me to see that movie. We laugh, remembering that between the two of us, we used up an entire package of tissues crying through the whole second half of the movie, all two hours of it.

"You know that I still have the movie program you bought me, with the pictures of the movie stars. Like Clark Gable!" I add, teasing, and she smiles shyly. Clark Gable was one of her idols. The pleasure of that memory suffuses her cheeks with a soft pink.

The memory book is perfect for this. It's obviously intended for a lovely white-bread kind of life, where budding young girls with shiny ponytails skip along manicured lawns and polite, bashful boys with carefully combed hair and pressed shirts hold their books for them after school. The kind of life I read about in my favorite books or saw on TV in programs like *Father Knows Best* and *Leave It to Beaver*.

Amid delicate floral borders curling up and down the margins of the smooth pages, my mother and I record the joys and sighs of her childhood. Mooning over a dashing Clark Gable or Robert Taylor. Dreaming of being as beautiful and talented as her particular favorite, Deanna Durbin. In short, the ups and downs of a normal life.

My mother's life started out like that. Add a few *cz*s and *rz*s, unpronounceable consonants that sound like you are gargling with razor blades, and you have it: *Tatuś Knows Best. Leave It to Lutka.*

This is just what I was hoping for.

Helena Beata Rosenberg was born at home on January 16, 1925. It was a Friday morning and the midwife in attendance fretted that she wouldn't get her *Shabbos* preparations done in time. She needn't have worried. Lutka, as my mother was always called, popped into the world after a quick labor, and the midwife was free to return to her pots.

Named after her father's mother, Berta Wolf, and said to look like her father, Josef, Lutka was very much her own person. One of her earliest memories is of the time she marched off to explore the fields near her home. She was about three years old. She came home to find everyone in a panic, thinking her lost. She's still indignant about it:

"*I* wasn't lost. *I* knew where I was. *They* didn't know where I was."

I smile indulgently at her still-defiant tone; I can certainly relate to her experience.

"Do you remember when I went to meet Roanna?" I ask her. She certainly does. I was in second grade, and decided to meet my best friend, Roanna Kettler, and walk her home from school, PS 114 on Jerome Avenue in the Bronx. The two of us came strolling nonchalantly home to find my parents and grandparents in a panic and the neighborhood police out in force, combing the stairwells and rooftop of my building and the park across the street, everybody looking for me. I was sorry for the fuss, but, as I told them over and over, *I* hadn't gone missing. I *had* told my mother my plan; she probably just hadn't heard me. To this day, she still insists that I hadn't said anything.

We shake our heads over the memory. Despite our shared chuckle, the tightening of her lips clues me in to the fact that traces of that trauma still linger. A mother myself now, I confess to having to suppress a sympathetic shudder. I get up to give her a quick hug.

"I'm sorry, Mom," I say, and she looks at me quizzically for a moment, then squeezes me back.

I sit back down and we continue.

She grew up surrounded by doting parents, and by a loving grandmother who sewed her clothes, baked her favorite poppy seed cake just the way she liked it ("no filling, just sugar sprinkled on top!"), always let her lick the bowl (she loved egg yolks beaten with sugar), and interceded on her behalf with her parents.

There were clear rules of deportment and behavior. She was expected to keep her room clean, take care of her dog, and do her homework. She did. She was supposed to be a lady. She was. But she was more. She found ways to push the limits of her upbringing, stretching its constraints quietly but resolutely. She may have toed the line and obeyed the rules ("bedtime at 9:00 p.m. during elementary school, 10:00 p.m. in high school") but she had her own very decided ideas about things. She was one spunky kid, who was "never scared of anything, not dogs, nothing."

Well, maybe *one* thing: She yanked out her own loose teeth rather than let Dr. Gryznowa, the dentist—otherwise a "very pleasant lady"—get near her. The few visits to the dentist she couldn't avoid she remembers, shuddering still, as a cacophony of pain and sound: the canary singing, the radio playing, the drill drilling, and the dentist shrilling away in her falsetto. As an adult, my mother consults only male dentists.

Eyes sparkling, she tells me how she ran before she could walk, from the age of thirteen months. She rode her tricycle down the flight of steps in front of her house, she reports with more than a touch of vindictive glee in her tone. Nothing deterred her. Not breaking her nose, tripping on a cobblestone passageway near her house. Not her mother's concern for her safety—or her bemusement over this unladylike behavior.

"My mother used to say I should've been born a boy, it would have been more suitable."

Her speed came in handy; she was always racing off to school in the mornings, getting there just in the nick of time. In high school, she fine-tuned her natural ability and became a runner, competing in track meets. Her best events were the one-hundred- and three-hundred-meter dashes.

She liked carpentry and disliked drawing. She loved math and science and planned to become an engineer and build bridges. She hated German, a mandatory foreign language, taught by a tough German master who struck terror into her heart. No matter how well she knew the lesson before it began, one question from him was enough to wipe out all memory traces and render her speechless. She got A's in written work, F's in spoken German.

"Every time there was a conference, you know, where the parents go to school to meet the teachers? It was the same story.

'I know she knows the material,' he'd tell my parents. 'But unless she says it right in class, I can't give her any other grade.'"

My mother just shrugs.

Listening to my mother sketch out her childhood, I find myself wanting to fill in all the outlines, flesh out the contours, get in there and experience it for myself. The sensation is familiar. It reminds me of the coloring books I loved when I was little. Coloring books were a forbidden delight: For my father, an artist and graphic designer, these books were anathema, the antithesis of creativity. But I remember clearly the quiver of anticipation and delight whenever someone, unaware of my father's mandate, ran the blockade of his disapproval and gave me one as a present: all those crisp white pages with heavy black outlines just waiting to be filled in, saturated with color.

I realize, also, that this is similar to the process that occurs as I work with clients. Listening to their stories, I allow my imagination to range and soar and doodle associations and scenarios in my head. Sometimes a soundtrack starts playing in the background. When I run these associations past my clients, we are often surprised and gratified by how on target they can be, highlighting important truths, opening portals into their inner worlds. It's no wonder that, as my mother speaks, the same associative process starts to happen.

"In elementary school," says my mother, "I went to a school run by nuns. It was a very good school, but very strict." But once, she continues, with an undercurrent of pride in her tone and a sly twinkle in her eye, she even defied one of her teachers.

"What!" I can hardly believe that my mother, paragon of obedience and decorum, ever stood up to such an authority figure as a nun. "What happened?"

"Well," she laughs, obviously still amused so many decades later, "she told me my skirt was too short, and I should tell my mother to make it longer. But I told her that my grandma made me this skirt, and if she says it's okay to wear, then it's okay."

"And—?"

"She called my mother to school. She told her that she wanted to punish me for talking back to her, but she couldn't. How could she say anything when I was defending my grandma?"

As my mother sketches out the story, my imagination starts whirring. . . .

It's Lutka's favorite part of the day: recess. In the big exercise yard behind the school building, she and her friends are jumping rope. It's her turn. They're chanting and she's just getting the rhythm right: JUMP-jump, JUMP-jump. The rope slaps against the ground. She loves the way her hair floats up into the air and her skirt puffs up like a bell every time she leaves the ground.

"Lutka."

At first, she's too busy counting her jumps to notice that someone is talking to her. She's going to set a record today, she can feel it. Then she notices that the rope is not swinging around anymore. There's something in front of her. Something brown. Something tall. It's the Sister.

The playground is suddenly still. Waves of quiet are spreading around her, almost as if she's a pebble tossed into a pond and the ripples are spreading out in silent circles that keep growing and growing.

"Lutka!" The nun's voice is louder now, sharper. "Look at me when I am speaking to you."

"Yes, Sister." She forces herself to look up. Her eyes slide past the belt at the waist with the tiny silver cross hanging down, over the dark brown of the habit, up to where a square bit of face looks out a narrow brown-and-white window.

"Tell your mother that your skirt is too short for school. You cannot come to school like this again. It is simply not allowed."

The nun turns and begins to move away. At each of their ends, Lutka's friends gently shimmy the rope between them, preparing to arc it over her head again.

"No."

Even Lutka can't believe the word has boiled out of her. Her friends stare, their eyes bulging, their mouths gaping like the fish sold at the market.

Sister swivels back at her. Everything, everyone freezes. The world falls silent.

The nun's eyebrows are like sharp mountain peaks, scraping the edge of her wimple. Her mouth had gaped open, but she pulls it into a tight line, like someone shutting a drawstring purse.

"What?" Her voice is as tight as her lips.

Lutka's stomach is one big knot. Her arms are hot and cold and heavy. Her cheeks are flames. Everyone is looking at her. Her lips are dry and it's hard to swallow.

She doesn't recognize her voice, all squeaky, like a very little mouse. "My grandma made me this skirt. If she thinks it's fine, it's fine."

No one moves. Even the Sister doesn't move. She just stands there, staring at Lutka, her face blooming from white to red. Lutka wishes the ground would open and swallow her.

The bell rings. Recess is over.

The nun draws a deep breath.

"Okay, children," she says quietly. "Back to class." She includes Lutka in her nod, and the girl runs for her life. She slides into her seat, ignoring the stares of her classmates. For the rest of the day, she doesn't dare lift her eyes from her books.

Later that afternoon, Lutka sits on her bed, feet scuffing the floor listlessly. Her dog, Jock, jumps on her bed, licks her face, trying to coax her to play his favorite games. She pushes him away. With a sigh, he curls up next to her on the bed and the two of them just sit, waiting. Her mother has been called to school for a special meeting with her teacher.

There are sounds outside her room. Footsteps. The handle turns and the door opens.

"Well," says her mother, standing in the doorway. "Your teacher has just been telling me what happened today at school."

Lutka doesn't move. She hardly breathes. Jock buries his nose between his paws and doesn't even twitch.

"She said you were disrespectful. She told you your skirt was too short and you talked back to her."

The girl keeps silent. The pattern of the floor suddenly looks very interesting.

"She said she really should punish you for your behavior. But . . ."

Her mother's voice suddenly sounds different. Lutka raises her eyes, risks a peek.

"She said you stood up for your grandmother. And respect for a grandmother is very important. Even more important than for a teacher."

What? She can't believe it. Her mother is actually smiling. She's trying not to, but she can't help it. Lutka's arms and legs suddenly feel

21

warm, as though someone is pouring deliciously warm water all over her for her bath. Jock is wriggling all over her, washing her face with his rough pink tongue.

"Come," says her mother, reaching for Lutka's hand. "Let's go to the kitchen. You can have a glass of milk and some cake. Grandmother just baked it. Your favorite. I'm sure she'd like to hear all about it, too."

I am tickled pink by this story with the nun. By all her stories. To me, raised in the concrete pastures of the Bronx, my mother's descriptions of childhood are like enchanting Currier and Ives paintings come to life. Imagine: throngs of red-cheeked, steam-puffing youngsters, their skates flashing over ice-hard streams or whirling and gliding on frozen water pumped over the vast concrete calisthenics area next to the high school. Imagine: troops of kids trudging up the neighboring hills, only to career down them a few moments later on their skis, their shrieks of delight carving the frozen air into ribbons of laughter. I see my mother tramping home in the fading evening light to a mountain of steaming boiled potatoes topped with homemade sauerkraut, biting and sharp, forked from the big wooden barrel in the cellar. Eating *her* special cake.

"Do you still have the recipe for the poppy seed cake—*your* cake?" I ask.

"I think I must have it somewhere, in the old papers, but I have to find it."

And dogs. My mother's crazy about them, and taught my brother and me to love them too. But we couldn't have one: my brother was allergic to them and my father thought keeping a dog cooped up in an apartment was cruel. What I only dreamed about—watching *Lassie* on TV, reading *Lassie Come Home*—my mother had lived: her terrier mutt, Jock (short for Joker), *did* wait for her at the end of her school day. Fiercely loyal to his young mistress, he liked what she liked, and woe to anyone who threatened her in any way. He hated her pediatrician almost as much as she did. Unfortunately, the doctor "with his fat, fat little fingers" was often summoned to the house because Lutka was prone to tonsillitis. (In fact, she missed most of the second half of first grade because of tonsillitis.) On those occasions, Jock, whining and protesting, had to be locked in another room or he'd launch his

22

wiry little body at the doctor to protect his beloved Lutka. And at day's end, he'd tunnel stealthily under the thick, down comforter on her bed, a trick he'd learned in order to leave no sign of his presence that might betray him to the Dog Police, my grandfather, whose fondness for animals did not extend to allowing them in bed.

"Intelligent dog," says my mother, smiling proudly, wistfully.

My mother only lacked two things as a little girl. One was braids.

My mother's curly hair was the envy of the town. Not just girls, she tells me, but grown women used to marvel at it. Some apparently interrogated the hairdresser: Was it true that all Lutka had to do was twirl her hair around her finger and it would hold a curl? Yes, it was true.

What *Lutka* wanted, however, and wanted desperately, was braids. Long braids tied with ribbons and bows, looped over the ears or sculpted into crowns around the head. Like the Ukrainian girls had. And Kasia, the Ukrainian maid, whose preparations to go out on Sunday mornings my mother loved to watch. But Lutka's hair was kept short. So she braided long lengths of string, adorned them with ribbons, and stuck them to her head with bobby pins.

I laugh gently, amused and moved by the image. My mother looks at me.

"You like this story, about the braids," she says, smiling.

I sure do. I love her inventiveness, her determination. This is the kind of story I was hoping for.

The other thing my mother always wanted was a baby brother or sister. She'd been told that storks brought babies, and that they liked sugar. So every night for months, she put cubes of sugar on the windowsill, hoping to seduce some sweet-toothed bird into delivering its precious package to her house. She was very upset when a baby arrived at a neighbor's house; she was sure the stork had made a mistake.

My mother never did get a satisfactory explanation from my grandmother as to why she'd been an only child. Many years later, my grandmother confided—to my father, not my mother—that she had had a miscarriage after Lutka. It didn't fully explain things.

There was another explanation, a secret that my grandmother once shared with me. She had been born with a birthmark, a large port-wine stain on her left cheek. She was terribly self-conscious about this mark and always wore a heavy layer of matte makeup to camouflage the purplish splotch. She told me that as a teen-ager, she had even left her home to travel, alone, to Vienna, for treatments that were supposed to remove or bleach the stain. She stayed there for several months, rooming with cousins, one of whom, Ludwig Schenker, teased her unmercifully. The treatments were painful and only partially successful: she returned home with the affected area only slightly smaller, and no less obvious. Her pain over this birthmark was intense. She was terrified of passing on this blemish to her children. When Lutka was born, perfect, blemish-free, my grandmother felt that she had been lucky once. She would not tempt fate again. She just wouldn't risk it.

Maybe she was right about her fear that her good luck might run out after the first child—but the critical mark would turn out to be not the purple one on her face, but the six-pointed one affixed years later on her sleeve. The rates of survival of an entire nuclear family during the Holocaust are infinitesimal. Who knows if another sibling could have survived? Or if my mother and her parents could have survived with an additional member of the family? Maybe my grandmother's birthmark extended its protection only so far—just far enough.

But these thoughts come later. For now, as I continue to inter-view my mother, asking about her childhood, about school, about friends, the room is full of light and promise. The girl I am getting to know sparkles with life, with zest, with vitality. And, occasion-ally, bristles with firmly held opinions. She was a fussy eater. She had few favorite foods, but definite dislikes. She hated barley soup, sure that the barley would never slip down her throat and she'd choke on it. Her mother tried to convince her to try it and see.

"*No!*" the word erupts from my mother, startling both of us. We crack up, but I wonder if I'm getting a taste of what my grandmother faced back then.

"And spinach," she continues, her whole face twisting into a grimace.

My mouth drops open.

"You forced *me* to eat spinach!" I accuse, remembering the time she threatened that if I didn't eat the pile of the vile stringy green mess on my plate one dinner, I'd face eating it again for breakfast—one of the endearing modes of child control apparently in vogue at the time. I can't believe she hated spinach, too.

"My grandmother loved to eat spinach with a sunny-side up egg on top. It was very, very mushy on the plate, and I couldn't *look* at it. It reminded me of cows'—you know!" she says, and my indignation dissolves into a giggle.

"And any meat that had fat on it, you had to cut away every vein and every piece of fat, or I wouldn't touch it!" she declares in ringing tones, and, bending over the tabletop, she pantomimes carving away, with a surgeon's precision, every last bit of offending stray fat on the imaginary piece of meat before her.

She'd obviously been a force to reckon with.

I love it. Her escapades remind me of the rambunctious child-hoods I used to read about. I listen to my mother spin tales of her youth, and my images are touched by an airbrushed softness into which I am more than happy to nestle. It dovetails beautifully with the pink-and-pearl sweetness of the memory book.

My mother slides a large black-and-white photograph out of a manila envelope. It's a family portrait of my mother's maternal family, taken in Potok, near Brzeżany, the area which, I now discover, was home to my ancestors as least as far back as my great-great-grandparents, Amalia (née Lempert) and Marcus Wolf Majblum, seated in the middle of the photograph.

My mother, who decries her poor memory, nevertheless remembers quite a lot. She remembers that her great-grandparents lived in Potok, managing an estate for a Polish nobleman there, and that Marcus Wolf was an ardent Zionist who attended the First Zionist Congress in Basel, Switzerland in 1897. She remembers being taken to visit her great-grandmother Amalia (Marcus Wolf had since died) and can still "see" the view from the apartment on Kolejowa Street down to the railroad station. To little Lutka, Amalia "was a little old lady, a *very* little old lady . . . like one hundred years old."

But when this photograph was taken, sometime around 1912, Amalia and Marcus Wolf were alive and well and holding court as matriarch and patriarch of the family. They would lease this farm from the Polish nobleman and send around a horse and buggy to collect all their children (they had eleven, though only nine lived to adulthood; the other two died of illness) and grandchildren and bring them out for a day in the country. According to my mother, my grandmother Agatha had fond memories of these occasions when the entire family got together on this farm.

Grouped around Amalia and Marcus Wolf, my mother's maternal family looks out of the photograph at me. Their expressions are serious, quiet, composed, as befits such a special occasion. Each one is carefully dressed and coiffed, the women's hair smoothed and molded, swept back, up, and high. Many of the men sport trimmed but luxuriant mustaches twirling up at the ends. Tall collars hold their heads erect. Their hands are folded, their carriage regal, ramrod straight. Looking at them reminds me not to slouch, and I draw myself upward from my center, the way I've learned to do in my Pilates exercise class.

My mother points to my great-grandfather, Mozes Schenker, one of the few Jews admitted to the Bar during the reign of Emperor Franz Josef. The emperor even bestowed a special honor on him in recognition of his legal expertise and services.

I pore over the photograph, looking for my grandmother, only to discover that she's not there; she was in Vienna having facial treatments when this was taken. But her brothers—my great-uncles—*are* there.

Leopold, or as we called him, Uncle Poldzio, is sitting on the extreme left of the front row; hugging his knee to himself. He was always "a character." I remember him from his rare visits to New York when I was a child: his thick, gray mustache, the round cherry cheeks. I especially recall how he used to make silver dollars appear from thin air; he'd perch one in his eye like a monocle and would then flip it through the air to my brother and me for us to keep. He wasn't really a gambler, my mother says, but he liked "to play." Horses. Cards. Dominoes. I think it's funny, even exciting, that someone in our family liked to gamble. *I* don't. Once, when Chaim tried to play a few hands of blackjack on a trip through Las Vegas, I dragged him away from the table after he'd won *four whole dollars* because "you have to quit while you're ahead." I must take after my grandmother.

My great-uncle Manek ("short for Emanuel, but we also called him Manio"), sits cross-legged right in the middle of the front row, arms firmly crossed. He was an incurable romantic. At some family wedding, he fell madly in love—at first sight—with Zosia (Sophie) Bardach. She cared for him too, but back then, Manek was merely a young medical student, without much to his name. Zosia bowed to family pressure to marry someone wealthy. Manek swore never to marry anyone else; he would wait for her, no matter what. Even when she had a child with her husband, Manek still waited. Eventually she divorced her husband and married Manek, who adopted her son, Richard (Ryszek). They later had a child of their own, Mietek, named after Mozes Schenker.

Manek stares out of the photograph. Peering into his eyes, I have a sense of Time, telescoped, kaleidoscoped. From my safe vantage point in the present, I see him in his past, I know his future: his suffering is still ahead of him.

My mother slides another photograph across the table to me.

"You should know," she says, "that you still own a building in Brzeżany, my parents' home town. *This* building, in fact." I bend over the photograph of an elegant, imposing, two-story building. I look up sharply—I'd expected a hovel—and my mother laughs at my stunned expression.

"Oh, yes. My great-grandfather on my father's side owned it. Leib Rosenberg. The family lived upstairs, and their grocery store was downstairs. The man who took the picture for me a few years ago even notarized a statement that the building had belonged to my grandfather. I could claim it, if I wanted to live in the Ukraine and establish residency there. Or you could."

I'm impressed. And cynical. "I'm a landowner. Wow." We laugh.

Our eyes caress the photographs. My mother spins a whole world into being. A dead tree stump is suddenly blossoming into life before my eyes: great-grandparents, great-aunts and -uncles, all those cousins—a close-knit clan whose members visited each other often. My mother smiles as she recalls climbing trees at her aunt Frederika's house ("we called her Frycia") in Zloczow during summer visits, getting running tips from her cousin Edek (Edzio) Majblum as they romped through the fields with his dogs.

I'm delighted with these stories. They sound like fiction, like something out of another favorite of mine, Louisa May Alcott's *Eight Cousins*, but these people and their exploits were *real*. And they are *mine*. These doctors, lawyers, and engineers, these business-men and -women, these romantics, adventurers, and gamblers, they are *my* ancestors. Imagine—tales of triumph, travel, achievement, danger, romance, and unrequited love—in my own family. Each detail is like a single note dropped one by one into what had been just a great, gray stillness. They begin to find each other, link together, swell like a symphony, surging and pouring forth. I ride the crescendo, crescendo . . .

"What happened to this one?" I ask my mother, pointing to one face.

"Killed," she says.

Silence.

Someone has switched off the music.

"And that one?"

"Killed."

This is the dark overarching awareness lurking, ever-present, behind the sparkle, the retroactive vicarious pride, the *naches*.

"And your grandfather, Leib?"

"Also killed. Shot by the Germans on the second day of Hanukkah, 1942. They came to deport him and found him in bed, ill. He refused to get up and leave with them. They shot him on the spot."

The conjugation of death:

"He didn't survive."

"She didn't survive."

"They didn't survive."

A shiver runs through me. And I realize: I'd actually thought I could get away with it. I'd thought I could interview my mother, take down some family history, preserve some cute "Hallmark Family Special" stories to regale the grandchildren with. I thought it would be quick, clean, simple. Even fun. And then I could run like hell, so fast the demons would never notice I had been tip-toeing around the periphery of their uneasy slumber.

What was I thinking? Was I so out of touch? Or just so desperate? How do I plead: Temporary insanity? An extreme case of wishful thinking? A folie à deux—my mother assuring me that her story is "no big deal," certainly nothing traumatic, and me wanting so much to believe her?

What's becoming clear is: The demons are stirring. The story has started growing. It's swelling, mutating into something dark and ominous. It's overwhelming my little yellow sticky Post-it Notes, darkening page after page of legal paper. We have obviously veered off the delicately calligraphed path and are lurching toward a gathering darkness.

Then: reprieve. It's time for my parents to return to New York. I tuck the memory book back in a drawer, all my scrawl-covered yellow sheets stuck between its printed pages.

Chapter Three

My reprieve lasts several months, until my parents' next visit. During that time, I struggle to understand how I've allowed myself to get sucked back into something I had hoped, even believed, that I could put aside, put to rest: the Holocaust. How could I have been so naïve?

I can no more easily put aside my legacy as a child of survivors than someone can change the color of their skin. Of course I didn't *always* think about it. I still don't. But it's always there. Like relatives who materialize only at holidays, births, and funerals. Something you just know. The way you know the smell of your own sweat.

I can't remember when I didn't know that my parents were Holocaust survivors. A cliché, for sure, but true. It's strange, the way I put it: a double negative. Not: "I always knew I was a child of survivors." Rather, that there was never a time that I didn't know. As though, if I worked at it long enough, I could part that darkness, that awareness of a strange and shattered past, and find something before it. Or besides it. Something light. Something easy. Something else.

But that was not to be. By second grade, I already knew how to get a powerful reaction, a sharply indrawn breath, kids around me drawing back in awe. All I had to do was mention, offhandedly, "My father was in The Camps." It was spooky. I didn't do it often. I still hate bringing it up.

Of course, that "power" came with a price tag: I—we—were different. From our neighbors in the working-class Highbridge section of the Bronx where I grew up. From my New York cousins, second-generation Americans, who seemed more comfortable in their skins, on their streets. From anyone who didn't grow up with parents and grandparents murmuring to each other in Polish so we kids wouldn't understand. (It was a good way to learn to understand Polish though, as I did—in self-defense, though I couldn't speak it.) From anyone who had four grandparents, two matched sets. I knew I was lucky to have any grandparents at all: my mother's parents.

My father hadn't been so lucky. His entire family had been wiped out: his father, his mother, his two younger brothers, his sister. They were all murdered, but not before having been humiliated and terrorized and starved for years. The Horror Roll in my house: Warsaw. Treblinka. Majdanek. Budzyń. Wieliczka. Plaszow. Flossenbürg. And finally, Theresienstadt. He survived slave labor. He escaped being executed by firing squad by the skin of his teeth. Then he lost his teeth when a German officer, enraged by the discovery that my father shared the same birthday as Der Führer, heaved a wooden stool into his face. What he's seen, heard, smelled, and touched would be anyone's worst nightmare. A catalog of nightmares.

My father was primarily responsible for The War being almost another member of our family. (The term *Holocaust* was around, but we didn't use it. For us, there was only The War.) Almost inevitably, he's the one who brings almost every conversation, every situation back to The War. The last meatball on the platter would set the stage for re-enacting the struggle for survival during the days in the ghetto. He'd push the meatball at me.

"You take it," he'd insist. "I can always get something cold from the fridge if I'm hungry."

I wouldn't want it, smothered with the sauce of memory: how his younger brother Shlomo snuck bits of his own miserable sliver of sawdust-bread into his mother's tiny piece so she could live just a little longer. Please, Dad, just eat the meatball.

Once, I asked him to show me how to plaster some holes in my hallway. We slopped gobs of plaster of Paris over the scars in the walls.

"This is a relaxing job," he said, scraping the putty knife evenly across the hardening white mound, first down and then across. Then, in a quiet, musing tone, he added, "The Germans used to seal the mouths of the prisoners with plaster so they wouldn't scream when they were sent to be gassed. They were still alive."

So much for relaxing.

Growing up, Life with Father wasn't all blood and death. It was also color and passion, creativity and temper, discipline and spontaneity. When I was little, my father used to take me with him to his art studio at 232 East 40th Street in Mid-Manhattan. I loved those visits, the shivery fear and delight of the subway ride, clutching tight to his hand amid all those pounding, rushing, flying feet. I loved the special lunches he would treat me to. Best of all was rummaging through the tumbled piles of crayons and pastels in his studio, holding rainbows in my hands. I loved the way scraps of paper of every color cascaded over the old blue daybed, spilled onto the floor like a chaotic mosaic, were stuck to the wall by silver pushpins where they shimmered like an exhibit of tropical butterflies.

My father would set me up at one of his two drawing tables, adjust the long-armed fluorescent lamp, put all my necessary drawing supplies within reach. For entire magical afternoons, I would draw, emerging at the end smiling, trailing clouds of pastel dust, scraping rings of paint from my fingers, brandishing yet another creation that was sometimes framed, and always saved.

Meanwhile, it was my mother who took me and my brother Barry, three years younger than me, ice-skating, to the movies. She made sure we learned how to swim, a brave move for someone who was almost phobic about putting her face under water. (As a child, she'd almost drowned when some well-meaning cousins tossed her into the local river; they hadn't believed her when she said she couldn't swim.) She hemmed our clothes, sewed our Purim costumes, and tested us before exams. She and her parents hardly mentioned The War. They were committed to transmitting the essence of the *life* they had left behind: European culture and etiquette. How to dress like a lady: white kid gloves and black patent leather shoes. How to hold a knife and fork properly, the European way. (American spies in wartime Europe had been caught and shot for getting this wrong.) Piano lessons, at our mahogany baby grand piano, purchased by my parents from George and Libby Silverman, next-door neighbors whose daughter Debbie had outgrown it. My grandmother, simply and neatly dressed, her thin reddish-brown hair held in place with rippling black bobby pins, practiced with me almost every day. Sitting beside me on the piano bench with its green-and-white cross-stitched cover, my grandmother would point to the time signature with her soft hands and their carefully manicured oval nails to help me keep track of the beats per measure.

Down in their small apartment one floor below ours, my grandfather loved to sit on the couch or in one of his armchairs, close his eyes, and listen to WQXR, New York's classical music radio station. Often he would sing quietly along with the music, his right hand gently arcing back and forth in soft movements, keeping time, conducting along with the piece. He'd often hold his hand up suddenly, for attention, and would ask me: "What's this piece?" And when I got it right, when I could tell Bach from Beethoven, Mozart from Mendelssohn, he would smile, delighting in my musical ear.

My grandparents didn't work, and lived very frugally. They must have scrimped from their disability pensions to treat me, every year, to two performances: Arthur Rubinstein performing at Carnegie Hall, and one grand opera at the Met. I remember the thank-you notes my grandfather wrote, in his feathery script, in his very formal English, to various box office agents who had helped him procure seats for these performances. Many years later, I would realize that they had probably just been doing a routine job, mailing him those tickets, but he greatly appreciated their help and made sure to tell them so.

And there was one unusual bit of American culture that somehow snuck into this European atmosphere: my grandfather's devotion to the New York Mets, despite the fact that we lived on Jerome Avenue in the Bronx, within earshot of the roars exploding each season from Yankee Stadium just a few blocks away. He never went to a game, his health did not allow for that, but he followed his team's exploits faithfully, watching the games on TV and listening to the radio broadcasts with the same rapt attention he gave to Brahms and Chopin, keeping track of the scores in a cardboard-backed notebook.

Behind the triumphant chorus of Beethoven's "Ode to Joy" and my prized 33 RPM recording of "How Much Is That Doggie in the Window?" was another soundtrack: scratchy Yiddish melodies, sad and otherworldly, broadcast by WEVD, "the station that speaks your language," to which my father was addicted. And the syncopation of my mother's resigned tones, imploring—eyes rolling, head shaking, shoulders slumping in anticipated defeat—"Morris, please! Not again!" when my father, talking Yiddish to some crony, would start in again: "*Gedenkst?* Do you remember?" The War was always there, crouching in the shadows, sometimes bursting out with a roar, sometimes snuggling down with a sigh.

Until the late 1970s. This intensely powerful, intensely personal Thing was suddenly blasted into the headlines, promoted to Psycho-Socio-Cultural Phenomenon. A seminal article by Helen Epstein made it official: our parents were Survivors, and we, their offspring, were Children of Survivors. We even got an official title: "The Second Generation."

Epstein's story appeared in the *New York Times Magazine* on Sunday, June 19, 1977. I remember the date because that was the day I married Chaim Zlotogorski, himself a child of survivors. I laughed at the timing of the piece, wondering what kind of omen it was, and asked my mother to save the issue for me before I ran off to get ready for my wedding.

At the time, I was in the first year of my doctoral program in clinical psychology at Long Island University in Brooklyn, New York. I was acutely aware of the debate raging between therapists, survivors, and us newly named "children of survivors": Had we been traumatized by our parents' experiences? Or had we emerged stronger, "hardier," more well-adjusted than our non-Holocaust-related peers?

As a fledgling psychologist and a daughter of survivors, I could take my pick of the proffered roles: therapist/patient, examiner/examinee, experimenter/subject. For each argument, I could serve as prosecutor, defense attorney, witness, and defendant.

Each side had merit and could marshal data and arguments to "prove" its position. However, I had already learned that what you believe can and does influence your data, even with supposedly objective measures. With so much emotional baggage attached to each position, so much riding on the outcome, I thought it unlikely that any definitive conclusions would be reached for a long time.

In this maelstrom, I formulated my own conclusions:

I doubted that I would be able to maintain clinical objectivity if this material came up in my practice. Not yet anyway. I decided to keep my professional, psychological world separate from my Second Generation world as much as possible. I never took on survivors or children of survivors as clients.

On the other hand, I believed that as a child of survivors, it was my duty to accept the burden of transmitting the legacy of my parents and other survivors to the world. So for the next five years, from 1977 to 1981, I was a "child of survivors activist," focusing on educational and communal activities. I served on the steering committee of Second Generation, a New York organization that ran commemorative, educational, and social programs as well as support groups—kinship groups, we called them—for children of survivors. I lectured on the "Second Generation" experience to civic and religious groups and in schools, and was interviewed on television and radio. I helped organize and eventually presided over the Second Generation program at the First World Gathering of Jewish Holocaust Survivors, an event that brought together over six thousand survivors and their children from Israel and around the world for four emotional days of reunion and remembrance in Jerusalem in June 1981. I also helped found the International Network of Children of Holocaust Survivors at the conclusion of that same Gathering.

Over and over in the kinship groups, children of survivors spoke of their sense of liberation. As they aired and shared long-suppressed secrets, theirs and their parents', it was as though they, too, were emerging from the closets and garrets and cellars and camps, all the places of hiding and death transplanted from Europe into their souls by well-meaning, still-mourning parents. They cried while recounting their parents' pain and their own. The tears turned to laughter as they realized that they were among people who not only knew what they were talking about but could match them, story for story, shtick for shtick. This newfound sense of kinship was heady, healing stuff. It was as though, after bobbing about in glacial waters, they had been thrown life preservers that were towing them back to warmth, to life.

In my naïveté as a budding psychologist, I believed in the power of catharsis. I hoped that my immersion in the Holocaust would somehow free me, through some dramatic climax like those you read about or see in movies, from the darkness that floated at times like a gray film around my family. But I did not reckon with the effects of sensitization and secondary traumatization, the fact that coming in contact with such charged, difficult material could itself be traumatizing. Talking about the Holocaust, hearing about the Holocaust, even trading sick Holocaust jokes with other children of survivors, did not liberate me from its influence. On the contrary, the more I dealt with it, the more it invaded my days, my dreams.

I still thought it was important for children of survivors to transmit the legacy of their parents, but I no longer wanted to be the one doing it, not "professionally" at any rate. I didn't want the Holocaust to be my life. There was more to my identity as a person, as a woman, as a Jew, than that of "Survivors' Daughter." And I didn't want to be perpetually involved with other "professional children of survivors."

After the World Gathering ended, I retired from what Chaim and I sometimes sardonically referred to as "Shoah business," never to return to it again. For both of us, it was time to move on, time to explore the rest of our Jewish identity, to build a family, and ultimately, to cast our lot with the Jewish State in Israel.

So how did I end up here, preparing to interview my mother about That Time? What was I doing now, tiptoeing toward the gates of Survivor Territory, teetering at the brink of this abyss?

I had thought I knew what I was doing. I thought I could stick to my narrowly defined path, illuminate just enough of the way to stay safe, and steer clear of the darkness I had sought to keep at bay all these years.

I was wrong.

It's like the time I went cross-country skiing. It was my second or third time out and I was bored with the beginner's trail meandering round and round the flat, snow-covered golf course.

I wanted a little more excitement, some snowy, dreamy vistas like those in a Robert Frost poem. Surely I could handle the intermediate track by now.

I found myself careening down a slope that seemed—to my terrified beginner self—geared to an Olympic downhill racer. It was a narrow tree-lined strip of road, one-lane wide. My instructor's voice sounded in my ears: *If you can't control the skis, just lean over and fall down.* That had sounded easy enough. Except that if I did that, surely I would be smashed into pulp against the trees on either side. I had no choice but to hunker down for the duration. I tucked myself into a tight crouch and bent low over the skis, the way I'd seen it done in the movies. I flew down the trail, the hard snow crackling below me, the air whipping into my face. My stomach was one big knot. After a few hours of what probably was a few seconds, the ground began to level and then even out, and I gradually slowed to a halt. I was still on my feet. Shaking. Proud of myself. Scared to death. I decided then and there: I'd never do that again.

Now I am doing exactly that again, without skis, without snow, with the same knotted gut. And again, there is no way out but through.

Chapter Four

It's time to continue. But not with the memory book. It's taken me—us—as far as it can.

During our last session, I'd skimmed it, finding the pages that coyly invited us to trip through my mother's adolescence. I'd read out one caption to my mother:

"My teenage years were: _____*,"*
and perched brightly with my pen poised over the three lines meant for her answer.

She said, "I don't remember ever being a teenager."

It was as though steel bars had clanged down.

My mother was a teenager, was fourteen in 1939. How could I have thought these elegant italicized questions could be relevant to the history we are exploring? The murky gray territory I am entering mocks the soft pastel shades of these pages, mocks me and my naïve wishful thinking. Sarcasm, like acid, wells up in response.

How are we supposed to complete this question: *My favorite foods were:*_____

    Do I fill in: *"anything edible"*?

Or this: *The fashion rage at the time was:*_____

    Do I write: *"a six-pointed Star of David on an armband"*?

So I have tucked the memory book back into my filing cabinet. My mother and I are on our own now. We'll have to navigate this uncharted terrain together. I'll have to be our guide.

Hey, I tell myself, *I'm a psychologist. I've interviewed people before. I'll just do it again. I'll pay close attention to what she tells me, and to my reactions to what she tells me. Just as I do with clients.*

Only this is no client.

This is my mother.

I usher her into the garden of my house and we sit across from one another at the white plastic picnic table, under the tangerine tree, its branches heavy with fruit, still green. A strong late autumn sun shines down and gently warms the edges of the breezes that rustle the leaves from time to time. My mother's lips and chin are lit by the sun, but her eyes are in shadow. I watch the dappled light and dark play over her face. Her eyes remain shielded by the softly moving silhouettes of the leaves. I think of how weak her eyes are, and I'm glad they're protected, in the shade. I want to protect her. Yet I'm about to dig into her past, into that darkness, to bring it back, to bring her back to it.

I balance my small tape recorder carefully on the tabletop. The table perches unsteadily on the uneven flagstones of the garden, and I don't want the tape recorder to fall over and break.

"You know," I say, working to keep my voice steady, neutral, as I reach for the record button. "I have mixed feelings about this. I really want to hear what happened to you, because if *you* don't tell it to me, no one will. But I hate bringing these things up and making you think of them again."

She shrugs.

"Let's go," she says.

Summer 1939 was a thrilling time. Martial music blared from every radio. Hearts thumped like patriotic drums. It was like the hundred-plus voices of the Metropolitan Opera Chorus thundering "*Guerra!*" in the opening act of *Aïda,* row upon row of gilt-armored chests heaving in proud, passionate unison.

"Everybody was very patriotic," remembers my mother, sitting up straight in her chair, tucking her chin in, like a soldier. "On the street, in school. All those fancy speeches on the radio! 'The Germans will *never* defeat the Polish Army!'" Her voice curls over "never," a whip snaking through the air. "The *glorious* Polish Army!" she amends, scornfully.

Lutka's father, a medical officer in the army, brought his uniform home and tried it on. She was jealous; if only she were a boy and could go with him! But she was stuck at school, sewing gas masks, day after day, after classes let out.

"You stitched together precut pieces of yellow flannel," she tells me, demonstrating with a couple of tissues pulled from the cellophane package on the table. Folding them into narrow strips, she lines them up carefully and exactly, explaining that "you stitched very carefully along predrawn lines, and you had to make sure they were *even!*" Even for my mother, herself a master of precision, the irony of the exactness required for these samples of stitched futility is too much, and her voice cracks with retroactive derision. "That's why you had to use a special foot on the sewing machine. Then you filled them with some sort of stones, like charcoal, that were supposed to absorb gas. There was a strap to tie over your head; they were supposed to cover your mouth and nose. We had to work like that every day after school, for two, three hours, for about a month, on those masks! During summer vacation! When they were all talking about the war." She pushes the tissues away from her.

"Nobody saw a single mask when the war broke out. When the bombs started falling, nobody knew what to do and nobody even thought about those masks. I don't know what happened to them. *I* never received one; I never saw one after that."

Everyone talked of war but no one believed it was going to happen.

Toward the end of that summer vacation, Lutka even traveled with her mother to Brzeżany, her parents' hometown, for the annual visit to her paternal grandfather, Leib Rosenberg. "My father said, 'Go, and if something happens, you'll come back.' It was so naïve: you go, you come, the war is someplace else."

Her fingers trace patterns on the tabletop, stray to the discarded tissues, fold and refold them.

I venture, quietly, "I guess it didn't seem real."

"I don't think anybody had any idea how strong, how well prepared he was." "He," of course, being Hitler. "All those fancy speeches on the radio. And the Polish government even hosted a delegation of German ministers who came to Poland to hunt. Can you imagine?"

I must look puzzled because she hastens to explain.

"Poland has very dense forests, east and north of Warsaw, famous for their wild animals, wild boars. So that summer, he sent his prime minister to Poland, to hunt, and he was received! They invited him! They let him in! In the summer of '39! So we thought, well, if they are coming to hunt, there isn't going to be a war!"

I think: *Obviously no one realized that Polish wild boar was only the appetizer.*

On September 1, 1939, all these illusions were shattered with the first air raids.

"The Germans were bombing us and shooting at us from their warplanes. By the time we heard the air raid sirens, the planes were already practically above us. I remember running with my mother and grandmother from our apartment to the park across the street to hide in the bushes until they passed by. We figured that being outdoors was safer in case a bomb hit the building and it collapsed. Nobody knew what they were doing. They were running, so we were running. You grabbed whatever you could— I grabbed my dog—and ran. Half an hour later, two hours later, the planes would be back. So we'd run back to the park." Josef reported to his unit in Lwów, as ordered. But the glorious Polish Army, hopelessly outmatched by the Germans, was falling apart at its meticulously sewn seams.

My mother starts laughing. "By the time my father got to his unit, there was nothing there. They didn't even know where to set up the army hospital. Everyone started running, to protect his own skin."

Anyone who could, deserted. "Officers, generals, they packed their wives, they packed their stuff, they took their cars and ran. Not the plain soldiers, some of whom didn't even have boots. I'm talking about the big shots. They were fleeing to Romania. You see, the Germans were coming from the west, the Russians were coming from the east, so they started running south to Romania, then through Romania, through Bulgaria, even to the Middle East. Some of them even got to London. That's how you got the Polish government-in-exile in London."

The officer in charge of Josef's unit suggested that he run away with them as well. But Josef wouldn't hear of leaving his wife, his daughter, and his mother-in-law behind in Żółkiew. He was returning home. "Well," they said, "then, be careful. You might be shot before you get there."

The uniform Lutka had been so jealous of now threatened her father's life. His medical insignia would not protect him from vengeful reprisals by either the Russians or the Germans. He buried the uniform, traded his officer's boots with some peasant for civilian clothing—"I don't even remember if he had shoes or not," says my mother—and began walking. It took him several weeks to get home. He arrived tired, sick, very hungry, painfully thin.

In the meantime, the Germans had occupied Żółkiew for almost a week, from September 18 to 23, 1939. Then, on September 24, under the terms of the Hitler-Stalin Pact of 1939, the Germans withdrew and the Russians moved in, beginning an occupation that would last two years, until June 1941.

I realize that I'd never thought about those first two years of the war under Soviet occupation. How narrow my focus has been. Now, with her words, it begins to widen. Her narrative continues matter-of-factly; my tension abates slightly. Maybe this won't be so bad.

"What was life like under the Russians?" I ask.

"Well, I was going to school. I *had* to go to school," my mother tells me, her tone implying that this should be obvious. "It was the same school as before, a state school. Some of our teachers remained, some were arrested and shipped away, some ran away, and we got some new teachers. And there were changes in the curriculum: Poland was out and Russia was in. We didn't learn Polish history or geography anymore. Now we learned *Russian* history and geography. We made maps of all the Russian republics, showing each one's industry, natural resources, topography. We also learned Russian, although the language of instruction in my other classes was still Polish. This they didn't deny us. Nobody wanted to study Russian; it wasn't patriotic. I actually didn't mind learning Russian, I even enjoyed it as a language, but I didn't learn that much since I'm always too shy to speak any language that I learn. We also still learned Ukrainian—I never liked Ukrainian—we had been learning that for years. And I think we still learned German at that time.

"The Russians put a lot of emphasis on sports and ran sporting competitions, *Spartakiada*, between schools and cities. They coached us. They taught us how to start and how to pace ourselves in order to save energy for the end of the race. They even gave us shoes with cleats. I participated in some of those events. My best event was the hundred-meter dash. And I also did the long jump and the high jump."

I'm visibly impressed, and she must see that because she adds, "I think I have something about this in Grandpa's papers. I found something when I was going through his desk after he died. I'll have to look for it and show you," she says.

"Did Grandpa continue to work?" I ask.

"Well, the Russians nationalized all the businesses, including my father's drugstore. At first, they allowed him to continue working there, but as an employee. Later, they transferred him to another pharmacy a little farther away from the center of town, on the corner of Lwowska and Turyniecka Streets, and made him the assistant to a Ukrainian pharmacist. At some point, we moved into an apartment above that pharmacy, which we had to share with the Ukrainian pharmacist because he came from Lwów and needed a place to live in town."

"How was it to live under the Russians?"

"Not easy. They took over two rooms in our house and we had Russians living with us until the end of their occupation.

"I was always scared of the Russians, because we lived under the threat of being sent to Siberia every day while they occupied us. Before the war, Poland had been very anti-Communist. And how! The Communist Party was illegal. Now, when the Russians came, all of a sudden some of the local population openly became communists. They had been suffering before, and now they tried to better their own position by insinuating themselves into the local government, by simply denouncing others as "rich" or "bourgeois." If your name was on one of their lists, the authorities could come and round you up at any time and ship you off to Siberia.

"They would come at four o'clock in the morning, knock on the door, and say, 'Out!' Sometimes they gave you half an hour to pack a suitcase. Sometimes they didn't even give you that."

"Why did you think that they would ship *you* away?" I ask.

"Because my father had a drugstore, we were considered bourgeois, not "proletariat," not "*robochy narod*," working class. So we were afraid we were on the list. One young guy, a communist, came to my father once or twice and warned him that we may be shipped. To Siberia. He said that he had seen our names on one of the lists. He tried to warn my father. I don't know what he thought we could do about it. There was nothing we could do. You couldn't move from one city to another just because you wanted to. You needed a place to live and a permit from the police. So my father just ignored the warning. He must have thought, Whatever happens, happens.

"My father warned me, 'This is the situation. We may be shipped away, so when you go to school, be prepared that when you come home, we might not be here. So have some clothes in your schoolbag. Just in case.' That way, you'd have clothing either to wear or to trade for food with the local population on the way to Siberia or once you got there. We'd learned this from letters we'd received from people who'd already been shipped away.

"I always carried a full change of clothing in my schoolbag. In the winter, I wore my ski boots, and two pairs of socks, and two sets of underwear, and a sweater. I had another sweater in my bag, and some food in case they took me out of school."

How would I feel if I had to send my teenage son to school not knowing whether I'd still be there to welcome him home at the end of the day? What would it be like for him to cram his backpack with spare clothes alongside his homework assignments and notebooks, to sit in class and listen to his teacher, all the while wondering what was going on at home, whether his family was still there, or whether they were being shipped to Siberia?

Yet is it so different from the way I live today? I send my kids off to school in the morning and wonder: What if they pass the local coffee shop just as some Palestinian terrorist decides to detonate himself at that spot? What if my walk to the grocery coincides with some Arab's attempt to make a political statement and earn himself, as he thinks, eternal salvation and sexual satisfaction by blowing himself up on the city bus rumbling past? Who will make it home in one piece today instead of in shreds? But I do send them off to school, and I do the shopping. Just as my mother loaded her schoolbag with homework assignments and "survival gear." I guess you get used to everything.

I push that aside and proceed matter-of-factly, methodically, searching for new angles to probe for information, to jog my mother's memory.

"How did your grandmother handle all this?" I ask.

"She died on January 22, 1941, after falling and breaking a hip. She was sixty-seven years old. I had just turned sixteen one week earlier."

This is the grandmother I am named after—my middle name, Laurel, after Laura Majblum Schenker. I was born on January 22.

"My grandmother was buried in the Lwów cemetery, near her husband. I didn't go to the funeral; I was never at a cemetery before the war."

Many people have qualms about including children in funeral rites. To this day, some parents—superstitiously, it seems to me—send their kids out of the synagogue when it's time to recite Yizkor, the memorial prayer for the dead. Not taking my mother to her grandmother's funeral: Was it simply the custom? A matter of logistics? Was she still being protected from death? My mother has no explanation; that's just the way it was. To me it seems particularly ironic, given how the world around her was slowly, inexorably, metamorphosing into one huge cemetery that would shortly engulf her.

"My mother sat shiva at her brother's house in Lwów. That was my uncle Manek. She was heartbroken. She had been very close with her mother. For her it was the end of the world."

"What was it like for you, when your grandmother died?"

"I missed her. She was my beloved grandma. But at least she didn't go through living under the Germans. She missed that part. Good for her." Her tone is defiant.

"When did the Germans occupy your sector of Poland?"

"On June 22, 1941. The Germans attacked the Russians, their so-called allies. At the beginning of the war, they had made a deal with the Russians, and gave them this part of Poland. Hitler wanted Stalin to feel secure and keep quiet and not join the United States and England, so that he—I mean Hitler—could do what he wanted to do in Europe. So he made this deal with Stalin for as long as it was convenient for him. And Stalin believed him. I was surprised because one crook and another crook shouldn't believe each other. But Stalin was fooled.

"We lived very close to where the Germans attacked, over the border near the River San, one of the big rivers that flows into the Vistula from the southeast. The Russians tried to bring in reinforcements, but Hitler's army was much more powerful, and the Russians were pushed back. It didn't take long. Before you turned around, the Germans were there.

"Some people fled with the Russians and some did not. And it was amazing: even though they had the chance, some of these newfound communists did not choose to run away with the Russians, after having lived under them for those last two years."

"And you did not retreat with the Russians."

As if I could still change history.

"We did not."

"Did you have a choice?"

Do I sound too accusing? I don't want her to think I am blaming her for not having suspected what was coming. For not having changed the course of her life—and mine.

"Technically, you did not have a choice. The Russians didn't ask you to go with them. People just tried to flee to the east, away from the Germans, even before the Russian army retreated from our town. Some were caught by the Russians, accused of being spies, and sent to Siberia. That was the chance you took. The Russian commandant of the town who used to come to our drugstore encouraged my father to pack and leave. He may have meant only my father, and not the rest of us, because everyone thought that maybe the men might be imprisoned and forced to do hard labor, but who would harm women? And children? But my father didn't want to leave. They didn't ask me for my opinion."

"What was your opinion?"

"I don't know," she answers. "In any case, my parents decided to stay. Whatever will happen to everyone else, will happen to us."

"What did people think would happen?"

"I don't know," she says again. "People were scared. I was scared. Of everybody."

Is this the same girl who had once declared, eyes flashing: "I wasn't afraid of anything, not dogs, nothing!"

"For two years I had lived under this terror that the Russians would send us to Siberia. So after living like that for so long, I thought—and many people did—that maybe it would be better under the Germans. Sure, we may have to do forced labor, maybe they'll beat some people up, like they did when they were in our town for that one week at the beginning of the war. They'd cut the beards off some of the old, religious Jews—"

"During that one week?"

I think: How much havoc can you wreak in one week? My mother sets me straight.

"During that one week. They sent some people to work, they beat some up, but at least they didn't kill them on the spot. So people said, 'Well, that's better than being sent to Siberia.' And after all, the Germans are very *cultured.*" Her face twists. Then she adds: "Aren't they . . . ?"

Her voice trails off.

I think of my grandparents and of how important culture was to them. It was everything good and exalted in life: poetry, music, literature, art, opera, philosophy, and manners. How could culture, German culture no less, countenance mayhem? Condone murder? Commit murder?

I feel helpless. My sympathy, my recognition of the irony, is all I can offer. It's no protection against the past.

"Once the Germans took over, it was complete chaos. They were constantly issuing decrees. Every day, there was a different order. Jews couldn't go here, couldn't go there, couldn't do this, couldn't do that. There was no more school. There was an ordinance that whenever a Jew passed a German on the street, he had to take off his hat and get off the sidewalk.

"One day, my father was walking on Bazylianska Street. I don't know if he didn't take off his hat fast enough, or if he didn't get off the sidewalk fast enough. But two German soldiers knocked him down and beat him, breaking several ribs. The injuries never healed properly."

She looks at me quizzically.

"Don't you remember how one side of Grandpa's back was higher than the other? And how he couldn't walk fast?"

Of course I knew that my grandfather walked slowly, that he often paused for breath, that he tired easily. But I thought that's just how grandfathers were. I thought they all walked slowly, deliberately, gravely. Especially European grandfathers. I never realized that his being at home, his not working, his having time to teach himself Italian from home-study textbooks and shortwave radio broadcasts, to surrender himself to classical music on WQXR, to devote himself to his beloved New York Mets, even the way he moved—all this was the result of beatings during the war, all this was his dignified way of living with constant pain. Now, hearing my mother's question, I feel like a fool. How could I not have known this before? Was this naïveté, or unconditional love?

"The Germans ordered the Judenrat to "assess" everyone. Several times. We had to turn in everything of value. Gold. Silver. Jewelry. Money. Personal objects, religious objects, like our candelabrum. In the winter, when the Germans were fighting on the Russian front and freezing to death, they demanded all the fur coats. Whatever they demanded, you had to give. You were buying your life.

"We had to turn in our radios. My father had bought a new one a year before the war, a Philips, I think, from Holland. We brought it to the municipal building next to the *Glinska Brama*, the gate near my school. A few days later, somebody told my father that he had seen our radio smashed on the ground behind the building. They had thrown them all out the window. They didn't even use them."

"So, if you had no radio, how did you find out what was going on?" I wonder.

"Some people had secret radios and would listen to Radio Free Europe, the London broadcasts. There were also German broadcasts. But I don't remember the broadcasts because we had no radio anymore."

"So you couldn't even hear their propaganda?"

"No, no. Nothing. Because if you could hear one, you could hear the other."

"No newspapers either, then."

It begins to sink in: how cut off you were from sources of reliable information, from the outside world, and how much I take for granted.

"And there were no more newspapers, only the German paper, and a Polish paper that reported only whatever the Germans allowed it to say. You only heard one side of the story: theirs. And they were always winning. Even toward the end, when they started withdrawing from the Russian Front, they kept insisting that they were winning and that they were retreating only for 'strategic reasons,' to 'straighten the front.'"

I appreciate her sarcasm. It offers a tiny respite. A bit of relief.

"So you learned to read between the lines."

She nods.

"Where were you living under the Germans?" I ask.

"In that apartment above the second drugstore on the corner of *ulica* Lwowska (Lwów Street) and Turyniecka. We shared it with the Ukrainian pharmacist, and with another pharmacist—a Jew named Stoekel—and his wife. Each family had one room. I slept on a couch. The kitchen was someplace in the middle. Everybody used it. There was also another tiny little room as you entered the apartment. I don't remember who slept there, but I know it had a bed in it because once, in the beginning of 1942, some German soldiers came to the apartment for some reason and I was sitting on the bed and hiding my dog under the covers. He didn't like soldiers any more than he liked doctors. I was afraid he'd growl, try to bite them. I was afraid they'd shoot him."

My eyebrows arc upward.

"You weren't afraid that they'd shoot *you?*"

"No, the *dog!*" My mother laughs. I join in, shaking my head. It figures, knowing my mother.

"Did he behave?"

"Yes."

"What happened then?"

"The soldiers talked with my parents and then left. I never knew what they came for."

The tape recorder clicks off. I stand and stretch. My mother's been talking steadily for a while now, so I suggest that we take a break. Carrying the tape recorder, we go inside the house to make ourselves a cup of tea. As always, she yanks her tea bag out of her cup after only a couple of dunks, "before it gets too strong," she says.

"That's not tea, that's *pishvasser!*" It's an old routine, and one that still makes us laugh. She reaches for the pitcher to add some cool water to her cup, so the tea's not so hot. While we sip, we chat quietly, about the kids, about my work, about how the rest of her visit to Israel has been going. She gives me regards from the friends and relatives—almost all survivors—that she and my father have been visiting, all of whom I've met over the years. I'm struck, as I've been so many times before, at how well they have maintained contact with all these people. But they are each other's family now.

My mother remarks, wistfully, that the visit is passing so quickly, and I nod, my insides tightening. I could raise the idea of their moving here yet again, and the words rise to my lips, but I catch them, swallow them back down. *Leave it,* I decide. *Just stay on track for now, bring it up another time.*

"Ready?" I ask.

"Ready."

We decide to sit inside now. As my mother settles herself in her seat, I bring in a new yellow legal pad and some pencils, freshly sharpened. Jotting things down while I listen helps me stay focused and keep the details straight.

I turn the tape over and slide it into place. One click, and we're back in War Time.

Chapter Five

My mother marks War Time temporally and spatially: before or after the ghetto was established. Inside or outside its boundaries. She's not sure when she and her parents actually moved into the apartment above the second pharmacy but knows it had to have been by the spring of 1942, when Jews could still live where they wanted, were still allowed to get together, as she did with her friends.

"I used to visit my friend, Muszka Zimmerman, that summer, when she still lived down the steps near the Ukrainian church. She was twenty-one, four years older than me. I don't even remember her real name, because everyone called her Muszka, which means a little fly, because she was so petite. Her parents owned a little villa near where we used to go skiing when I was little. Muszka and I worked together in that garden."

"What garden?"

"When I worked for the Germans, growing vegetables for them."

My mother's tone is so matter-of-fact. She takes it for granted that I already know that she did forced labor for the Germans. But this is the first I've ever heard of this.

"Tell me about that," I ask, speaking matter-of-factly in return.

"This was in March 1942. The Germans decreed that everyone had to work. The Judenrat sent me to work at a house on Lanikiewicza Street. This was a very nice street beyond the Zwierżyniecka Gate."

I take careful notes, making sure to get all the spellings correct. Does just about every Polish word have a *w* or a *z*—or both—in it?

"Before the war," she tells me, "the sports club, the Sokol, had been located there, as well as the post office and the military barracks, *koszary*, where our division of the cavalry kept their horses. Oooh, I loved watching the horses parade down the street." And I love watching her face light up as she remembers the horses. Her whole carriage shifts, she straightens unconsciously, as though she, too, is perched on a prancing steed, cantering smartly down the avenue in full view of the admiring crowd.

"Many prominent people lived along that street as well, both Jewish and Christian. During the war, the *Ortskommendantur*, the German military command for the Wehrmacht, kicked out all the Jews living on this street, and set up their headquarters in a two-story villa there.

"We worked from about eight o'clock in the morning until four or five in the afternoon. For the first two or three days, we had to clean chickens and geese. It was the first time in my life I ever did that. Plucking chickens wasn't so bad, but ducks and geese were hard. My fingers hurt.

"Then the Germans decided they wanted to have fresh vegetables every morning. They could've gotten them from the surrounding farms, but no, they wanted their own. So a group of about twenty of us, only young women, were ordered to set up a garden for them on the grounds of one of the houses along the street that had been under construction and had never been finished. My friend Muszka was in that group with me.

"This was in the early spring. For a few weeks, we cleared the stones, turned over the earth, hoed and raked and prepared the beds for planting. A local Polish gardener, Koszycki, supervised us and selected the vegetables we were to plant. Before the war, he had owned a plant nursery near the edge of town. I remember he had one eye.

"Once everything was seeded, the Germans decided that only a small group should continue working in the garden. One of the officers was in charge of supplying the kitchen with provisions. He was in the Wehrmacht, not the SS, which was a little bet-

52

ter. But I still thought of him as a vicious dog. He also had one eye—the other was glass. He liked my friend Muszka; she was very pretty, with a very nice face and blue eyes. He asked her to choose those who would continue working there. She picked me and another three or four girls and he put her in charge of us. We were responsible for maintaining the garden, weeding, watering the garden—the well was nearby—picking the vegetables, cleaning them, and bringing them to the cook."

My neck prickles at hearing how this officer liked Muszka, the pretty, petite one. I'm afraid, almost embarrassed, to ask, but I do:

"Were you ever worried about some kind of sexual attack from this officer?"

"Yes, I was. But nothing happened. As it turned out, we were lucky to have a steady job until the end of the summer. The others had to report to the Judenrat every day and were always being assigned to different places.

"You know," she continues, "after the Russians retook the town, I never went there to see what happened to that place. Would you believe it?"

I can. I can understand never wanting to go back there, wanting only to put it all behind her. Nostalgia could come later, as the sharp edges of experience are—sometimes—smoothed and softened by time, distance, and safety.

"What about the rest of your friends? Did you see them?"

"We could still meet at each other's houses. About ten to fifteen of us would meet at my friend Rozia Fisch's house. She lived across the street from us, in a very small apartment. Once— I was probably about sixteen and a half—we were all there, and someone had one cigarette and everyone was trying to smoke it. That was my first and last try at smoking cigarettes."

As she grimaces at the memory, I am transported back to my own first—and last—puff. I was probably about six. I entered the living room to find my father lounging on the black-and-white tweed couch after some guests had left. Everything about the scene was unusual: my father rarely lounged—he was too charged up for that. And he also never smoked. Yet there he was, puffing contentedly on a cigarette taken from the pack left behind by one of our guests.

Seeing my intense curiosity, he beckoned me over. Smiling, he asked, "Want to try?" Of course I wanted to try. It looked so grown-up, so special, who could resist? He held it to my lips. The next thing I remember was hacking my lungs out, tears spurting from my eyes, and my father laughing.

Imperceptibly shaking my head to clear it of the smoke of memory, I bring myself back to the present and take a moment to decide which thread of the story to follow. I'm still trying to get at what my mother thought, and particularly, how she felt *about everything that had been happening, but that's proving elusive. She insists that she doesn't remember. That may be, though whenever I reread these pages and prepare the transcripts, I am struck by how much she does remember. But when I tell her so, she brushes off the compliment. This fits, because her style is not to mull things over, as I do. She is much more matter-of-fact: deal with something, and move on. Finished.*

I wonder: Does she really not remember what she had thought then? Is she just disregarding it because it doesn't seem important enough to bother with? Does this reflect her mode of survival: not thinking too much about anything, just keeping her head low and trying to stay out of sight?

Maybe I can get more information if I inquire indirectly, the way I sometimes try to find out about my son's day at school by asking how his friends are doing, hoping that would net me more than a monosyllabic "fine."

"Did you talk about the war with your friends?"

She shrugs.

"We did talk about it, but who knew what would happen? We were all scared. Once the Germans started rounding people up and shipping them away, people were saying, 'we could've been in Russia, we could've run away.' Could've and could've, but we didn't so we were stuck. And later, even when we knew what the Germans were doing, there was nothing we could do. We were just waiting and hoping: maybe young people would have a better chance of surviving than old people. Maybe they wouldn't catch you, not this time. Maybe you'd make it through another month. Maybe the war would end. After all, how long could he hold out against America and England and Russia, against all these countries! How can he survive? Well, he managed very well! He almost accomplished what he wanted!"

Her voice rises sharply, cutting into the stillness cradling us. The edge in her tone is unusual, so different from her usual mode of simply and quietly relaying the facts. It also dissipates just as quickly. I feel the air stirring around us and settling back down.

These are the sounds of preserving history: the hiss of the tape recorder, the click of one tape ending, another tape snapping into its place. Chairs creaking, bodies shifting, voices rising and falling.

"When was the ghetto established?"

"In December 1942."

"Was there a wall?"

"No wall. Just a fence all along. We didn't have a high wall. We just knew where the Jewish quarter was and that was all. The building where we now lived, above the second pharmacy, was on the corner of Turyniecka and Lwowska Streets. The Germans made that corner one of the borders of the ghetto. Until then, Jews lived all along both sides of those streets. But now the buildings along one side of these streets were inside the ghetto, and the other side of the street was outside the ghetto.

"There was a terrible commotion. People who lived in houses on the wrong side, outside the ghetto, had to move. So they moved all over, grabbing whatever space they could find, wherever they could squeeze in.

"I lost touch with almost everyone. You couldn't keep track of where anyone moved unless you bumped into them. I can't even remember if I knew where all my friends from my class went. I did manage to stay in touch with one of my friends, a boy named Jozek Taub. Jozio, we called him. But I completely lost contact with my friend Rozia. I didn't even know where she and her family ended up living. We had very little contact with anybody. I didn't go inside the ghetto area much. I didn't even know how far it extended. Anyway, we didn't go out much. Nobody did. We tried to stay home, to be off the streets and out of sight as much as we could, because we never knew when they'd come in and round up people. Everybody was so absorbed in surviving another day.

"Many people just disappeared. People ran away from the ghetto and hid in the villages or in the forests, joined partisan groups. Some apparently went into hiding in the town, although I didn't know it at the time. Some were taken away. Some ended up in work camps. And a lot of people were sick with typhus. Many died of that. You didn't know who was where, who remained, and who didn't. It was chaos."

I feel confused and disoriented. The street names swim together. I keep losing my bearings, struggling to grasp how the ghetto area was demarcated, which corner, which side of the street, which buildings. Is this a reflection of my mother's experience: the chaos, the disorder, people being shoved and thrust from place to place, appearing, disappearing?

My mother tries again, patiently, to explain, to create some order.

"The *buildings* along one side of these streets were inside the ghetto, but the *sidewalks* in front of the buildings were considered outside the ghetto. Jews were not allowed on them anymore. To get from house to house, we had to walk through the yards behind the houses—every house had a yard, with gates or openings from one to the next.

"So we were no longer allowed to walk in front of our own building. But the Ukrainian pharmacist was allowed to enter and leave the building through the main door. After all, that's where the pharmacy was. And Christians continued to come to the pharmacy.

"Maybe because of the pharmacy and the Ukrainian who lived there, our building was sort of excluded from the ghetto. That's what saved us, later. Maybe the Germans didn't even realize that there were Jews in the building. The Polish and Ukrainian police certainly knew, but somehow, they left us and the other Jewish couple sharing our apartment, the Stoekels, alone."

"What happened to them?"

"I don't know."

"Did you have food?"

"We were not starving. We got some food by selling off some of our possessions, some small pieces of jewelry or items like linens. There was a black market in the ghetto. Poles, peasants, would sneak things in to trade with the Jews."

"What did you do in the house all day?"

"Nothing. You just sat there. Just passed another day and another day and another day. We just stayed upstairs. The Ukrainian pharmacist let us stay in our room. We were lucky that he didn't kick us out. We tried to stay as invisible as possible so the police or the Germans wouldn't remember we were there and force us into a more interior part of the ghetto."

I hear a commotion: The garden gate slams. Voices. Footfalls on the flagstones, in the entryway.

"I think the boys are home," I say, reaching over to switch off the tape recorder.

"Ah!" my mother sings out joyfully, beginning to rise.

Before she's fully on her feet, the door bursts open. Yonatan and David, home from school, throw their backpacks down in a heap and swarm all over my mother, pushing her back into her seat. She hugs and kisses them, and they're all three talking at once.

"How was your day?"

"Look at this, Grandma!"

"Are you staying for lunch? Can we play a game?"

"You know how much homework I have? It's not fair!"

"Will you read to me?"

She laughs, she clucks sympathetically—she also had tough teachers, only hers were stricter!—and of course she's always ready to play a game or read a book. They run to get their selections and my mother follows them out of the kitchen. I move our things out of the way, the tape recorder, the mugs, the pad on which I've been doodling and scribbling notes. In a little while, I'll have to pick up Yehoshua from kindergarten. In the meantime, I start to prepare lunch to the sounds of voices excitedly chattering and giggling in the other room.

Chapter Six

The following morning, I putter about the kitchen, washing the cereal bowls, wiping the placemats, straightening out the messes left in the wake of the preschool rush. I feel ripples of tension in my belly and try to reason them away. It hasn't been so bad so far, really. No horror stories, just like she promised. Nothing to be nervous about. Okay, so today I am going to ask her about the Łozińskis, the Poles who hid them. I don't know what to expect. Or how she'll handle it. But she's been fine so far, calm, her usual "Just the facts" self. It should be fine.

My mother arrives, hangs her coat on the tall red coat-tree in the hallway, kisses me hello, and seats herself at the table. I pour us each a mug of tea with its splash of milk—"British style," as my father calls it (though my British friends would beg to differ). And continue to fuss about the kitchen, aware of stalling, of not being quite ready to settle down. I move more dishes around, straighten out papers. I put a fresh tape in the tape recorder, check the batteries, draw the legal pad closer to myself. My mother waits quietly. Finally, I sit down. Take a careful sip of my tea, feel the sharp warmth biting the back of my throat, feel it flowing down my throat and into my belly, and breathe it out in a silent sigh. I reach for the tape recorder.

"Tell me about the Łozińskis. Who were these people, and how did you get to them?"

"My father knew him," my mother answers. "He was a retired railway official."

"How old was he?" I ask.

"He was in his eighties—"

"Even then?" I burst into her speech. This is so different from what I had been expecting.

"Well, at least in his seventies. He was an old man. At least, that's how he seemed to me, like a very, very old man. He was retired, for many years already. His wife was much younger. She was probably about sixty. We found out later—when we were already sitting there—that she came from Brzeżany, where my mother and father came from, and she remembered our family, my grandmother, my mother. My grandfather too, because he was a lawyer, well-known in town. And it was a small town. How they met each other, I don't know."

"What did he look like?"

"I think he was a little bald but he had gray hair, a-round face. He wore glasses. I guess he was probably about my father's height. He was a very pleasant person."

"What were their first names?"

"His name was Emil. Hers was Maria."

"But you never called them anything but *Pan* and *Pani*, Mr. and Mrs.?"

"Of course not."

"Of course not," I echo, muttering to myself. "How silly of me."

I know full well the rigor of Polish etiquette. Always address people in the third person, except when speaking to very close friends or family, or children. I am just testing limits here, to see if close confinement in hiding might have softened those iron-clad linguistic relationships. It did not.

"Did they have any children?"

"They had no children."

"No relatives?"

"Well, she had a sister, and a Volksdeutscher brother-in-law. They still lived in Brzeżany."

"What's a Volksdeutscher?"

"A Pole of German descent."

"What was your connection to Łoziński?"

"We knew him, because he was practically a fixture in my father's drugstore, the first one, the one on the *rynek*, the town square. Łoziński was friendly with another Jewish man, also retired, whose name was Berger. Berger and Łoziński used to meet every day at my father's pharmacy. There were chairs inside the pharmacy where people could sit and wait for their prescriptions. These two guys would come in around noon, sit down, and discuss politics. They always had something to discuss.

"My father sometimes got upset. He said: 'These guys are sitting there and talking, getting into heated discussions, and people coming for their prescriptions don't want to hear that.' Sometimes he'd ask them to go outside, so they'd stand in front of the pharmacy and talk."

"Did you know Łoziński too?"

"I knew him too because I'd see him at the pharmacy when I'd stop in to visit my father. You see, often when I would go for a walk through the town with my dog, I would stop in to say hello to my father and get some candy from him. He had these hard clear honey candies that I liked. He kept them in a big glass jar on the counter. *Slazowe cukierki*."

"What does that mean?"

"*Slazowe* means soothing, and *cukierki* is candies. They were some kind of cough drops, made of honey and something else. They looked like little square pillows. I always got one, and my dog Jock got one. He loved them, too."

These are some of the sweetest memories she can share with me: her marching proudly across town, her dog trotting at her heels, visiting her father's pharmacy, crunching cough drops between her teeth, feeling confident, on top of the world.

And, interestingly, cough drops seem to hold some intergenerational status in my family: if I concentrate, I can still conjure up the sweet-bitter hardness of the dark, oblong lozenges my grandparents used to give me when I was little. These days, my mother is the Cough Drop Lady, supplying our stash of Luden's cherry and honey-lemon cough drops in response to my kids' plaintive telephone entreaties to Grandma to save them from their current epidemic of coughs, earnestly reproduced over the long-distance telephone line.

"If Łoziński was in the pharmacy, I would say hello. But I didn't know him well. More people knew me than I knew them. I didn't pay attention to older people."

"How did it come about that you were hidden by them?"

"Because we knew a big *akcja*, a big roundup of Jews, was coming. There had been several *akcje*: one on November 22, 1942, and one before that during the summer of 1942 that we called 'the wild *akcja*' because it had been so violent. During that first one, we had hidden in the cellar for a whole day and only came out in the evening, after dark."

I am, once again, confused.

"What's an *akcja*?"

I mimic her pronunciation carefully: "Ahk-tsyah."

"A roundup of Jews."

"Wasn't it called an *Aktion*?"

"*Aktion* is German. *Akcja* is Polish, that's what we called it. *Akcje* is the plural."

"And which cellar are you talking about now?"

"The cellar of the building on the corner of Lwowska and Turyniecka, where we now lived, where the second drugstore was. Every building had a cellar where people stored potatoes and fruit for the winter. Anyway, after that last *akcja* in November, my father asked Łoziński if he would permit us to hide at his house for a day or two during the next roundup. Łoziński said he had to talk to his wife. He came back a few days later and said, okay, we could come over if we had to, but we would have to be very careful."

"What did you think would happen after that *akcja* was over?"

"I don't know what we were expecting would happen after that, that the ghetto would survive forever? I don't know. Everybody thought they would have some warning that the Germans were planning something, either because you heard that the Gestapo was coming—which always spelled trouble—or because someone you knew in the Polish police might tip you off to "be careful," so you could hide. Nobody imagined that this time they would clean up the entire population of the ghetto."

"Why should you have suspected anything worse than another raid?"

"Because everything the Germans said was a lie, and by now we knew it. When they started taking people away, in 1942, they said they were resettling them in work camps in the East. In the beginning we didn't know what to expect, so that was different. We thought the Germans were only rounding up people who didn't have ID cards and putting them to work. Nobody had any idea that they would be murdering them. At first. But then you start to think, logically: Why would they be 'resettling' old people? Or sick people? Who do you take to work, young people or old people? Where is the logic?"

She pauses, sighs.

"How naïve and stupid we were."

I hate it when she is so hard on herself, as though she should have known better. How obvious everything looks in 20/20 hindsight. Her harsh, self-disparaging tone grates on me, probably because I also feel helplessly angry that there was no way for her to have known what was coming, and no way out even if she had.

"Are you saying that by the time you went into hiding you should have known it would be for more than just a few days?"

"No. I don't know what we expected."

"Well, what do you think you'd have done differently if you had known you'd have to be in hiding for the next year and whatever?"

"I don't know," she replies, shaking her head. "Probably wouldn't have gone anywhere. Or maybe we'd have tried to run away. To the forest or something. Łoziński certainly wouldn't have agreed to hide us for such a long time. His place was not the right place for a long stay. Or maybe because it was not the right place, it was safer than some of the others."

"Because nobody expected anyone to be there?"

"I guess so. Actually, people were hiding everywhere: in barns, under the straw, in lofts, under sheds. The cows and animals were on top and the people were hiding underneath."

"Did you discuss going into hiding with your mother and father?"

"Yes. Yes. My father told us that he had spoken with Łoziński and he had agreed that we could come over, in an emergency."

"What was your mother's reaction?"

"She was afraid to leave, but my father convinced her that there was no other way. You either wait for them to come and get you, or you try to do something. And I said I wouldn't go away by myself."

"What do you mean, 'go away by yourself?'"

"One of our maids had wanted to take me with her and hide me. This was Kasia, the Ukrainian maid with the braids, the one I had always liked to watch as she got ready to go out on Sundays when I was little. This must have been before the ghetto was closed, when she could still come to see us. She knew already that people were being grabbed from the street. They all knew where people were being sent.

"I still don't know how she thought she would save me," she continues, her voice rising slightly. "Where would she stick me, in a village full of Ukrainians, when I didn't speak Ukrainian? Where everybody knows each other and here she comes with me? What would she say, 'This is my niece?' What was she going to do with me, keep me under the bed? Or maybe put me in the stable, with the animals. I don't know what she had in mind, how she thought she could save me.

"My mother thanked her and said she'd think it over and Kasia left. My parents were not sure what to do." Her tone is sharper. "Of course they weren't sure. They wanted the best for me. Maybe going with Kasia would save me. But I said, 'I am definitely not going with her.' I didn't distrust *her*. But I did not trust her husband, a Ukrainian, because I didn't know him at all. And going to a Ukrainian village was risky. Although some people did survive that way, many Ukrainians helped the Germans, and turned in Jews. And that was *my* decision," she concludes, her voice ringing out.

My mother's unusually strong declaration catches me off guard. So often I've felt frustrated at my inability to get at how she felt, what she wanted. And yet, now that my mother gives me a glimpse of her decision-making process, I feel guilty. What if my

questions seem to imply anything amiss in how she held herself
together in the midst of that murdering madness? This was not some
assertiveness drill. This was a matter of life and death. Compared
to that, my queries shrink into insignificance, and my efforts feel
weak and insipid.

In our next session, several days later, we again settle back into
our spots at the round table in the kitchen, with our customary
mugs of cooling tea, the tape recorder once again propped close
to my mother. The pages in the yellow legal paper in front of me
are filling up with names, carefully recorded in neat print block
letters. As additional backup, I transcribe them into the computer
immediately after each session, using the Polish language program
to capture that language's unique accents.

I feel a tremendous sense of responsibility to get the names
right. Not because of some need for perfection, although I do share
this Germanic, *yekke*, trait with my mother. And not out of fear
that some linguistic misstep could instantly identify me as Jewish
and get me killed; those days, thankfully, are over. No, this is my
way of paying respect: to a world that is no more, and especially,
to people who are no more. This is the only gravestone they will
ever have.

We pick up the thread of the story with the Łozińskis and
their decision to allow my mother and her parents to seek refuge
in their house during the next German roundup, if necessary.

"When Łoziński told us he would take us," my mother explains,
"we packed a small bundle with the few things we thought we
would need for a few days in hiding. Then, one evening, before
curfew, I took the bundle and left through the gate to the building, which was the drugstore gate. You see, our building, like all
the buildings, had gates we kept locked from the inside, for our
own protection. We didn't want anyone walking into the building
uninvited, particularly the Germans and the Ukrainians. When I left
the house to deliver the bundle, I unlocked the gate with our key
and walked out onto Lwowska Street."

Her voice is very quiet, her words slow and measured.

"It was about a fifteen- to twenty-minute walk. I had to be
very careful that nobody saw me. Luckily, it was still winter, and

it got dark very early, so I could still be out before curfew. And it was cold, so there weren't many people around. Still, I took a risk." At the word *risk*, her voice rises, almost breaks. "I *knew* I took a risk."

I am almost breathless, listening. I hate suspense, even when I already know the end of a story.

"I didn't go through the center of town, through the town square, because one of its sides was the border of the ghetto. I took a route I had never gone before, through side streets, which the Germans didn't usually bother patrolling at night anyhow. I just hoped I wouldn't meet any soldiers.

"The Łozińskis knew I would be bringing some things over, although whether they knew I was coming on that particular day, I don't know. This was the first time I met her, Łozińska. I didn't stay long; I ran back, to get home before curfew, so I shouldn't get caught on the street. Because nobody was allowed on the street after curfew, not just Jews, but even Poles. I think I went twice. Yes, I went twice."

"Did you wear an armband?"

"I didn't wear it. I took it off."

"With a yellow star?"

As I speak, my mind is already painting a picture of tattered yellow stars, stitched loosely onto armbands, slipped over coats.

"We didn't have a yellow star. We had a white armband with a blue star."

I'm startled. My mind's eye quickly erases the initial images and redraws the amended version.

"It was just an outline of the star, not a solid blue star. The band had to be a certain width. It couldn't be too narrow, or too wide. Yes, it was a prescribed width, maybe ten centimeters wide. And it had to be clean, it shouldn't be dirty. It shouldn't look like a rag." Her lip curls with sarcasm. "And it had to be visible. I don't remember if we wore it on the left arm or on the right arm."

"You had to make this yourself?"

"Everybody made them by themselves."

"What did you make the blue out of?"

"You either took a very narrow strip of blue cloth and stitched it on, or you embroidered it. I think I embroidered it."

"Embroidered it! Like you monogram a towel?" My voice cracks.

Like cross-stitched linen tablecloths? His and Hers terrycloth robes?

"Yes," she answers. "I used the chain stitch, I think. Yes. The chain stitch. In blue thread. It was just the outline, that blue. Not a solid. Just the outline."

I imagine: A snowy-white piece of fabric. The sharp point of a needle suddenly piercing through, stabbing upward like a shark's fin breaking the froth. A row of tiny blue loops, evenly spaced, tightly worked, marching upward on a slant, turning smartly, marching downward . . .

"You mean the same stitch you used to put my name on my gym uniform in high school?"

"I don't remember what I did for you in high school."

But I do. In ninth grade, girls were required to wear gym uniforms, silly little royal blue one-piece outfits with short sleeves, elastic waists, snaps down the front, and ballooning baggy shorts. Like abbreviated bloomers. Our very first gym assignment that year was to embroider our names on the breast pocket. As if it wasn't enough to wear the damn thing.

I didn't know how to embroider, so I asked my mother for help. The next morning she presented me with the finished product: my name swooped and soared in pure white chain-stitched perfection over the flap of the pocket.

I was awestruck. And uneasy: it was too beautiful for such a ridiculous outfit. In the shark-infested waters of my competitive, cliquish class, it was risky to stand out, and this was too perfect to be missed. This was an era when possessing a skill like needlepoint marked you as hopelessly bourgeois, when taking school rules about gym uniforms seriously stamped you as irrevocably "square." Besides, it wasn't cool to be anything but at war with your parents; but my mother's love was stitched there for all to see. I felt exposed.

"Anyhow, I didn't wear it. I left without it."

"Did you have identification papers on you?"

"I had nothing on me. . . . I couldn't have any papers on me."

"What were you supposed to tell them if you were stopped?"

"I don't know what I was supposed to tell them if they caught me. If they caught me, they'd either ship me somewhere or shoot me."

She's so matter-of-fact.

"Were you scared?"

I'm *scared just listening to her.*

"Sure I was scared. But there were no people out, and it was a dark night. I was moving in the shadows. I took back streets to get home. I didn't know exactly what street I was on, but I knew where I was going. The town was not that big."

"How did you choose what to take with you into hiding?"

"We only took a few things. The package had to be small enough to carry, and be inconspicuous, and besides, we knew we'd only be there two or three days. We packed some clothes, and some things that the Łozińskis could exchange with the peasants for food, like linens, tablecloths, pillowcases. You couldn't buy those things anymore, and the peasants were very anxious to get the stuff that the city people had."

"Were these things meant as payment for the Łozińskis?"

"No, no, no." She is adamant. "We didn't pay them to hide us. He didn't demand any money, and we didn't pay him. He agreed to take us for the few days without any payment."

"They didn't ask for any payment?"

I want to make sure.

"They did not ask for any payment."

She is sure.

"Did you pack anything sentimental?"

"I don't remember taking any photographs, because if I did, I would probably still have them."

"What about books, or diaries?"

"No."

"Or stuffed animals?"

"No, I never owned any. I had many dolls when I was little, but no stuffed animals. I just always had my dog, Jock."

"What about him?"

"He wasn't alive anymore."

"Why? What happened to him?"
"He had died; he ate rat poison."
"When?"
"I don't remember."

I wonder: What would I take with me if I had to go into hiding? My mind begins to hum, setting a stage, building a set, peopling it. . . .

Dusky maroon curtains part heavily and swoosh to the wings, revealing a small bedroom. The lighting is dim, amber-hued, cast by a small lamp on a little table off to the left. A drab blanket hanging on small rusty metal nails conceals a small window, the outlines of which can just be discerned. To the right is a bed, piled with a variety of men's and women's clothing, obviously worn, in shades of brown and black. Next to the pile is a stack of white tablecloths and sheets folded neatly. In the somber darkness of the room, the linens seem to glow. A small valise lies open on the bed.

To the left of the stage, on a small easel, a white placard reads: Winter 1943.

Two women enter from stage left. One is young, an adolescent, of medium height, with dark hair cut in a short, curly style. She is wearing a long woolen skirt, a blouse under a thick sweater, stockings and sturdy shoes. She strides purposefully across the room. She stops to survey the bed and its contents carefully, hands on hips, her head cocked to the side, biting her lip in concentration. Her name is Lutka.

She is followed by an older woman, slightly taller, with light brown hair, dressed casually in slacks and an oversized sweater. She enters the room somewhat hesitantly, watching the younger woman closely. Her name is—why, it's me, my middle-aged self, meeting my teenage mother.

> DIANE, *speaking almost to herself*: What would I take with me, if I had to run away? (*She stands, thinking, her brow slightly furrowed.*) Ah! (*She nods.*) I know what would be really important to me. Photo albums.
>
> LUTKA: Don't be ridiculous, they're too big. And too heavy. (*Her tone is distracted, and somewhat dismissive. She's only*

half-heartedly paying attention to the question right now; she's too busy studying the items in front of her.)

DIANE: Maybe just the negatives, then. I save negatives, in these non-PVC folders, more or less in order, just in case something happens to the originals.

LUTKA: This is 1943, Diane. Those things don't exist yet, remember? We only have a handful of photos anyway. *Mamusia* is such a stickler for those.

DIANE: *Mamusia?* Oh—you mean Mother. I remember.

LUTKA, *nodding*: Yes, that's right. Anyway, she's always saving things. You obviously take after her. She always wanted me to keep things for sentimental reasons: ticket stubs, lists of books I've read. I never did. I was too busy playing with my friends, skating, skiing.

(*As she speaks, she is striding toward the bed. With quick movements, she selects a sweater, pulls it over her head, works to settle it properly, comfortably, over her hips, under her armpits, around her neck. She chooses another one and sets it aside, near the pile of clothing.*)

DIANE: What about a notebook? To write things down, like a diary?

LUTKA, *reaching for an article of clothing and beginning to fit it into the valise*: I'm not a writer. That's my father's department. (*She stops in mid-movement, shooting the older woman a quick, sharp glance.*) What do you think is going on here, anyway? This is a war, not a writing class.

DIANE (*her face flushing*): I'm sorry. I'm just trying to understand. Too many Anne Frank movies . . . (*Her voice trails off.*)

LUTKA (*frowning*): Who? (*She shrugs.*) Oh, never mind. (*She resumes putting things in the valise.*) Look, it's only for a few days. We've had these *akcje* before. They're terrible, but then they're over and life goes back to normal. (*She laughs, harshly.*) Some normal. But maybe, if you stay out of the way, and are lucky . . .

(*As she speaks, she sits down, pulls off her shoes, pulls an extra pair of socks over the stockings she is wearing, shoves her feet back into her shoes.*)

I can hardly move, I'm so bundled up. Good thing it's winter and still so cold outside. Otherwise, I'd melt. As it is, I'm sweating.

DIANE: Aren't you scared?

LUTKA (*Her chin juts out.*): I'm not scared of anything. Not dogs, not anything. (*Her voice falters a bit.*) Well, I never used to be. (*Then, recovering somewhat.*) Anyway, there shouldn't be many people around. It gets dark early now and it's too cold and dark for anyone to be out. Lucky for me. Otherwise, I'd have to wait till later and then I'd be breaking curfew and that would be too risky.

Pass me those tablecloths over there, would you? (*Diane bends down, gathers up two or three and hands them over. Lutka lays them carefully in the valise.*) Mamusia told me to take them. Maybe they can trade them to the peasants for food. We sure don't need them. . . . (*She strokes them with her fingertips, smoothing them into place.*) Aren't they beautiful? I remember the dinners we used to have, with my aunts and uncles and cousins and friends all around the table, and all that delicious food. . . . My grandmother was a marvelous cook. And a great baker. She'd make the best cake—my favorite. Just for me.

DIANE: I'm named after her, you know. My middle name. Only they named me Laurel; someone told them it was more American than Laura.

LUTKA: Well, she was wonderful. She used to sleep in my room. She had a trunk full of old-fashioned dresses she'd brought with her from Brzeżany when she came to live with us. I used to try them on. Her waist was so tiny that I could never fit into them even when I was little! Like this, her waist was! (*She curves her fingers into a circle in front of her.*) Look at my waist now! (*She laughs, poking at the padded layers of clothing. Then she sighs.*) I miss her so much. But I'm almost glad she's dead. I'm glad she can't see what's happening now. This would kill her, for sure. She'd never be able to take this, running to hide in a hole in the ground like some hunted animal. (*She folds some of the sheets and pushes them into the valise, but it's filling up and it's harder to squeeze things in. She struggles, getting frustrated.*)

I *hate* this. I *hate* the Germans and I *hate* the war and I *hate* running away and I *hate* packing! (*She punctuates each* hate *with a sharp jab into the valise. Sweat beads up on her forehead and red splotches appear on her cheeks.*)

DIANE: What else do you need? What about personal stuff, like toiletries?

LUTKA (*Stops abruptly, stands upright, and stares at her.*): Toiletries? For what? There's no toilet! You really don't get it, do you? Look, this is not one of those assignments in school: "What would you take with you to a desert island?" We've been living like animals for years now. All those things you're thinking of, they don't exist anymore. There's nothing left of anything. You're talking about luxuries. We don't have the most basic things. Do you know how long it's been since I've had a bath, a real bath, not just wiping some damp rag on my face and arms? Or some new clothes, something that fits, and that's really clean, and not mended and mended over and over? (*She thrusts out her arms. Her hands and wrists jut out past the ends of the sleeves by several inches. She yanks at the skirt, holding it up so the many places where it has been mended are apparent.*)

DIANE (*She holds up her palms in a gesture of appeasement.*): I'm sorry. I'm just trying to understand. The things you're talking about, I've never lived them—

LUTKA (*interrupting*): Well, you're lucky—

DIANE (*She continues speaking, barreling through the interruption.*): I've just read about them. I keep trying to imagine what it would be like.

LUTKA (*She stops shoving things into the suitcase, straightens up and looks at the older woman, frowning.*): Why? Why do you want to? You should be glad you're safe, and clean, and none of this is happening to you. Isn't it enough that I have to go through this? What do *you* want to get into this for?

DIANE: I'm not sure. I *need* to understand. Maybe to understand you better . . .

LUTKA (*speaking brusquely*): What's to understand? We're in a war. They hate us. They want to kill us. It's simple. Only— (*Her voice falters, becoming softer, more tentative.*) I don't really understand it either. What do they want from us? We never did anything to anyone. Sometimes I get so mad. I hate them. (*Her voice hardens, becoming more intense though she doesn't raise the volume.*) But it's not just the Germans. You think the Germans would know who's Jewish and who isn't, unless someone told them? And who tells them? Our own neighbors. People we've known for years. Otherwise the Germans would have a much harder time finding us. (*She looks around secretively, and lowers her voice to a loud whisper.*)

I know I shouldn't be saying this, but sometimes I even hate being Jewish. In Hebrew school, they taught us that we were the Chosen People. Ha! Why doesn't God choose someone else for a change? (*She leans down, pressing hard on the lid of the valise and forces the snaps shut.*) There! I'm ready. This is full and I can't carry any more. (*She struggles into her old coat, buttoning it as she speaks.*) I've got to go. You stay here. It's too dangerous for two of us. You stay where you are, safe. I have to go by myself.

The scene fades and I'm back in the present. But the scene lingers. It felt so real. I remember my questions and squirm. How silly, how naïve I sound. Still, only by entering into the fantasy do I become aware of how many preconceptions stand between me and my ability to grasp what my mother went through.

When I think of packing, it's for trips, or summer camp. (Though I can hardly bring myself to say "camps" anymore.) Whenever I travel, I promise myself that this time, I'll travel light. And I mean it. And then I start tucking in: Band-Aids. A flashlight. A box of matches. A spare bottle of water. A sandwich. All kinds of "Just in case" stuff. It's like the Boy Scout logo—which really speaks to me: Be Prepared. Some survivor must have made that up.

When I think about it, I realize that real security doesn't mean having everything you might ever need, like Mary Poppins's magic carpetbag (oh, for one of those!). Real security means knowing, down to your bones, that you can make do without, and that you'll be okay no matter what happens.

From out in the garden comes the metal clang of the front gate. Footsteps approach. My father's voice rings through the open window.

"Where are my girls?" he sings out. He's spent the last few hours with some of his cronies, fellow survivors all, talking and reminiscing in *mameloshon*, literally, the mother tongue, meaning Yiddish, giving my mother and me time alone for our work.

My mother gets up to greet him and I start clearing the table. I pull close to me the shoebox housing my growing collection of sixty- and ninety-minute cassettes carrying my mother's voice, her story. Each clear plastic cassette case is dated, in permanent black marker. Before sliding today's cassette into its case, I label it carefully and snap off its tiny recording tabs to make sure nothing can be accidentally erased.

Chapter Seven

"You know," I say to my mother, the next time we sit down together, "we should go to Poland."

"What for?"

"To see your town."

"It's not in Poland anymore," she corrects me. "It's in the Ukraine."

"Okay, so the Ukraine."

She grimaces.

"Well, wouldn't you like to see Żółkiew again?" I keep pushing.

She says yes. Her tone says no.

"What's the problem?"

This is not the first time I've brought up the idea. In the early 1980s, she had accompanied my father on his first trip back to Warsaw.

"What about Żółkiew?" I had asked back then. She refused. She was afraid. What good would her American passport do her if the authorities decided to make trouble?

"What trouble?" I'd asked. My naïveté is born of my faith in the American Way and countless recitations of the Miranda ruling on "Law and Order." But my mother has lived through a crucible that reduced naïveté to ashes. The effects of two years under the Soviets, four years under the Germans, and sixteen months under a floor are still etched deep into her nervous system. Her fear outweighs her wish to revisit her hometown.

I dropped the subject.

In 1989, the Berlin Wall came crashing down. Several years later, so did the Iron Curtain.

"Now can we go?" I asked.

"No."

I dropped the subject again.

Now it's 1994. Still more time has elapsed. And now that we are in the thick of this emotional archeological dig, I bring up the idea of traveling to Żółkiew again.

"Wouldn't it be amazing to actually see the place again?" I ask. *And I would love to see it with my own eyes, not just what's refracted through hers.*

I can see the longing in her face. But she is still leery.

"It's not safe," she says, her tone determined. "Not if we traveled alone. I don't trust them."

"Don't trust *whom?*"

"The Ukrainians. The Poles." She's getting edgy just talking about it.

I drop the subject. Again.

In the meantime, we continue to haunt the sites in our minds, her words transporting us back to wartime Żółkiew.

It's February 1943, the dead of winter, and the fleas are thriving. No matter how hard you try, no matter how often or how diligently you check the wooden frame of the bed or the seams of your clothing, cornering the tiny, light-colored creatures, cracking their shells between your fingernails, there are always more. Biting you at night. Sucking your blood. Spreading typhus.

My mother ventures into the interior of the ghetto to visit her friend Jozio, one of the few people whose whereabouts she knows. He was just recovering from typhus. Back home, to her horror, she discovers fleas on herself. Are they carriers? If they are, there is nothing to be done. The disease takes two to three weeks to incubate. Only time will tell if she has caught the dread disease.

She did.

"You develop a high fever," she tells me, "over one hundred and three degrees Fahrenheit, and you get pink spots all over your body. That's why it's called *tyfus plamisty; plama* means spot. Sometimes you lose consciousness or develop a brain infection. In the ghetto there was no treatment. You either got over it or you died. For many, it was probably a blessing to die of that rather than what came later.

"Luckily, my parents didn't get it," she continues. "They took care of me. I think they had one of the doctors in the ghetto come and check me, although there wasn't much anyone could do for me. My father had nothing in the pharmacy to give me.

"We kept my illness secret from the Ukrainian pharmacist we lived with; we were afraid that he would throw us out, because it's very contagious. It's a good thing we didn't have much contact with him.

"I was sick for weeks. I got over it only two, three days before we ran away into hiding. The day we went into hiding was the first time I was on the street, out of the house, since I'd gotten sick.

"That day—it was March 25, 1943—we were awakened at five o'clock in the morning by screams, loud noises. We ran to the window and saw the Germans chasing people on the street in the direction of the Christian cemetery. It was terrible. You didn't think about anything. You just wanted to get away, to hide. If you could dig a hole under the floor and hide, you probably would have.

"We couldn't go out anymore. We couldn't even go to the bathroom, because the outhouse was across the backyard where the fence was all open, and if you left the building you would be seen by the soldiers alongside the fence, who were standing there and grabbing people. The only thing we could do was run up to the attic. The building had a pointed roof, supported by poles. We squeezed ourselves behind some of the poles, behind some boxes that were up there, and hid.

"At one point the Germans entered the backyard of the building and asked the Ukrainian pharmacist, 'Who lives here?' And he said, 'I live here, this is my drugstore, and I'm not Jewish.' He didn't tell them about us, although he knew we had to be in the building. He saved our lives. Because the Germans left without searching the building."

"Do you know why he did it?" I ask.

"I don't know." She shakes her head, and shrugs. "Maybe he just didn't want to be the one to betray us."

"Did he have a good relationship with you?"

"It was mainly a professional relationship with my father.

"When it got darker and a little quieter outside, we came back down to our room, and this Ukrainian told us that the Germans had been there, looking for Jews. He had been able to save us because the ones searching the building were members of the Gestapo and didn't know who was Jewish. 'But,' he said, 'the Polish and Ukrainian police are helping the Germans, telling them where the Jews are. *They* will know you are here. You are not safe and you have to get out.' So we had to get out.

"That's when we went to the Łozińskis' house. We were lucky it was March, and that at six o'clock it was already dark. And curfew was shortly after that. We left right before curfew. We left in two different directions. We split up: my father going one route, my mother and me walking a different way, staying in the shadows, until we reached the house. I don't remember who got there first, my father, or us. And we couldn't enter the house. The door was locked, they were not home, and it was dark."

"And this was after that whole day of shooting," I prompt.

"After that whole day of shooting. And it was not over, because the Germans continued the next day. They didn't do it at night, but over the next few days they continued liquidating the entire ghetto. At first they kept I think about sixty to seventy Jews alive to go through the ghetto, digging for God knows what the Germans thought the Jews had left behind, and then they killed them too. Some on the spot, others they shipped away to camps and they were killed there. And a few, I found out later, managed to run away."

"And you had to wait—"

"We had to wait in the outhouse, which was attached to their house. We knew that since it was night, and after curfew, he must be away. We didn't know where he is, we had no idea when he would come back, or *if* he'd come back. We didn't know anything. We had gone there because we were hoping he would keep us there. And here we arrive and it's locked. We knocked on the door a few times, but we were afraid to call out, in case the neighbors would hear us. And we were afraid we'd be seen, three people standing in front, so we went into their little outhouse and hid there. It was the only thing open. We locked it from the inside and stayed there."

"Can you describe the outhouse?"

"It was squeezed between their house and the tiny shed next to it. It was just a shack with a big, big hole in the ground and a bench with a hole in it, over the hole in the ground. That was the toilet. The three of us had to fit in that shack. One person could sit on the board on one side of the hole in the board, and another person on the other side, and one person had to stand.

"We stayed there all night. The next morning, Łoziński still wasn't there. In the afternoon, a neighbor's son came along and knocked on the door of their house, and there was, of course, no answer because they weren't home. Then he came and stopped in front of the outhouse and called his name. I guess he thought that if Łoziński was not in the house, maybe he was in the outhouse. When nobody answered, he walked away. Luckily he didn't try the door.

"We stayed there till the evening. In the evening, the Łozińskis arrived."

"Where had they been?"

"They had been in Lwów. It turned out that she had had an operation on her eye; she had cataracts. They were away for a few days, and that day he brought her home, with a patch over her eye. Because they had been away, they hadn't realized what was happening in town. They only found out when they got back.

"We saw them coming into the house; they were also hurrying to be home before curfew. We waited until it got very dark, and then we snuck out and knocked on the door and he let us in. And we were very glad to get inside the house, I can tell you that.

"They gave us something to eat. We had had almost nothing to eat for almost a day and a half. When we had run out of our apartment, we were hiding a whole day in that attic, and I think we had some bread or something with us, and we ate that. And then at night we ran to the Łozińskis and hid in the outhouse all that night and all the next day. So we were hungry. And we were cold. It was March and the outhouse is outside, and the wind blows right through."

"Did you go right down into the cellar, or did you stay upstairs?" I ask.

"No, we didn't go down at night. We stayed upstairs. There was a couch and I think it opened, and my parents slept on that, and I slept on blankets on the floor.

"We only found out over the next few days what had happened to everyone else. We had seen the Germans pushing people in the direction of the Christian cemetery. Behind the cemetery there was a small wood, called a *borek*. *Bor* means a big forest and *borek* is a little wood. There were some trees, some sand, a pasture where people used to take the cows to graze. That's where they took the Jews, lined them up in front of trenches that had been dug earlier, and shot them. They shot all the thirty-five hundred Jews of Żółkiew."

Chapter Eight

In one of his short stories, Edgar Allan Poe masterfully describes the harrowing account of a young sailor being sucked into a massive maelstrom off the coast of Norway. That's how I feel now: I'm trapped and being pulled, slowly, inexorably, into an exquisitely slow-moving whirlpool, moving closer, ever closer, to the funnel.

"Tell me about the Łozińskis' house."

"It was a corner house on a very narrow street, right across from the Jewish cemetery. It was just an old wooden shack, made out of planks. It stood right on the ground. I don't think it had a solid foundation. You could probably kick it and it would fall apart. It was very low, maybe two and a half meters high. Seven, eight feet high," she adds, in deference to my frown indicating that I still think and visualize in yards and inches rather than meters. "And attached to it was the outhouse and then the shed."

"Wait. Can you draw it for me?"

I know my mother's penchant for precision. In fact, one of her jobs as a new immigrant in New York—the job she enjoyed—was as a draftsman in a company that specialized in water treatment systems. I bring in a few sheets of unlined white paper and push a pencil across the table at her. She pauses for a moment, thinking, eyes narrowing in concentration, trying to visualize the house. Then she starts to draw. The sound of the pencil tip softly brushing against the paper fills the room. She draws several diagrams, motioning with the pencil, pausing, considering, erasing, correcting, and resketching as she talks, sometimes almost to herself, sometimes to me.

"The back wall of the house came right up to the street and had no windows. There were a few windows in the front: a small one in the front door, with a little curtain over it, and two more, one on each side of the door, and one other window in the living room.

"The only entrance to the house was that front door. You entered a little square hallway. The main room, the living room, was to your left. Straight ahead, through another door, was the kitchen.

"The kitchen was tiny, maybe two meters square. About six feet by six feet," she says, recalculating for me again. The sketch is a top view, looking down, and she fills it in as she goes. "There was a stove on one side, here, and a sink, and a little table. It was very dark; you had to keep the light on to work there. At the back of the kitchen, there was a door to the corridor. That connected the main room on the left and the storage area on the right. The corridor was very dark since it was in the back of the house where there were no windows. The trapdoor to the cellar was in that storage area.

"The main room was divided into a living room and a bedroom by two closets with a curtain hanging between them. Behind the closets, up two steps, was their bedroom. It had two little beds, placed head to head, along the wall.

"The living room was in front of the closets." Another drawing. "They had a couch, a few chairs, and a table placed under the living room window. In front of the curtain they made an altar for a statue of the Holy Mary, with a step where they could kneel and put some flowers. Real ones in summer, artificial ones the rest of the year. They prayed there every morning and every evening. They owned a few religious books.

"Beyond the storage area with the cellar beneath it, were the outhouse and the shed. These were on the outside of the building, not connected from the inside. The shed had a loft, with a ladder going up to it, where he had some straw, although I don't know what the straw was for, he had no animals. At one time I think he had had a goat. And he had some garden tools. The whole thing was very tiny.

"In front of the house, they had a nice-sized garden, bigger than the whole house. Some potatoes were growing, and some fruit trees. But it was very neglected. A garden requires a lot of work and they were too old to do it themselves. They couldn't carry pails of water. And she had problems with her eyes. They couldn't hire anyone to work there because of us, and also because they couldn't afford to pay. Nobody would come for nothing. So basically, whatever grew, grew."

She puts down the pencil. The sketches are spread across the tabletop. I pick them up in turn, studying them, trying to will the house into three dimensions, to see it for myself. I'm also playing for a little more time before I ask what I've been waiting to ask, dreading to ask.

"What was the cellar like?"

Sketch of Łozińskis' house, front view.

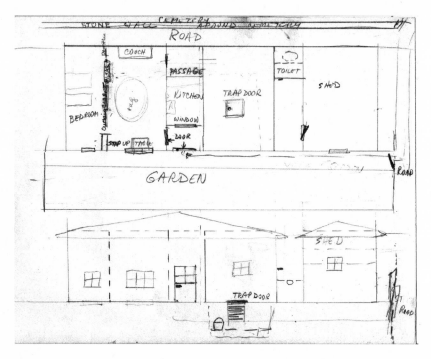

Diagram of Łozińskis' house, top view.

"It was a dug-out hole in the ground. The floor was packed-down earth. All cellar floors were like that, even in houses like ours from before the war, where the walls were brick. Here, the walls were wood."

"Was it square?"

"I don't remember . . . Don't remember."

"How high was the ceiling? Could you stand?"

"You couldn't stand, you had to sit. It was lower than your height. Just a hole in the ground. I think we sat on something. Maybe a piece of paper, maybe a piece of cardboard. It was unfinished dirt. I think all around the walls there was a raised area out of soil, like a bench, and the rest of the cellar was a little lower in the center."

"It must have been very cold in the winter," I realize.

"You put a coat on and you were sitting." Her tone is matter-of-fact.

The thought of being stuck in a cold, dark cellar makes the back of my neck prickle. I am very sensitive to cold. In fact, the significant temperature differential between me and Chaim and the boys has become a standing joke. When they're hot, I'm comfortable, and when they're comfortable, I'm usually donning—to their amazement—extra layers of clothing.

Conjuring up images of my mother and grandparents huddled in their coats on the hard-packed earth triggers a memory of taking my son Yehoshua to his judo class one winter. It was a forty-five-minute class, too short to drive home and turn around again to pick him up, so I'd often wait, perched on the stairs, reading.

The building was constructed of cinder blocks, poured concrete, and pale Jerusalem stone, economical construction that insulates nicely against the harsh summer heat. But in winter, the cold seemed to congeal within the walls and seeped into my bones through my down coat and even through Yehoshua's, pillowed beneath me as an extra layer of insulation.

I drag my attention back into the cellar.

"Was the cellar big enough for three of you to lie down, three across?"

"I think you could lie down, one next to the other. We could squeeze."

"I'm trying to get a sense of how big this place was."

I'm apologetic . . .

"You are forgetting that my perception of big or small changed over the years," she says.

. . . but not letting up, either.

"Did you sit across from each other, or next to each other?"

"Good question . . . however we could, I guess. I don't remember."

"Could you stretch your legs?"

"I really don't remember. I'm sorry, I just don't remember."

"That's all right. . . . Did you sit next to your father, or your mother?"

"I don't remember."

"Was there any way into the cellar from outside the house?"

"There was no way into the cellar from outside, only from inside, through the trap door in the storage area off the hallway."

"Did the trapdoor have a handle?"

"There was something that you pulled it up with, a ring or something. Łoziński put all kinds of things over it to cover it. Although the trapdoor was open most of the time."

"But you just said he put things over it."

"He did that sometimes when he was afraid, when his neighbors were around, or they heard that Germans were in the neighborhood. Not every day. When nobody was coming, he didn't bother that much."

"Could you open it from inside?"

"I think you could push it out. You have to realize that this was not intended as a hiding place. It was just a cellar. Everyone had one under their houses, to store fruits and vegetables, because it was cold down there.

"And even when we knew we would be hiding there, we didn't do anything to prepare it, and neither did he. It wasn't like other cellars, where people dug them out, brought in straw, supported them with poles. Our cellar was not intended for that purpose. Łoziński just agreed with my father to let us hide there for a few days."

"What did they keep down there?"

"They didn't have much. A few potatoes, some vegetables, I think. Not much. Don't forget this was already three-and-a-half years since the war started. Supplies were very low for everybody."

"To get into the cellar, you climbed down a ladder?"

"Sort of a short ladder, maybe a bit wider than a regular ladder. It had three or four steps. You couldn't jump down, you needed something to step on to go down."

"Did you have to turn around and go backward?"

"Yes."

"Were you wearing pants or skirts?"

"I think skirts. The only pair of pants I had owned then was the pair I wore to go skiing, and I don't remember if I had them with me then, or if they even still existed. I had a coat, shoes, stockings, but I don't remember what else. We had few changes of clothing."

"What did you do in the cellar all day long?" I ask.

"Nothing."

I'm thinking: Well, maybe it wasn't so bad. Maybe you could read, or write. Keep a journal. I ask her.

"You couldn't even read. It was too dark."

"Was it pitch black?"

"It wasn't pitch black because it wasn't airtight. The cellar was partly under the shed, which had a window, so some light came in through the cracks in the floor of the shed, and some came in between the boards of the trapdoor."

"There was no electricity?"

"They had no electricity down there. There was electricity in the house. That they had."

"No candles or anything?"

"No."

So, there wasn't enough light to read. Or write. Anyway, my mother doesn't like to write much; I should know that.

"So from seven, eight o'clock in the morning until dark you sat—"

"Until it got dark. About seven o'clock at night. In winter, the days were shorter. And it was safer: she kept the doors and windows closed, and the windows were covered anyway because of the war. Summer was a pain in the neck because it was hot, you want to keep the windows and doors open! But anybody can just walk by, so you have to be more careful than in the winter."

"Did your parents talk between themselves down in the cellar?"

"Yes, they would talk, but very quietly. In a whisper. They had to, there was nothing else to do."

"What did you talk about?"

"We were so scared, we were so shocked, we were in such a state that we didn't talk much. We were just trying to push the days ahead, another day, another day, another day, and that becomes a week, and then a month."

What did you do in the cellar all day long?

you just sit you just sit you just sit you just sit you just sit you
just sit you just sit you just sit you just sit you just sit you just sit
you just sit you just sit you just sit you just sit you just sit you
just sit you just sit you just sit you just sit you just sit you just sit
you just *stare* sit you just sit you just sit you just sit you just sit
you just sit you *at the wall* just sit you just sit you just sit you just
sit you just sit you just sit you just sit you just sit you just sit you
just sit you just sit you just sit you just sit you just sit you just sit
you just sit you just sit you just sit you just sit you just sit you
just sit you just sit you just sit you just sit you *cracks* just sit you
just sit you just sit you just sit you just sit you just sit *of light* you
just sit you just sit you just sit you just sit you just sit you just sit
you just sit you just sit you just sit you just sit you just sit you
just sit you just sit you just sit you just sit you just sit you just sit
you just sit you just sit *what time is it?* you just sit you just sit you
just sit you just sit you just sit you just sit you just sit you just sit
you just sit you just sit you just sit you just sit you just sit you
just sit you just sit you just sit you just sit you just sit you just sit
hungry you just sit you just sit you just sit you just sit you just sit
you just sit you just sit you just sit you just sit you just sit you
just sit you just sit you just sit you just sit you just sit you just sit
you just sit you just sit you just sit you just sit you just sit you
just sit you just sit you just sit you just sit you just sit you just sit
you just sit you just sit you *cramp* just sit you just sit you just sit
you just sit you just sit you just sit you just sit you just sit you
just sit you just sit you just sit you just sit you just sit you just sit
you just sit you just sit you just sit you just sit you just sit you
just sit you just sit you *cold* just sit you just sit you just sit you just
sit you just sit you just sit you just sit you just sit you just sit you
just sit you just sit you just sit you just sit *what time is it?* you just
sit you just sit you just sit you just sit you just sit you just sit you
just sit you just sit you just sit you just sit you just sit you just sit
you just sit you just sit you just sit you just sit you just sit you
just sit you just sit you just sit you just sit you just sit you just sit
you *stiff* just sit you just sit you just sit you just sit you just sit you
just sit you just sit you just sit you just sit you just sit you just sit
you just sit you just sit you just sit you just sit you just sit you
just sit you just sit you just sit you just sit you just sit *stare* you just
sit you just sit you just sit you just sit you just sit you just sit you
just sit you just sit you just sit you just sit you just sit you just sit
you just sit you just sit you just sit you just sit you just sit you

just sit you just sit you just sit you just sit you just sit you just sit
you just sit you just sit you just sit you just sit you just sit you
just sit you just sit you just sit you just sit you *waiting* just sit you
just sit you just sit you just sit you just sit you just sit you just sit
you just sit you just sit you just sit you just sit you just sit you
just sit you *stare* just sit you just sit you just sit you just sit you just
sit you just sit you just sit you just sit you just sit you just sit you
just sit you just sit you just sit you just sit you just sit you just sit
you *cold* just sit you just sit you just sit you just sit you just sit you
just sit you just sit you just sit you just sit you just sit you just sit
you just sit you just sit you just sit you just sit you just sit you
just sit you just sit *waiting* you just sit you just sit you just sit you
just sit you just sit you just sit you just sit you just sit you just sit
you just sit you just sit you just sit you just sit you just sit you
just sit you just sit you just sit you just *what time is it?* sit you just
sit you just sit you just sit you just sit you just sit you just sit you
just sit you just sit you just sit you just sit you just sit you just sit
you just sit you just sityou just sit you justsit you just *hungry* sityou
just sit you justsit you just sit you justsit you just sit youjust sit
youjust sit you justsit you just sit you justsit you just sit youjust
sit you just sit you justsit youjust sit youjust sityou just sityoujust
sityou justsit you justsit you justsit you just *cramp* sityoujust sityou
justsit youjust sityoujust sityoujust sityoujustsityoujustsityou justsit
youjustsityou justsit youjustsityoujustsityoujustsityoujustsit youjust
sityoujustsityou justsityoujust sityou justsit youjustsit youjust sit you
justsityoujustsityou justsityoujustsityou justsit youjustsit *waiting* you
justsit youjustsityoujustsit youjustsityoujustsityou justsit youjustsit
youjustsityoujust sityoujustsit youjust sit youjustsityoujustsityoujustsit
youjustsit *stare* youjustsityoujustsityoujustsityoujustsityoujustsityou justs
ityoujustsityoujustsityoujustsityoujustsityou justsityoujust sityoujustsity
oujustsityoujustsityoujustsityoujustsityoujustsityoujustsit youjustsit you
justsityoujustsityoujustsityoujustsityoujustsit youjustsityoujustsit youj
ustsityoujust sityoujustsityoujustsityou justsityoujustsityoujustsityouju
stsityoujustsit*hungry*youjustsityoujustsityoujustsityoujustsityoujustsityou
justsityoujustsityoujustsityoujustsityoujustsityoujustsityoujustsityoujust
sityoujustsityoujustsityoujustsityoujustsityoujustsityoujustsityoujustsity
oujustsityoujustsit youjust sityoujustsityoujustsityoujustsityoujustsityo
ujustsityou justsityoujustsit youjustsityou justsityou justsityoujustsity
oujustsityoujustsityoujust sityoujustsityoujust*waiting*sityoujustsityoujust
sityoujustsityoujustsityoujustsityoujustsityoujustsityoujustsityoujustsi
tyoujust*whenwillthisbeover*sityoujustsityoujustsityoujustsityoujustsityou

"Okay, but—What *did* you do in the cellar all day long?"

> *She already answered me.*
> *I know she did.*
> *She has nothing more to say.*
> *I try to comprehend.*
> *I remember heroes of fiction: the Count of Monte Cristo, acquiring an entire education in the bowels of the Chateau d'If. Prisoners of Conscience in the Soviet gulag, doing mental arithmetic, learning poetry.*
> *Did she think about her life and her childhood, about her dog? Did she think at all? Maybe you just stare yourself into a stupor.*
> *Was it at all like "sitting meditation"?*

Over the past few years, in my never-ending quest for more techniques to help my clients—and myself—reduce anxiety and stress and be calmer and healthier, I have been exploring meditation and mindfulness practices. In addition to practicing meditation regularly at home, I have, from time to time, gone on meditation retreats lasting from a few days to over a week.

The idea of a retreat is literally that: to retreat from the hustle and hassle of everyday life and nourish yourself spiritually and emotionally in an atmosphere of quiet and contemplation. Participants are expected to refrain from speech throughout the retreat, both when practicing formal meditation and when carrying out routine activities such as sweeping the rooms, preparing meals, eating, and washing the dishes. The silence is broken only when the teachers offer guidance and instruction, and by the reverberating chime of tiny brass bells signaling the transitions between activities. The deep stillness calms your body and mind and lets you explore your internal landscape and the messages of your heart.

If you've never been on a retreat, it probably sounds bizarre. If you have, you know that even with prior experience, retreating from the world in this way is not easy. It's challenging to slow down, to get still, to stay still.

I'm carried back in time. . . .

About ninety of us are gathered in a large hall in a kibbutz in the northern Negev. It is evening, the end of the first day of the retreat. Outside, the earth is breathing out the warmth of the day in a last sigh and the shadows are lengthening. Inside the hall, the overhead lights are off. A few tea candles flicker in round tin holders and one elbow-joint halogen lamp pours a narrow cone of light into the dimness. Otherwise, the quiet of the room is a deep gray. In every direction, on mats covering the entire floor, people sit cross-legged, folded into themselves. Snuggled into assorted shawls and throws, they look like round-edged pyramids of body and blanket. Everyone is still. Now and then, someone quietly shifts position, carefully resettles a bent leg, eases a cramped shoulder. A muffled sneeze. A restrained cough pressed into a palm.

It's hard for me to settle. I squirm against the piece of wall I've staked out for myself. The wall's touch is beginning to chill me and I carefully, quietly, ease a pillow behind my back, a warm buffer zone. There. Now maybe I'll be able to get comfortable. I settle into position again. I remind myself to pay attention to my breath. Breathing in. Breathing out.

The still shroud of the room envelopes me.

One minute.

Another minute.

More minutes.

My eyes slide open slowly, like window shades being raised inch by inch. Moving slowly, silently, I bring my watch up to my face, curving down to meet it, straining to see. I cup my right hand over the face of the watch and my index finger presses the Indiglo button. The LCD screen flares into a tiny blue square of light caught within the protective cage of my fingers. I can't believe it; only a few minutes have passed.

I lower my hand to my lap, settle back into position, and bring my focus back to my breath.

In.

Out.

In.

Out.

Is time even passing?

The darkness, the quiet, the silence of the bodies, press on me like weights. How much longer? I want this to be over already. I want to be able to move. Freely. Without taking stock of every twitch and every swallow. This is endless.

Breathe in.

Breathe out.
When will this be over?

I snap out of the memory. I'm back in the present, thinking of my mother, sitting in the dark, squirming, silent, waiting for it to be over. I flush with shame at my associations.

Sitting meditation!

"You are ridiculous." I wield the judgment like a whip.

I struggle to excuse myself. To apologize—though I'm not sure to whom: to her? To me?—for this desperate groping in the dark. But what else can I do? I have no context for her experiences. What do I know of real hunger, of being in hiding, of sitting in darkness for months? I am trying to make contact with what cannot be contacted, trying to relate to my mother's experiences through my own.

I understand all that.

No. Actually, I don't understand anything.

"What did you do in the cellar all day long?"

"What did you do in the cellar all day long?"

"What did you do in the cellar all day long?"

The question keeps jabbing at me like a woodpecker let loose in my brain. I can't get it to stop. My mind is racing anyway; like slipping the reins off a hyperactive horse, I let my imagination go.

The trapdoor descends slowly over their heads. The light is cut and reshaped, from trapezoid to square to slit to black. The wooden boards thunk into place. There is a rustling of garments as they settle into position, once again. Heels scuff against the packed dirt. One more day. One more.

The darkness presses into her eyes like a heavy shroud. She squints, trying to pierce it. Here and there, on the opposite wall, a slice of lighter gray, a tiny slash in a dark gray skin, stares at her like a blind eye. Someone shifts. Fabric rubs against fabric. She hears the long release of a sigh, the strong initial rush of air, the soft slide into silence. Someone swallows. It reminds her of water gurgling soapily down the drain.

She feels out gently in the blackness for her father's arm. He starts.

"Co jest? What is it?" His whispered words clatter into the stillness like sharp bits of gravel.

"Nothing! I just want to know what time it is."

"But it's too dark. You can't see!"

Nevertheless, he lets her move his arm, bend it, bring his wrist up to her face. It is too dark to make out the features of his watch. But she doesn't really need to; she knows them almost as well as her own. She remembers the ivory-colored face, the delicate black Roman numerals, the XII, the III, the VI, and IX. Minuscule diamond-shaped black dots indicate the other numerals. The hands are also black, slender, with filigreed points, the crystal, buffed to a soft shine, unmarred by scratches or fingerprints. The dark brown leather watchband is smooth, except for the tiny squintlike wrinkles where it's bent to tuck into the gold-toned buckle.

When she was little, she used to watch her father winding it every morning, deliberately, ceremoniously, carefully rotating the golden knob between the pads of his thumb and forefinger. If she was very quiet, and held her breath, she could hear the faint clicks of its orbit.

Now she bends her head, bringing her ear to the watch. At first she can't hear it at all. The silence is too loud. Then, as she holds her breath and stills her movements, she finds it. The gentle tick . . . tick . . . tick . . . tick. . . . She strains to see, but the darkness defeats her. The ticking continues. Like the tenderest flick of a fingernail against your thumb. Like a pencil tapping thoughtfully against an unwritten page. Like first hesitant raindrops. Like the dog's toenails on the wood floor as he sneaks into the room in the morning. Like a heartbeat . . .

I strain to see, but the darkness defeats me.

I'm trying to see in the dark, into *the dark. To see—what?*

Suddenly, an image: my mother's hand, moving restlessly, constantly. Her right index finger, endlessly tracing shapes, "writing," forming letters, curlicues, numbers, patterns. On her thigh as she sits. Hovering and "sketching" lightly in the air, skimming over tabletops, as it often does as we sit and talk together. Sometimes the sight of her finger looping and air-sketching makes me edgy. Once, feeling the tension rising in my chest, I asked her why she did it. "I don't know," she replied, shrugging, a little self-conscious. "Just a habit, I guess." She stopped for a while. And then continued.

Another time, when we were together and her finger began its nervous dance, I put my hand lightly over hers. I could feel the bony fingers, the bumpy network of veins protruding through the soft skin. (These are a legacy from her father, sculpted in bas-relief on my own hands as well. "Rosenberg Veins," my father calls them.) I wanted to soothe the hand, to still its restless flight. I held it until the zigzagging quieted down.

Now I wonder . . . I "see" my mother, sitting on the floor, leaning against a rough-planked wall. Her knees are drawn up before her in the almost-black, and she is writing, drawing shapes, on her knee. Over and over. In the dark. In the endlessness of that Time.

Like an infinitely patient inquisitor, the question calls to me yet again:

"What did you do in the cellar all day long?"

Sitting
Sitting and sitting
Still and silent
    on the hard-packed earth
Cold creeps like a slowly spreading stain
    into my back, into my butt,
Wrap my skirt tight around my legs like a bandage
Draw them up and hug my knees to my chest
Sitting
Sitting and sitting
Sitting and staring
Counting—
    glints of light through the cracks in the wall
Counting—
    days in this place
Counting—
    hours since food
    hours till food
Not enough food.
Never enough food.
Potatoes again.
Potato soup again.
Water with potato peels again.
Have to be thankful.

I hate potato water.

Memories of great big mounds of boiled potatoes topped
with sauerkraut . . . Grandma heaping my plate full
when I came home from ice-skating on the frozen
river with my friends. Steaming and delicious . . . That
heat, that sour-softness flowing all the way down to my
toes . . .

My toes are cold.

Wiggling my toes. First the right, then the left. Then the
left, then the right.

Like the folk dances we did in school.

I tilt my head to hear the music.

I hear

my mother's sigh

my father's grunt

the creaking footsteps of the old lady above

our savior

our jailer

our lifeline

our noose

Chapter Nine

I continue to probe, trying to force the darkness to part, to see what it was like to pass the time down there.

"How did you wash?"

"Washing was a big problem. They had no bathroom facilities. You heated water in a kettle on the stove, poured it into a metal cup, splashed a little on yourself, and you were washed. Face and hands you washed more often, I think every day, but not your body because you needed too much water for that."

"How did you go to the bathroom in the cellar?"

"We had a pail and she had to empty it every night. Took it out."

"What did you do for privacy?"

"What privacy?" she snaps.

Her sharpness hurts.

"Well, that's what I'm asking."

"No privacy. You had to go, you went."

"That must have been strange for you." *The adjectives I have in mind are much stronger: Awful. Humiliating. I swallow those.*

"Sure it was. But I think by that time you were used to anything. Nothing shocked you anymore."

"So if someone had to go, you just turned your back and went?"

"Yes."

"What was that like for your mother? It must have been very hard for her."

*I'm thinking of my delicate grandmother. She was always coax-
ing me to rub cream into my hands and elbows, especially the
elbows. It's important for a lady to have soft skin, she used to tell
me. She'd urge me not to sprawl, not to walk around barefoot, or
my feet would swell, become big and ungainly, like a peasant's. To
laugh softly. Eat only with utensils, "never with the fingers." Even
chicken drumsticks. Always act refined. Be a lady.*

"I think it was harder for *me!*"

My mother's vehemence catches me off guard.

She continues. "It bothered me, the whole thing. Everything
bothered me." She pauses. I wait. It's a long pause. Her eyes stare
off somewhere, somewhere I can't see. When she speaks again,
it's very quietly, and very slowly.

"I gave my parents a hard time. . . . I blamed them for being
born . . . especially on some days, bad days, when I was in a
bad mood, when it looked like we would never get out, and the
Germans would catch us. I blamed my parents for having me, for
living, for having to go through this. I told them I would've been
better off had I never been born. I was glad my grandmother
wasn't alive."

"How did they react when you'd say things like that?"

"What could they say? I know they were very upset, very,
very upset. About my statements. They were suffering. I made them
suffer. They were suffering because of me. I was mean."

She's blinking her eyes very fast. The tears don't fall, they
glisten like mirrors. *I have to do something to ease her pain. I have
to do something to ease mine.*

"You don't think they understood?"

*Sure. Take cover behind some lame Universalizing Statement.
Brave move.*

"I think they understood, but I don't think it made them
feel better, that's for sure. It was mean on my part. Why would I
blame them for something they didn't do on purpose? I also said,
'Why did we have to be born Jewish? Why do we have to be the
"chosen people"? Why us and nobody else? Why do we have to
be persecuted?'"

"You must have been pretty angry, to be stuck down there."

*I hate the way I sound. Like something out of the Therapist's
Basic Empathy Primer. Why don't I just shut up?*

"Yes." She sighs. "It wasn't easy for our landlords, either."

(That's what she calls them as we speak, but she is not happy with the word. Reviewing these notes with me later, she crosses out the word *landlords* and writes *protectors*.)

"It was very, very hard on them too. They were very pious people who wanted to help, but they didn't realize what they were getting themselves into. They had volunteered for three, four days, five days, but not sixteen months. It was terrible. Nobody knew it would be like that. If we had asked them to hide us for even a month or two, I don't think they would have agreed. But once we were there, they were stuck. The only thing they could do was to kick us out, tell us: "Go!" Which they did, once. But then they changed their minds. They were scared. They were scared that if the Germans caught us, they'd find out where we'd been hiding, and they'd go after them. And they also felt that if they throw us out, it was like murdering us. Because sooner or later, we'd be caught and killed. And they didn't want that on their consciences either. So they were stuck.

"It was hard to feed three additional people. They hardly had enough for themselves. They traded whatever they had for food—their things, our things, the few things we had brought with us. But they didn't like to deal with the peasants. For one thing, the peasants also didn't have much. Everyone was suffering at that time, nobody ate well. It wasn't safe to ask for more than a little food, or people would start wondering why two old people needed so much. Besides, many of the peasants in the villages around us were Ukrainian, and the Łozińskis were scared of them.

"From the peasants, they got potatoes, some vegetables, a bit of flour. Łozińska would mix the flour with water and make a sort of flat bread. Every once in a while she'd get an egg and if she also had some flour, she'd mix that together to make some kind of noodle, and you ate potatoes and noodles, and were very happy you had that. I didn't eat a whole egg once in sixteen months. Mostly, she'd make a big pot of soup out of whatever vegetables she had, some potatoes, some cabbage, beets. At least it was a hot meal. We were not starving but most of the time we were hungry, because it wasn't enough and you couldn't expect more."

A sudden loud click calls us back to the present. Side A of the tape has finished. My mother is surprised—didn't we just turn the tape recorder on? I am also amazed at how fast the time has flown. I flip the cassette over.

Something that she mentioned earlier nags at me.

"I don't understand something," I say. "You said you slept upstairs in the living room. Wasn't that just the first night when you arrived at their house, when you went into hiding?"

"No," she replies. "At night, we stayed upstairs. My parents slept on the couch in the living room, and I slept on blankets on the floor. We had to clean the couch often because it had fleas. I was often awakened by bugs biting me. Luckily, they were not infected fleas. Anyway, we went to sleep very late and we got up very early, cleaned up our stuff right away and went back into the cellar."

Growing up, it was always my father who served as my family's Holocaust Heritage spokesman, presenting his story, and my mother's, to anyone who would listen. She'd be standing quietly, slightly off to the side, looking shyly downward and away, while he'd declare: ". . . and my wife and her parents were hidden in a cellar for sixteen months." All these years, I imagined this silent black hole into which my mother and her parents had vanished for those entire sixteen months. I've been burrowing into that hole from every angle I can think of, twisting it like a pretzel, inquiring about it, imagining it, and projecting onto it. Now I am shocked to discover that the hole has shades of blackness, nuances of gray. I have to readjust my thinking. Because they didn't stay in the cellar all the time; they came up at night to sleep in the tiny living room.

I recalculate, subtracting time upstairs from cellar time downstairs. Sixteen months minus one-quarter, figuring six hours of sleep a night out of twenty-four hours per day. I feel strange and off-balance: Do I feel cheated? Misled? Had the drama been less than I'd imagined? Then I feel guilty. How can I begrudge their sleeping upstairs in the flea-infested living room? Wasn't the experience tough enough as it was? The darkness may not have been as complete as I'd imagined, but it never lifted for that entire sixteen-month period.

More than ever before, I am in awe of the decency of this elderly couple who allowed my mother and her parents to be upstairs with them whenever possible, maintaining some semblance of normalcy.

Then again, I can't believe that any of them would take such chances.

"Wasn't that terribly risky?"

"It *was* risky."

"I would think you'd be safer staying in the cellar."

"How could you stay in the cellar?" she demands, indignantly.

Her innocent, almost naïve reaction knocks me off guard. I feel stung, as though my preposterous suggestion is responsible for putting her there. But wait a minute: I've read the books, seen the movies. I know what people endured. My idea is not so far-fetched. In fact, it seems rather prudent. Why am I on the defensive?

"I don't know, but wasn't it safer? What if someone saw you?"

What I really want to say is: "Are you crazy? What do you mean, 'how could you stay in the cellar?' The same way you can sit in a cellar. You take your blankets and huddle up and sleep. How could you not stay in the cellar?"

To her, it seems obvious.

"At night, there was a curfew. Nobody was out. The windows were always covered, because of the blackout. They covered the small window in the bedroom with papers. They hung blankets over the window in the living room, on hooks."

"Well, what about German patrols?"

"Actually, the Germans didn't usually go from house to house, especially Polish houses, unless they were looking for someone specific, if someone denounced you, or they suspected that you were a member of the Polish underground. It was different from the way they hunted for Jews. Even so, we took a chance. I know we took a chance."

There. She said it. What am I after, my pound of flesh? To force her to admit that what they did was reckless, irresponsible, even stupid? Is it so difficult for me to tolerate the retroactive suspense, the risk, even so many years after these events were safely concluded?

"Still, we tried to get out of the cellar as much as we could. Even during the day, especially in the summer. Whenever we felt it was safe, we would come upstairs and sit in that little corridor leading to the kitchen. Just to stretch a little, to have a little daylight. And we tried to help her as much as we could.

"My mother, for instance, helped with the cooking, made some soup, although there wasn't much to cook. And I did the laundry. Łozińska put a big round washbasin in the little passageway behind the kitchen, and I would wash the clothes there, using a washing board. Not often; there wasn't much water, and not enough place to dry them, especially in the winter. You wore the same clothes for one or two weeks."

"I don't understand how it was safe enough for you to be upstairs."

I can't let go of this.

"It *wasn't* safe enough, but she needed some help, especially in the beginning after she had the eye operation. A neighbor came over and offered to help her, because she had a patch over her eye. So Łozińska thanked her, but said, no, she was managing, her husband was helping, and besides, how much do two people need, after all? She obviously couldn't have anyone come over. You had to be very careful; every little detail could give you away."

"Did anyone ever get suspicious?"

"No. Thank God. It was just neighbors being polite. I guess everyone had his own problems and was concerned about himself."

"Could someone see you in the kitchen?" I worry.

"No. Because the kitchen was on the inside of the house, and it was dark. There were no windows on that side of the house."

"Could someone passing by the house hear you, hear water running in the kitchen?"

"Nobody could just pass by. You didn't just walk up to the house; there was a little walkway from the fence to the door of the house. Łozińska would stay in the garden, and if she saw anyone coming she would start talking, greeting them. We'd hear her voice and knew someone was coming and we'd run back down."

"That would give you enough time to jump down the stairs?"

"Yes. And close the trapdoor."

"Did you ever have such a narrow escape?"

I vacillate between being terrified for them even now, and being titillated by the drama of such a narrow escape.

"No."

"Did you have a password?"

Too many war movies on the brain.

"No, we did not."

Give it a rest. This is not a novel.

"Very few people came by. People mostly stayed to themselves in their houses. Which was good for us. And the Łozińskis didn't have many friends. They had a few neighbors who would stop by once in a while, stand outside and talk over the fence, or even come in for a bit, but she didn't have people over for meals.

"Some of these good neighbors—Poles—were very grateful to Hitler for solving the problem of the Jews. One of these, an officer of the Polish Army, lived next door. He would come in from time to time, bringing news about the war from his underground contacts and making big speeches about how the Poles should put up a big gold statue of Hitler for the one good thing he did: getting rid of the Jews."

"You could hear this from where you were sitting?"

"Yes. I told you, it was a small hut. Just thin boards, thin walls. You could hear everything. And this guy certainly wasn't hiding his feelings about Jews. That didn't add to the Łozińskis' feeling of safety. Or ours.

"He wasn't the only one who felt that way. Łozińska had a sister who lived in Brzeżany whose husband was a Volksdeutscher. He was a *gauleiter*, which was a high-level official under the Germans, a kind of head of a local branch of the Nazi Party. Once he was in our area on some official business and he stopped in to see the Łozińskis. He didn't stay long, just an hour or so, bringing regards from her sister and boasting about what a good job he was doing, cleaning up his district of all the Jews. And we were sitting right below them in the cellar; we could hear everything they said. Łoziński also repeated the conversation to us later. He and his wife were not happy that her sister had married him. They didn't like him. They said he wasn't a good human being.

"Going back to that neighbor of Łoziński, the officer," she continues, "once, in the winter of 1944, a group of the Polish underground army, the *Armia Krajowa*, the AK [which she pronounces "Ah-Kah"], was retreating from the Warsaw region, fleeing south, to Hungary. As they moved, they fought the Germans, on the one hand, and killed Jews, on the other, if they found them hiding in the forests.

"This neighbor was in contact with the AK. One day, he came over and announced to Łoziński: 'A group of the AK will be passing through our town and I have to hide them in private homes for two, three days so they can rest a bit before they move on. Poles have to help them out. You have to take in a few of them.'

"Łoziński didn't want to. 'How can I take anybody in? You know my wife is sick, we are old, I don't have the space, I have just one little room. And you can't expect my wife to sleep in the house with young guys, with soldiers!' But the officer insisted. Łoziński couldn't get out of it, because it would have been unpatriotic and suspicious. Finally he agreed to let one person stay in the house during the day and sleep in the loft, under the straw, at night.

"So this soldier came. He stayed for three days. We couldn't move at all during those days, because he was right above us, in the house. She prepared some food for him, breakfast, something at lunchtime, and let him stay inside to keep warm. At night, while he slept in the loft, we would tiptoe upstairs to sleep and early in the morning we ran back to the cellar.

"One day, Łoziński and his wife went out shopping and to church. This soldier was right over our heads in the house. All of a sudden we heard some banging and noises upstairs. We were scared; we didn't know what was going on. So very quietly I came out from the cellar, peeked through the tiny window in the kitchen door, and I saw him lying on the floor, having an epileptic fit! Then Łoziński came back and found him like that. He ran straight to this neighbor, this Polish officer, and told him, 'The guy is sick, I don't want him in my house.' So they moved him somewhere else; I don't know where. And then the whole group left."

"If the Poles had found out that Łoziński was hiding Jews, would they have reported him to the Germans?" I ask. "Would they have considered them traitors?"

"I have no idea. But I know it was very dangerous for Łoziński. He had us, and he had the Polish underground. Had the Germans discovered that he was hiding a member of the Polish underground, they would probably have searched the house, or burned the house and found us, the Jews. So I can't blame the Łozińskis for being very nervous."

This story with the soldier makes it even harder for me to grasp: How could they have risked coming out of the cellar at all with a hostile soldier bunking under the straw in the adjoining shed? Maybe living with constant danger numbs you, like being immersed in frigid water. After a while you don't feel anything.

"I also sometimes came upstairs to play with the cats."

"Cats!"

This comes as yet another surprise. Not her love of cats—and dogs—which she transmitted to us. But my mind-reel of war movies certainly never included pets.

"Yes, cats. Because on top of everything else in that little shack, she had a cat. A very pretty cat with long fur, like a Persian. They kept the litter box under the table.

"Łozińska was very fond of that cat. Once I stepped on its tail and she got mad. She started yelling at me.

"Then the cat had kittens. Four of them. She kept one, and drowned the others. And then that one died. And she was angry at me. She said it died because of me. I don't know what happened to the kitten, it just died . . ."

. . . One summer when Barry and I were little, my parents sought to escape the sweltering heat of a New York City summer and rented a tiny apartment on East Olive Street in Long Beach, Long Island. My father joined us every weekend as part of the great gray-suited fatherly migration heading seaward on the Long Island Railroad.

The apartment belonged to Joszi ("Yoh-zhee") Deutsch, a wiry, bronzed Hungarian Jew and fellow survivor. Joszi was a gifted car mechanic whose passion was deep-sea fishing. Besides treating us to a "voyage" in his fishing boat, Joszi was happy to let us play with the family of stray cats—two mothers and their four kittens—that he fed and sheltered in the backyard. This was a rare treat as we didn't have pets at home.

The kittens were adorable. They rough-and-tumbled all over each other by day, and one, whom I named Friendly, sometimes curled up next to me in bed at night. My mother encouraged and enjoyed their antics as much as Barry and I did.

I remember clearly the pleasure those kittens brought me. Considering, now, the bleak misery of those long months of suspense and agony, of hiding someone and being hidden, I am grateful for any fleeting moments of joy and normalcy generated by Łozińska's feline family. I feel for the old woman's distress at the death of her kitten but bristle at the accusation leveled at my mother. I wonder how I might have felt if it were me who was being unjustly blamed.

My mother says, simply, "I don't know what happened to the kitten, it just died. . . . I liked the cats. And there was nothing else to do. Just sit and hide, and hope for the best."

She shakes her head slowly.

"I really don't know how we could survive. I don't know how we managed, not only in that period, but during the whole war.

"The other thing I did when I'd come upstairs," she says a few minutes later, "was read some of their books. They had these thin little books on religious topics. I read anything I could put my hands on. There was nothing else to do. And they were interesting stories. Some were from our Bible. Like Daniel being thrown into the lion's den and coming out alive. There were lots of stories about fish because Peter was a fisherman. And about the different saints and the early Christian martyrs who were thrown to the lions in the Roman amphitheaters."

Listening to her takes me back to one of my favorite places as a child: the Highbridge Branch of the New York Public Library in the Bronx. "My" library. I remember a huge, airy room, hushed into respectful silence, rich with the smells of print and paper and thick white paste, the dull polish of brown wooden shelves bursting with books like a treasure chest spilling forth its jewels.

During one point I went through a "mythology phase." I devoured the myths of the Greeks and the Romans and then moved on to the early Christian saints. I remember names like Beatrix and Joan, and words that filled my entire mouth, words like beatitudes *and* salvation. *I read these stories voraciously, repelled and fascinated by images of arrows sticking out of innocent, sanctified flesh, of saintly upturned gazes. Dying for the Lord. Like lambs. The holiness of the meek, the suffering, the nobility.*

"But I was amazed," my mother continues. "After all the Christians suffered at the hands of the Romans, they never had anything against the Romans, or the Italians. Just the Jews."

Just as I used to wonder: Why did Christians get to die like lambs, sweet and holy and noble, while Jews are said to have gone to the slaughter like a mindless herd of stupid sheep?

"You didn't bring any of your own books with you into the cellar?"

"No. Didn't think of it."

"A siddur, a prayer book?"

"I think my father had one."

"Did he use it?"

"Yes."

"When?"

"During the day, I think."

"He prayed every day?"

"Yes. And he was fasting every week."

"Grandpa?" My voice cracks.

"Yes. From the day we went to their cellar."

My grandfather? The grandfather I knew was cynical about religion, mocking it as a vestige of a ghetto mentality. He never made kiddush on Friday nights, and my grandmother lit candles only on major holidays.

The one exception to this attitude was Rosh Hashanah and Yom Kippur. My grandparents were too frail to go to the synagogue, so they prayed at home, dressed in their most formal attire, my grandfather in his dark suit and tie, my grandmother in a dress of dark cloth with tiny multifaceted buttons that caught the light of the small army of Yahrzeit memorial candles set out on the sideboard in the living room. Even in bright daylight, you could feel the silvery radiance of those tiny flames trembling inside their glass enclosures.

As a small child, I would come down to my grandparents' apartment on Yom Kippur, hoping at least there to find some relief from the seriousness of the day. But they'd shush me gently and keep reading from dark, somber prayer books. I was disappointed.

This was no fun. Why were they being like this? Why were these days different?

And now, to discover that he prayed, that he fasted, *during his captivity . . .*

"Why did he do that?"

"He thought it might help. I guess he believed there was a God that could save us. Hard as it was to believe that, with all these people murdered, burned, massacred. I think he even continued fasting once a week for a while after we came out of hiding, until we went to Katowice after the war."

"He started from the time you were in the cellar, not before?"

"Right. He decided that until we would come out alive, he would fast every week. We didn't have that much to eat anyhow. But he was fasting. Like on Yom Kippur."

"On any particular day?"

"I don't remember. But he was fasting once a week."

"What did your mother say about this?"

"She didn't say anything."

"Did she pray, also?"

"I didn't notice."

"But you noticed your father."

"Yes."

"Did he have *tallis* and tefillin?" I ask, thinking of the prayer shawl and phylacteries usually worn during morning services.

"No. Who had those things?"

I feel chastised. Guilty of that most awful crime: stupidity. Especially about this. Because being stupid means truly not understanding what they went through. And that means leaving them out in the cold, alone, abandoned. Again.

But wait a minute. How was I supposed to know?

"Do you mind if I ask? I didn't know you had a siddur down there until today!"

I'm still recovering from her snappishness, and mine.

"Was the siddur in Polish or in Hebrew?"

"I don't remember. It usually had two languages, Hebrew on one side and Polish on the other. Or maybe it was German. Now I don't remember if his siddur was in German or Polish."

"Was it the same siddur you gave me, the *Modlitwy?*"

"No. The siddur I gave you had been my grandmother's. That's why my mother cherished it so much. We found it on the floor of our apartment, thrown among other papers and scraps of things, when we went back after the war."

Every Yom Kippur, my grandmother prayed from her little Polish-Hebrew prayer book. Embossed in faded gold letters on the worn black leather cover was the word Modlitwy, *prayers. A few front pages had loosened from the binding and peeped out from behind the covers like feather-soft lace. The little book shook slightly in her soft hands. One survivor holding another.*

"Did you ever say any prayers yourself?" I ask.

"I think I did, in my mind, in my heart."

"But nothing formal."

"No."

"How did you know when it was Yom Kippur or Rosh Hashanah?"

"We knew it was sometime in September, but we didn't know when. So sometime in September we fasted on one day for Yom Kippur. We didn't know if that was the right date. How could you know? There was no one to ask; there were no Jews!

"My mother always tried to keep track of when she had a *yahrzeit*," she continues. "But it was very hard."

"How did you know what date it was at all?"

"I think Łoziński had a calendar. He knew when it was Sunday. We knew the seasons were changing; we came in March, then it was summer, then fall, then winter. Christmas, of course they knew, and New Year's."

"What about Passover? You knew when that was because of Easter."

"Yes, but we didn't celebrate Passover. Any other questions?"

"Yeah—" I begin, but her voice overrides mine.

"I'm sorry I can't help you, but I really don't remember."

Pause.

I try to regain my bearings. I reach for another strand of the story.

"You said you were pretty angry at your mother and father. Were you angry at God too?"

"I was. I couldn't understand why their God was better than ours."

"With all this anger about God and your situation, and the books you were reading about saints, did you ever think of converting?"

"Good question. You know, Łoziński wanted us to convert."

"You mean, to save you?"

"No, he wanted us to convert after the war. He said that if we survived, it was only because the Holy Mary was protecting us."

"What did your father say? What did you think?"

"I just thought about getting out of there. To be free, to be able to move, to survive.

"You know," she continues, "before we went into hiding, my father had somehow contacted some Poles from Warsaw, a man and a woman, who were selling false papers that every non-Jew had to have: birth certificates, baptismal certificates, and *Kennkarten*, which are German identity cards. With these, you could move around and hope to get by. Otherwise, you couldn't move. Later, when we were already sitting in the cellar, and we realized that we couldn't go back to the ghetto, and we were afraid we might not be able to stay there any longer, my father asked Łoziński to contact these people. The woman came and my father paid her and gave her some papers so she could prepare false papers for us. I don't know where my father wanted to go and how he figured we could get by as Christians, with our looks. She felt that I was the least Jewish looking, because I don't have dark eyes. Mine are hazel; they were even more greenish at one time.

"She was supposed to bring us the papers and take us by train to Warsaw. But she took the money and never came back. We were all very, very scared. Because she knew where we were. I was very angry at my father. Very angry. I told him, 'You are endangering us and the Łozińskis. How can you trust Polish forgers? They can tell the Germans where we are!' It was such a stupid thing to do.

"After the war, when we were in Katowice, my father actually went to Warsaw to look for these people. That was also a stupid thing to do. I don't know how he traced them, but the man warned him he'd kill him if he didn't leave them alone. My father said he was lucky to get back alive. I told my father to forget about it, that we were lucky that they just took the money and never denounced us."

"Just imagine if they'd gotten you the papers and you'd have ended up in Warsaw!" I say.

What a tightrope of fortune they were walking.

"One miracle after another," she says.

"And I thought you don't believe in God," I tease.

"No, no," she protests, shaking her head. "I keep saying all the time there's something there. I don't know what you call it, I don't know what it is, or who it is. But there's something that watches over you. Definitely."

"But you thought their God was stronger than our God?"

"Well, they were not killed like we were. Not for their religion. They were killed because they were Poles, fighting for their country against the Germans."

I am used to my mother's critical questions and skepticism about religion and God's presence in the world. Her comments often irritate my father, who, despite all he has been through, still holds close to his faith. He often calls her a religious rebel, accusing her of tainting me as well.

As if I needed my mother's doubts. I have enough of my own.

I remember a recent Yom Kippur. This most serious day of the year, the Day of Judgment, of Atonement, is about to begin. Just before sunset, I light the yahrzeit *candles.*

I light in memory of my mother's parents, Agatha (née Schenker) and Josef Rosenberg, the grandparents I grew up with, who survived the war and lived to see the continuity of their family after the destruction.

I light in memory of my father's parents, Dobe (née Blajfeder) and Chaim Boruch Wyszogród, the grandparents I never knew, murdered in the Treblinka death camp.

More candles: for my father's brother, Pesach, killed during the Warsaw Ghetto Uprising of April 1943. For his other brother, Shlomo, and his sister, Esther Raizel, murdered in Treblinka.

In recent years, I adopted my mother's tradition of lighting on behalf of those who had nobody left to light for them, orphaned souls who became part of my extended family.

I light one in memory of my father's old friend, "Uncle" Shlomo Janowski, who survived the war and found himself all alone once it was over, who carried his pain and the memory of his murdered young wife and infant child in his broken hunched back.

I light one in memory of Leib Lensky, the actor, who broke the fast with us every Yom Kippur and vehemently fought to keep the Yiddish language alive.

I light one in memory of David Grynberg, Hebrew scholar and educator.

I light one in memory of Victor Goldstein, who broke out of the infamous Pawiak prison in Warsaw in a daring escape, and his delicate, elegant wife, Wanda. Their postwar years in New York were both a tribute to human survival and an example of post-traumatic suffering.

I strike one last match. Holding it over the wick of the last candle, I hear someone say: "And this is for God." And gasp in surprise: the voice that spoke was my own. I think of "taking it back," the way kids do. Too late. The words have already been uttered.

Walking to the synagogue, I gird myself for the challenge of yet another Holy Day. At the appropriate moments in this penitential service, along with everyone else, I'll bang away at my breast, thumping out the cadences: "We have sinned, we have trespassed." I can do that readily enough. God knows—as I certainly do—that I have sinned and am guilty of many things. But so is God. And I'm angry. I want an accounting. I want an explanation. I want an apology. I will not grovel, call myself dust, before a God who watched so many members of my family, so many families, scorched into dust, who answered their prayers with silence. I want answers.

And, yes, I know there are no answers, at least none readily apparent to us mere mortals with our limited understanding. All the great philosophers teach us that we can't possibly grasp the overarching patterns of the universe, can't understand the purpose underlying the events we can see, any more than we can see the gnarled knots on the underside of a glorious hand-woven rug. Who are we to judge?

On the other hand, how can I not judge? How can I accept without understanding? And, if I accept, what does that mean: about the Janowskis and the Goldsteins? About my father's family? About my mother and her parents, crouching in a dark hole in the ground for months? Do I forgive? Do I acquiesce?

Another part of me groans and rolls its eyes around: "Who are you to challenge God?"

I am reminded of a Calvin and Hobbes comic strip: Little Calvin is taunting a potted plant, teasing it with how he just might—or might not—water it. And then the skies open up and it pours. So much for his little tantrum. So much for mine.

Besides, I have some nerve, complaining. I have a lot to be grateful for, starting with my mother and her parents and my father, who did survive, and going on down the line to include my husband, my children, my health, and many other blessings. Hasn't God also been good to me?

I walk to the synagogue feeling as though I'm skating on thin ice, my emotions brooding, flexing, just under the surface. What will my prayer be like tonight?

Chapter Ten

Several quick jabs of the bell announce my mother's arrival at the garden gate. I dash out into the sunny winter morning to greet her and rush us both through the chill into the house. Despite the ambient warmth supplied by the ever-faithful kerosene heater, each of us is wearing extra layers of clothing in order to feel comfortable and keep our fingers from turning blue, a sensitivity to cold we share.

Observing my mother in sweatpants and sweatshirt, I marvel yet again at how her style of dressing has changed with time. Growing up, I never saw her in pants, except when we went sledding or ice-skating. Hers was a classic look: tailored dresses, pleated skirts, matching blouses, simple and elegant jewelry. She despaired at my "dressing like *that*" when, after high school with its strict "skirts-only" dress code, I wanted nothing more than to live in jeans and sweats, anything loose and unconstructed and comfortable. I called it heaven. She called it "shlumpy."

In recent years, her tastes have changed. I kid her about it sometimes when we place orders together for sport knit pants from the Lands' End catalog, twitting her about how far she's come from the patent-leather-and-white-glove look she extolled when I was little. She laughs and repeats one of her favorite expressions, *Jajo jest mądrzejsze od kury*, the egg is smarter than the chicken. I laugh with her, at times wistfully: I find her sartorial shift a bit disconcerting, wondering what it signifies and why *I* feel some sense of loss.

We settle down to work. I want to go back to something that's been bothering me.

"You mentioned that at one time the Łozińskis wanted to throw you out," I prompt.

She nods.

"I think it happened sometime in the winter, 1943 to '44," she says. "The Russians were still far, far away, fighting the Germans, and there was no end in sight. We had very little hope. And wintertime was very, very hard. There was hardly enough food for all of us. The pressure was too much for the Łozińskis. They were old. They were tired. They just couldn't take it anymore."

"Did they threaten to get rid of you?"

"They were not threatening. They just had a 'discussion' with us." Her tone puts sarcastic quotation marks around the word.

"It wasn't angry?"

"No, it wasn't angry. They just couldn't take the constant tension anymore. Any knock on the door, they were shaking: 'Who's coming?'"

"When did you have these discussions?"

"In the evenings, before we went to bed, so we could 'think' about it." More edgy quotation marks.

"And then what?"

"I guess they hoped that when they got up in the morning, we would have disappeared into thin air."

"Did you have to convince them to let you stay, or did they come around by themselves?"

"My father spoke to them. He told them that of course we understood their situation, that we had also never imagined it would be like this. But now we had no place to go. If we left and the Germans caught us, they would also be in danger. Maybe they also realized that throwing us out was like murdering us, because the Germans would catch us, sooner or later. They didn't want that on their consciences. They talked it over, and she went to church. When she came back she said, 'Okay, stay. Whatever will happen with you, will happen with us.' And they never asked us to leave after that."

The Book of Ruth 1:16–18: "And Ruth said: Entreat me not to leave thee, and to return from following after thee, for whither thou go, I will go; and where thou lodge, I will lodge; thy people shall be my people, and thy God my God; Where thou die, will I die, and there will I be buried; the Lord do so to me, and more also; if aught but death part thee and me."

"Then, in March 1944, we heard that the Russians were advancing, with help from the Americans and the British. You could sense it was only a matter of time. Whether we, or the Łozińskis, could last that long was a different matter. But at least we had some hope. Although every day from then on was a nightmare. The Russians were advancing, but not fast enough. We were expecting them to liberate us already in April. But they had to retreat—several times. Each time they did, it was terrible. Łoziński was going crazy. He was waiting for that liberation just as much as we were! My father tried to calm him down, telling him that maybe the British and the Americans would liberate us first.

"And then came May First. May First is a big Russian holiday. The Russians attacked Lwów from the air. They bombarded the city with such force, such power, that, thirty kilometers away, we could see the whole sky lit up at night. The flares. The explosions. It was like fireworks. Maybe they even were; at any rate, that's what Łoziński called them. Ooh, I liked that." Her eyes sparkle, her whole face lights up as she speaks.

"Wait!" I interrupt. "You *saw* that?"

"Łoziński let us come up from the cellar to see what was going on. We stayed in the house but we could see it through the windows.

"The Russians were close, but they still weren't there yet. The Germans were retreating, retreating, but they still hadn't been cleared from our area, yet. We had to wait until July. It took until July. In the meantime, everyone was waiting. Another day, and another day." Her voice suddenly rises. "Do you know what another day meant? Not only for us but for all the others? A lot of people got killed during that time, waiting for the Russians. Because every day meant life.

"When Łoziński finally came and said, 'The Russians are here, in the town,' we were still not sure we could come out. He told us to wait, not to come out yet. Who knows if the Russians will have to retreat again, if the Germans would return, you never know. So we waited another day before we dared to come out."

"Do you remember what you and your parents talked about at that point, now that it was almost over?"

"I don't remember. I know we were very happy that we managed to survive, that we might be able to go out."

115

"Could you finally relax at least? It was only a matter of hours now."

"I think it was an anticlimax. You'd waited so long and now you feel lost."

"Did you plan what you would do after liberation?"

"No. We didn't think at that time, somehow. Didn't make plans for after. We couldn't imagine what it would be like, after. You just want to be free, to be able to go out, to know that the Germans will not come and kill you if you stick your head out the door and somebody sees you. We were hoping to be able to come out and have some sort of normal life, but what 'normal life' meant at that time I don't think I knew, or anybody knew.

"And we also didn't know who else had survived, how many Jews would still be alive. We thought: maybe we're the only ones who'll come out. Maybe we're the last ones. And we didn't know who else had survived from the family. We had very little hope for anybody. But we still hoped. The family was pretty big. Maybe someone had managed to escape.

"We knew that my uncle Manek, my mother's younger brother, and his younger son Mietek were dead. They had been killed at the Janowska concentration camp. We knew that his wife Zosia had been killed, in Bełżec. We knew that their older son, Ryszek, was dead. He had been living in Warsaw, posing as a Christian. The Germans came for him and he threw himself out a window. Killed himself.

"We didn't know what happened to my mother's other brother, my uncle Poldzio and his wife Jadzia. We had lost contact with them."

"What was your first reaction to the news that you could come out?"

"We were crying. We were crying and we embraced Łoziński, he blessed us, and we thanked him, and we kissed him."

"And Łozińska?"

"Yes, yes. Her, too. And they felt like heroes. And they were, there's no question about it. We owed them our lives."

"At what time did you actually come out of Łoziński's house, go outside?"

"Daytime. Daytime. I know it was daytime because I was practically blind from the sunshine. It was July. Summer. We had been away from bright light for so long that our eyes were affected. We

116

couldn't see straight. The daylight bothered me very, very much. I am still very sensitive to bright sunlight.

"Before we actually came out, we checked carefully to make sure there was nobody on the street. Then we each came out separately and went in different directions, so that nobody would see that we came out of Łoziński's house. He didn't want anybody to know that we had been hiding in his place. He was scared of his neighbors, of the Polish underground. He begged us not to tell anybody. So we didn't."

"Who was the first one out of the cellar?" I ask.

"I don't remember. But I remember that we couldn't walk. We were not used to walking. And I was afraid to be out, walking on the street. I was afraid to look at people. What would they do to me? I was supposed to be dead, right? So what was I doing here in the street? I was afraid they'd hurt me, they'd say something nasty. I didn't know what to expect."

"Did you think that you could still be in danger from the Poles?"

"Well, when Łoziński told us that he didn't want anybody to know where we were hiding because some Poles may not like it, we didn't feel very secure. But I never expected that the Poles would actually go and attack Jews. Although we found out later that some did."

"How did the townspeople react to you? Did they talk to you?"

"Yes. People came over, congratulating us, saying they were happy to see us. I don't know how happy they were on the inside, but they *said* they were happy to see us, happy that we had survived, that we were back."

"Did they ask you how you survived? And where?"

"Yes, and we said that we had been in the forest, here, there, all over. We kept it very vague. We never told anyone we had been hiding in Łoziński's place."

"And you feel so weird," she says. "You come out and you think you're the only Jews left. Nobody else. Just the three of us. Nobody else. Only later did we find out that some other people had survived."

"When did the other survivors start to appear?"

"I don't remember who were the first ones to come out. I think everyone came out more or less at the same time. Slowly, slowly we all got together. I don't know how we all met, we just did."

"What was that reunion like?"

"I don't remember too much about this reunion. I just know everyone was very happy to see each other. And bewildered. We couldn't believe it. 'You are alive!' 'You are alive!' And then you started crying for the others who didn't survive. They were no more.

"Over time, a few others came out of other hiding places, like from Lwów. They came back to Żółkiew, to see if anybody else had survived."

"Did any of your friends survive?"

"None of my friends survived."

"Rozia?"

"No."

"Jozio?"

"No."

"Muszka?"

"No."

She adds, "I met some of my non-Jewish school friends after the liberation. I don't remember their names. We would get together every once in a while."

"How many Jews survived?"

"One group survived in a bunker in Żółkiew. That was my friend Clara Schwarz's group. Eighteen people. And the three of us made twenty-one. Giza came with her mother, Sala Landau, that's twenty-three. Żenia was twenty-four. Leiner came back, twenty-five. Waks, Mrs. Strich's brother, came back with his wife and daughter. That's twenty-eight. So maybe forty, fifty people.

"By the time my parents and I left one year later, there were a few more Jews living in Żółkiew. They'd lived in the little villages and towns around Żółkiew before the war. They never went back to their villages after the war; it was too dangerous. They came to Żółkiew because it was bigger, and they wanted to stick together. So altogether, a year later, there were maybe seventy Jews living in Żółkiew. That's it."

"What percentage of the Jews of the town survived? How many Jews were there in Żółkiew before the war?"

"Before the war there were probably about five thousand Jews. And now there were about seventy."

Seventy out of five thousand.

1.4 percent.

Chapter Eleven

"What was the first thing you did after you left the cellar?"

"The first thing we did was go to my father's pharmacy, the one on the *rynek*, the town square. It was still standing, even still functioning. Then we went to the second pharmacy, on Lwowska Street. The ground floor of the building was in ruins. The Germans had thrown a grenade into it as they were retreating, and everything was burned, destroyed. The apartment above the drugstore, where we had lived, was empty; the Ukrainian pharmacist was gone. In the mess, we found some of our prayer books, the *Modlitwy*, that had belonged to my mother's mother. The ones I gave you, that you asked me about.

"Anyway, we couldn't stay there so we went back to the building with my father's pharmacy. There was an empty apartment above the store. My doctor, Milo Rauchfleisch, had lived and worked there before the war. He's the one neither I nor my dog had liked."

"What happened to him?"

"I found out later that he survived the war in Russia. But his wife and their child were killed."

"So you moved into that apartment?"

"Yes. We didn't ask any questions, we just moved in. Over the next months, until we left Żółkiew, we shared the apartment with many people, including some Russian officers on their way to and from the front."

"Did you have any food? How did you manage?"

"I really don't remember how we managed that first day, the second day. We had nothing, just whatever we wore on our backs, maybe an extra change of clothes. Nothing else. We had no money and no food. I don't remember how we were fed. Somebody must have brought us something, maybe the Russians, because we somehow survived."

"Do you remember how you felt that first day, that first night?"

"I really don't know how I felt. Can't describe. I don't think I was really aware of what was going on at that time. I think we were all so mixed up, so bewildered, that we didn't know in which world we were living. It was like a fog. All I was interested in was that I could move, that I could move around. It takes some time, you know, to readjust to something that you would maybe call normal. It wasn't normal because the war was still going on. And I don't know if anyone was normal. Because if you live through that horrible experience, and you come out, and you see the total devastation of your city, and you think of all the people you knew, who will never return, how can you be normal? And you see all those poor people, barely walking on their legs, undernourished. And then you realize that you're one of them. We didn't look like skeletons, not like the people who came back from the concentration camps, that's for sure, but we were also very weak. None of us had had enough food. I don't know how we had the strength to walk around. You didn't know what was happening. You were just free from that fear hanging over your head."

"Did you believe it was finally over? Were you afraid that the Germans might come back?" I ask.

"By the time we came out, we felt more sure that they would not be back because they were in full retreat. Of course they might have managed to stop at some point and counterattack. I guess we figured that if that happened, we'd run with the Russian army."

"How did you feel about the Russian soldiers this time around?"

"Well, this was the second time they occupied us. The first time, from 1939 to 1941, we'd always felt threatened by them, especially when they were shipping people to Siberia. Also, because they had come from such a completely different system, communism, where they didn't have anything, they were stealing left and right, grabbing anything they could put their hands on. This time around, their behavior was a little better and maybe our attitude was also different because they came as liberators.

"That didn't mean that they liked Jews," she laughs, wryly. "In fact, we met two Jewish officers serving in the medical unit of the Russian army, attached to the unit that had liberated us. One was a major, the other had a lower rank. They lived in the apartment next to ours for a while. They warned us, 'Russians don't like Jews either. Don't say that you are Jewish if you don't have to.' So we didn't advertise.

"The war wasn't over for another ten months, until the following May. We still had a curfew in the evening, at about eight, nine o'clock, and we still had to cover the windows. But for us, maybe a week or two after we came out of the cellar, we felt that the war was over. The Germans were gone. That period was over. They would not hunt us down anymore.

"We *were* still afraid of the surrounding Ukrainian population. But for the most part, they were too scared of the Russians to do anything to us. The Russians were taking revenge on anyone they suspected of having collaborated with the Germans. They would raid the Ukrainian villages, shooting and burning and killing. So the Ukrainians kept pretty quiet.

"The Russians organized some sort of government. They provided some supplies for the drugstore and let my father work there, under the supervision of a Russian pharmacist named Alexandra, Shura for short, who came from the Russian Ukraine. My father even got a small salary. I worked there, too, helping him, although I had never liked this type of work, filling prescriptions, rolling those little pieces of paper with medicines and powders.

"Many peasants, Polish and Ukrainian, began to stop by the pharmacy, just as they had before the war, asking my father for advice, ointments, pills. They seemed to prefer coming to him than going to doctors or even to the hospital clinic. In exchange, they brought us food: a little cheese, a piece of bread, an egg, whatever they could scrape together. They also did not have much.

"About eggs: I should tell you that after we were liberated, the first time I got a chance to eat eggs, I ate nine of them at one sitting. One after the other. I thought I would never get enough. And butter: in the beginning, I used to cut slabs of butter and put them on my bread. I wasn't eating bread with butter, I was eating butter with bread.

"The Russians even opened a school which I attended from the time we were liberated until the end of the war. It was a real mishmash. Everybody was in the same class, younger kids, older kids. We had all lost so much time from school. It was not a great education, just something for us to do. They even organized sporting competitions, *Spartakiada*, for the young people, like they had before, during their first occupation. I took part in those.

"One of our former Polish maids, Mania, came to greet us. She claimed that after the Germans had blown up the building on Lwowska, where the second drugstore was, she'd gone into our apartment and found some photographs of ours which she had kept. Now she brought them to us. Why she picked them up, I don't know. Maybe she had a sentiment to us. I don't know what else she found that she *didn't* give back. You know, I really didn't care at that time. It just didn't mean anything to me. Because everything else was gone. My mother was happy to have the photographs, though. She always was more sentimental than I was."

"Was there any kind of Jewish religious life, any communal life in Żółkiew?" I ask.

"Not much," she answers. "People just got together to socialize. My parents were pretty friendly with Waks, who returned with his wife and daughter, and another two couples."

"What about the Łozińskis?"

"Of course we stayed in touch with them. He started coming back to the drugstore just like he had done before the war, coming in to talk. He didn't have his companion, though, because Berger didn't survive. And we would visit them."

"I thought he didn't want anyone to know that they had saved you," I ask, puzzled. "How could you be in touch with them without people noticing?"

"People knew that we knew him from the pharmacy. And Łoziński and his wife were old, and not so healthy, so there was nothing wrong if we went to visit them from time to time. We didn't go so often that it would be obvious."

"Were they happy to see you?"

"Oh, yes, they were always happy to see us, happy that we were managing, that we were adjusting. They always hugged us and kissed us. And we helped them as much as we could, while we were still in Żółkiew. At the beginning, we couldn't share much with them because we didn't have anything ourselves. But after a while, when people started bringing my father food as payment for medicine and advice, we always shared it with the Łozińskis."

"Did she behave differently now that you were out?"

"No, she was always pretty reserved, never too warm or friendly. She didn't talk much, and she was involved with her prayers. He was a much warmer person and much easier to get along with."

"What was the end of the war like? V-E Day, I mean."

"There was a lot of excitement, a lot of excitement. People were crying and carrying on. The end of the war, after six years. It was a long war. Nobody predicted it would last so long.

"For us, though, it wasn't the big day. Our big day had come a year earlier, when we were finally free to come out of hiding. When we were free of that fear that someone would come and find us and kill us.

"The only thing that changed with the end of the war was that we had to decide what to do next. Żółkiew was no longer part of Poland. It was now part of the Soviet Union, the Ukrainian Republic, along with the rest of eastern Poland. Unless the Russians decided to retreat. But the Russians don't like to retreat." She laughs.

"How long did you stay in Żółkiew?"

"Until the summer of 1945. That summer, the Russians announced that anyone who was a former Polish citizen could repatriate to the western part of Poland. And about that time we also found out that my mother's brother, my uncle Poldzio and his wife Jadzia had survived and were living in Katowice, which was western Poland, in Silesia, not far from Auschwitz."

"How did they survive?" I ask.

"He was posing as a Christian. And she was hiding under his bed the whole time."

"What?"

"That's all I know," she says.

"How did you find out that they had survived?"

"I can't remember. I guess there were Jewish committees where people were registered so relatives looking for them could find them. Once we found them, we were in touch with them by mail. They invited us to come and stay with them.

"My parents decided that we would go. In fact, most of the people who survived went west, the first chance they got."

"What about the Łozińskis?"

"My father asked Łoziński to come with us. We wanted to help them, we didn't want to leave them there with the Russians. But they didn't want to go. He said, 'I am old, my wife is not well. Where am I going to go? I don't have that much longer to live. Here I have my house, my garden, the few people that I know. I'm not moving.' So we had to leave them behind. We left them some supplies, some money, whatever we could spare, and said good-bye."

"Did you stay in touch with them afterward?"

"Oh, yes. My father even sent them packages, in the beginning. But Łoziński was afraid that people would find out that he had hidden us. He asked us not to send any more. My father sent two more letters, and never got an answer. So we stopped. I don't know what happened to them after that."

"Tell me about leaving Żółkiew."

"There were two big transports. The Russians gave us a date, provided us with the necessary papers, and freight trains. They allowed us to bring along whatever we owned by then, which was not much. A few valises with some pots and pans, some clothing. We stuffed our valises and ourselves into a corner of a freight car, crossed the border into Poland, and went to my uncle in Katowice."

124

This latest session with my mother has come to an end. I feel reasonably satisfied. I think I've gotten most of the information I wanted.

I label the tapes, put them away safely until I can transcribe them, and prepare to say good-bye to my parents as they once again leave Israel for New York.

Chapter Twelve

March 30, 1995

I am finally going to Żółkiew.

After all those years of bringing up the idea, and my mother refusing to hear of it, suddenly it's going to happen.

Several survivors from Żółkiew have been financing the construction of a memorial on the site of the murder of the town's 3,500 Jews on March 25, 1943, the day my mother went into hiding. The dedication of the completed monument is scheduled for mid-July and a group of my mother's townspeople, with their families, is planning to attend the ceremony. Now that a group is traveling directly to her town, with all the land arrangements attended to, my mother feels safe enough to make the trip. She and my father will be joining the group.

"Do you want to come?" she asks me, over the phone from New York.

Do I want to come!

I am overwhelmed. I don't know what to feel first. I am so excited. I can't believe this is really going to happen. I thought I would never have the opportunity to make this trip. And I'm afraid: How will my mother react? Such trips back to the past, to the sites of murder and loss, have pitched other survivors headlong into major depressions. Could that happen to her?

And how will I react? Will I come home a wreck, emotionally drained? Or choking on "reaction-overload"? Will I feel numb, dead? I try to imagine the trip. The survivors I will meet. I know some of them, the ones from America whose names served as a backdrop to my childhood, like music playing faintly in another room. Now I'll meet the Israeli contingent, the survivors and their children, my peers. *Landsmen*. Fellow countrymen. Could they become part of a new, extended family? I still struggle with the feeling that I haven't really "cracked" Israeli society, that most of my friends are "Anglos," that I haven't made enough Israeli friends. Maybe this group will open a new avenue into my adopted country for me.

My mind starts racing. What will I pack for the trip? A few changes of clothing, as little as possible. A skirt for Shabbat services. The video camera. Spare batteries and battery packs. My 35 millimeter camera. Lots of film. Notebooks, pens, and pencils. What if streams of thoughts and reactions gush out so fast I can't write them all down? Okay, take a tape recorder. Audio tapes. More spare batteries. What if I am so overwhelmed that I go blank, and nothing comes out at all? What if I give in to the impulse to simply experience everything as it happens, and then I forget it all? What if it's an anticlimax? What if, after all this buildup, I react perversely, just shrug, and move on?

What's it going to be like, traveling to Poland, "this accursed land" as my father calls it. I want to have as little to do with the place as possible. Spend not a cent more than I have to. I don't even want to eat their food. Not just because I keep kosher. Because I don't want to ingest anything of a place where everything that springs from the earth is fertilized by ashes and blood. But can I actually manage not to eat their food? I'll take along cans of tuna fish, packages of crackers, some juice packs. It's not just the food, I realize. How can I tread on that ground and later trot through the supermarket back home in those same shoes? Maybe I should wear one pair of sneakers on the trip and then discard them at the end, like used-up surgical garb. A cynical part of me rolls its eyes. *"How dramatic. A martyr's field day!"* The thoughts persist nevertheless.

The tradition is that when Jews leave a cemetery, they wash their hands. What do you do when you leave an entire country that's a Jewish cemetery—dip into a *mikvah*? Take a shower? (Oh my God. What have I just said!) Are there special prayers to be said? *Birkat Hagomel*, the prayer of gratitude for having come safely through some trial or danger, is usually recited for present-day events; does it also apply retroactively?

I keep adding to my packing list: Siddur. Make sure it contains the special Holocaust kaddish. Shabbat candles. Memorial candles. Matches. Basic health care supplies: Aspirin. Imodium.

Sunday, July 16, 1995

My packet of travel documents arrived a few days ago: my passport with the Ukrainian visa, the plane tickets, the printed itinerary. The details are finalized. My brother Barry, who lives with his family in Rehovot, Israel, will join me and the handful of Israeli "Żółkiewites" at Ben Gurion Airport for the flight to Warsaw. There we will meet my parents and some of the others, arriving from North America. From Warsaw, we will fly to Lwów in the Ukraine, where we will meet the final contingent. Altogether our group will be comprised of about twenty people, survivors and their children, which sounds funny because these "children," like me, are adults, young and not-so-young.

All this time, I have been preoccupied with preserving my mother's story, with interviewing, recording, transcribing, processing. A whole world has been seething and living and dying inside me, and I've hoarded it almost entirely to myself. And now, similarly, hardly anyone knows I am going on this trip. At the clinic where I work part-time, nobody asked for details when I told them I would be away for a few days, and I didn't volunteer any. I haven't wanted to deal with anyone's reactions, not the raised eyebrows, not the suddenly hushed tones or questioning inflection that so often shades people's voices when discussing the Holocaust. Just like when I was in second grade, acutely conscious that I could control the flow of awe and fear of my classmates by turning on and off the tap of Holocaust material. I feel too vulnerable to chance anything; this odyssey is like a delicate fledgling that could get hurt by too much handling, however well-meaning.

I try to imagine what I will see in Żółkiew. I imagine Łoziński's house as a low, little hut of some dark color, brown maybe. I see the main room, roughly partitioned by two big, old-fashioned dark brown wooden wardrobes, with some faded swath of once-colorful cloth hung like a curtain between them. I imagine the two narrow beds, end to end, each with an immense square feather-filled pillow, the kind that, when you lean back into it, billows around your face like two enormous extra cheeks. They're encased in some stiff, almost threadbare, yellowed fabric that is clean but feels rough against the skin.

I picture a narrow dark corridor with some sort of big chest, heaped over with blankets or ruglike throws, hiding the wooden trapdoor beneath. And underneath—the cellar. I can barely get a sense of this dark, hard-packed hole in the ground. Will I ever begin to grasp what it was like? My mother was such an active kid. Always moving, running, doing. How could she tolerate just sitting and waiting and sitting and waiting? Will I be able to climb down into the space, shut the trapdoor, and sit there for a while to see for myself?

I recently read *The Bunker* by Charles Goldstein, an account of how seven people survived the aftermath of the general Polish uprising in Warsaw in 1944, by hiding in an underground bunker off the city's sewers. I read the detailed description of their day-to-day, minute-to-minute existence. Physical details. Psychological details. I still cannot comprehend what they went through.

And why do I even want to, for God's sake? Maybe I'm trying to reach back in time to provide comfort to that little girl, now my mother, and to my grandparents, to hold them and "make everything all right." I ought to know better. There is no way to penetrate the unalterable otherness of someone else's experience. Maybe that's the only way it can be. Each of us is alone. All I have are shadows, as they touch my own.

I have to try anyway.

I think back to the tail end of my last conversation with my mother, several months ago, the tape recorder whispering between us.

"It was a very nice property," she had mused, speaking of the Łozińskis' house. "The garden was a very nice size, bigger than the whole house. I wonder what is standing there today."

"Do you think the house is still there?" I had asked.

She'd shrugged. "I don't know."

"Do you remember the address? Where it would be?"

"In general, yes," she had replied. "The general direction, I know. Or maybe it changed so much I wouldn't recognize it. Maybe it doesn't even exist; that whole area could have been razed and new buildings put there. Who knows?"

"Is the cemetery still there?"

"The cemetery is still there. Destroyed, but the remnants of the wall are still there."

"Because if the wall is still there, it shouldn't be that hard to find the house," I had offered, hoping.

"Yes, I guess so. I know in general where the house would be. Although you can get completely confused. The center of town I would recognize, my street I would recognize, the apartment I first lived in I would recognize, the school and the convent, all those things remained. And I know the Ukrainian Church is still standing, I'm sure they didn't destroy that. But the side streets . . . I know in which direction to go, in general, but it is still a big question if I would be able to get there. It's fifty years ago? Fifty years exactly since we went out of that place.

"I think it would be interesting, after fifty years, to see it again."

Chapter Thirteen

Tuesday morning, July 19, 1995, 1:00 a.m.

The cab I've ordered is due any minute. The boys are sleeping. I tiptoe into their rooms, kiss them softly, blessing each one silently, before hugging Chaim good-bye at the door. Quickly pulling the feelings back inside, I climb into the cab and we are off.

The moon hangs like a half-closed yellow eyeball in the sky. It is dark and peaceful all around. My mind is racing. I feel buffeted by thoughts, by feelings. The cab speeds through the night, rocking gently along the highway, and I realize how tired I am after a long day of pent-up emotion.

All day, I had felt very much at loose ends. Morbid thoughts kept biting at me: What if, God forbid, something happens to me on this trip? Will it have been worth leaving my husband, my kids? In several farewell phone calls, close friends helped me laugh these fears away, and I hug their warm parting wishes to me like a soft, fluffy shawl. Just in case, though, I had dashed off several overdue letters, straightened my files, and gone over the kids' schedules with Chaim. He'd laughed when I showed him the containers of frozen soup stockpiled in the freezer, and the stacks of frozen casseroles. I was deadly serious.

Now, riding through the night, I feel myself trying to absorb Israel into my skin, through all my senses. There isn't much to see in the dark, and the minutes pass in silence. Just once, as he swings onto the highway, the cabby asks me where I am headed. When I say, "Poland" he merely grunts. I suddenly wish he would ask me more. After my self-imposed silence on the subject, all of a sudden I feel like telling someone what I'm about to do. But he stays mum. So do I. The forty-five-minute ride down the hills of Jerusalem to the airport passes wordlessly.

Walking through the terminal, I feel like an overloaded coat rack with bags hanging off every possible hook. A pouch is cinched around my waist. The video camera digs into my shoulder. My backpack is crammed with notebooks, pens, my small tape recorder and cassettes. The overnight bag is stuffed with a minimal change of clothes, rolls of film, spare batteries, memorial *yahrzeit* candles, a siddur, Shabbat candles and wine, and a small stock of kosher food: packets of crackers, cans of tuna fish, containers of fruit juice.

I suddenly realize that I forgot to bring along a hat. Will I need one? What will the Polish sun be like? Will the daylight blind me behind my sunglasses? How will I manage with all my bags and the cameras if I have to also shade my eyes from the sun?

How ironic. Here I am, flying to see my mother's birthplaces—the house in which she was born, and the cellar, the womb from which she emerged to rejoin the living. When she came out, the light blinded her. Now I'm worried about not being able to see straight in Żółkiew.

I spot my brother already on line at the LOT Polish Airlines check-in counter. Yosef Hirschhorn, our travel agent and group leader, is also already there, formally attired in a suit and hat, helping his fellow "Żółkiewites" through check-in. We exchange warm greetings and he begins to introduce us to the others.

As names and bits of biographical data rain down on me, I smile and shake hands and smile again. I feel my identity—even my age—shifting. I am Lutka's daughter, the granddaughter of Josef Rosenberg, the town pharmacist. I suddenly feel like a precocious youngster being taken along on an adult outing. I almost forget that I am already in the middle of my own life, a professional, a wife, a mother with school-age children. I seem to have gone back in time to being the same age as my mother, that smiling teenager in the few remaining pre- and post-war photographs in the album at home. The survivors in the group seem much younger than their sixty or seventy years, perhaps because of their vibrancy, or by virtue of this trip back into their past.

Hirschhorn tells me that my grandfather's pharmacy is still standing. I hadn't known that. I can't believe it. "Yes, yes," he insists. He's seen it on his previous trips to Żółkiew with other groups. I'm relieved that he's familiar with the territory we'll be covering. On the other hand, his having been there before makes it sound almost disappointingly routine. But maybe that's what this trip will be like: periods of the mundane interspersed with moments of drama. Maybe that's not unlike what my mother lived through during the war, and what makes it so hard to grasp. The dramatic parts of her wartime experience seem more familiar, having been brought to us already in those tightly edited documentaries with their tense highlights, professional voice-overs, and evocative music. What's hard to imagine is the day-by-day, minute-by-minute existence.

Barry and I inch down the check-in line, joke with the young security officer conducting the standard preflight interrogation, clown around. Just another trip. Just like when we were little, on those rare family vacations. I'm suddenly back in the rear seat of our old silver Rambler Classic, rolling through Buffalo on the way to Niagara Falls, listening to the Beatles sing "Love, love me do," eating huge, soft, glazed donuts. Or taking off in a fierce thunderstorm on our very first trip to Israel in 1966, courtesy of my father's first reparations check from the German government. We were heading for a reunion with his first cousin, Abraham (Abie) Wyszegrod. Abie, the sole survivor of his nuclear family, is the only one left alive from my father's entire paternal family. That trip began, I realize, on July 19, 1966, exactly twenty-nine years ago today.

It's time to board. How can I be full of such turmoil on the inside and still look the same as usual on the outside?

Staircase. Bus. Steps up to the plane. I mount them slowly, reluctantly. I don't want to leave Israeli soil.

The cabin lights dim as we prepare for take-off. The plane picks up speed, a long, narrow cylinder hurtling through the night. The enormous rush of power as the plane throws off earth's gravity is frightening; I close my eyes for a moment and fervently pray for a safe journey.

I watch the lights of Israel drop away. I feel immensely sad and lonely; I don't want to leave my country. "Don't go! Don't go!" I cry silently, not sure who's leaving whom. At times like these I am particularly conscious of how connected I am to this land, notwithstanding my other bone-deep identity as an American.

I leaf through the LOT in-flight magazine. I pause at an announcement of a Chopin festival scheduled for this week. "Oooh, let's go!" I think, and then I remember what kind of trip this is. The brilliant green and blue plumage of Papageno in another ad, this time for Mozart, stops me cold. It takes me a second to realize why: it's in color. Vibrant, living *color*. I realize that my mind screens Poland only in black and white.

I doze for a while and wake up somewhere over Poland. A patchwork of long, narrow strips of cultivated land lies below us. Like matchsticks of tawny yellow, brown, dark fir-green, and light grassy green, the fields are laid out in perpendicular and parallel patterns. Fuzzy dark-green bumps, forests, rise between the flat fields. Long farmhouses. A few cars scuttle below us. I look at the soft, green, pastoral scene rising toward us and think: at one time this place was one giant murdering bloody cage from which there was no escape. The plane dips lower, swaying softly. A city skyline up ahead pokes through some kind of gray cloud. Two long thin smokestacks pierce the fog, smoke rising from them.

The wheels touch down.

July 19, 1995, 8:00 a.m.
Okęcie Airport, Outside Warsaw

This is the same airport where my father did forced labor for the Germans for two years during the war. From this spot, he watched the Warsaw Ghetto—with his middle brother, Pesach, in it—go up in flames. Today, Okęcie Airport is a modern, state-of-the-art airport, all glass and metal. We exit the plane and make our way to our connecting flight to Lwów in the Ukraine.

As we finish with ticketing and seat assignments, I spy my parents through the glass doors separating us from the next corridor. They had flown in earlier from New York. My parents, brother, and I rush toward each other, full of excitement. Just like on a normal trip.

Another group of travelers suddenly rushes toward ours. They grab the people we've been traveling with in an ecstatic reunion, exchanging cries of joy, hugs, kisses.

My parents, my brother, and I stand off to the side. My mother seems unsure of herself, shy. I ask her if she knows these people, who obviously know each other. She is not certain. She recognizes some, is not sure about the others. She thinks they are all somehow related, to each other and to the survivors who will be joining us tomorrow in Lwów.

I feel left out, like we are crashing a private party. The warmth and love they feel for each other is evident. Their reunion is lovely. It's also painful. I had been fantasizing about bonding with this group of people with whom we would be sharing this experience, almost like finding a new surrogate family. Now I find that it's an exclusive club and we're not members. It's a familiar, unhappy feeling: the sense of almost, not-quite, belonging.

Our flight on Ukrainian Air is called, and we board the small plane.

After an hour's flight, we begin our descent toward Lwów. The city is surrounded by large stretches of farmland, spreading out in varying shades of green and yellow. Closer to the city, blocks and blocks of gray housing units become visible, reminiscent of public-housing developments I'm familiar with from New York, or Israel. But the scale is larger here, with wide streets or expansive strips of green between them. They must be Russian-built.

After disembarking, we are ferried the twenty-or-so feet from the plane's gangway to the terminal in old, yellow buses. One building serves as the all-purpose arrivals/departure/customs terminal for the city of Lwów. It has obviously seen better days. The entrance is surrounded by an intricately carved lintel painted a shade between beige and salmon, which contrasts strongly with the gray stone facade. We enter a long hall and are thrust into darkness. Immediately to our left is the duty-free shop, a small booth featuring a selection of bottles of hard and soft beverages whose contents glow faintly in the dim light. There are no customers, and no sales clerk. I take a picture of it, finding the sharp silhouettes of the Art Deco panels and the soft jewel-like radiance of the bottles particularly pleasing. But something about the atmosphere, dark and menacing, makes me put the camera away after only one shot. It feels as though everything is forbidden, although nothing actually says so. Uniformed airport personnel in dark, khaki green uniforms scrutinize us in stony, slit-eyed silence, reinforcing my feeling that I have entered a police state. Watching them watching us makes me uneasy, so I look elsewhere, wondering whether even looking around is allowed.

The white ceiling towering above us is crisscrossed with wooden beams painted in highly detailed, multicolored beauty, like *pisanki*, those intricately colored Easter eggs that Ukrainian and Polish peasants are famous for. These beams obviously predate the communist regime. However, the influence of Soviet, party-controlled art is unmistakable in the huge mural covering the entire opposite wall. Larger-than-life youthful figures—wholesome, apple-cheeked, robust young men and women—are earnestly, resolutely, engaging in Work. Numerous embossed five-pointed red stars and emblems of the hammer and sickle march around the dome of the ceiling.

We are all edgy, having heard of cases of mistreatment at the hands of customs agents in countries of the former Soviet Union. We complete the customs forms, carefully recording every valuable item with us. I even list my engagement and wedding rings. Just in case.

At Passport Control, cold eyes dart back and forth between our real-life faces and the images in the passport photos. Eventually, our papers are appropriately pounded. We drag our bags through the narrow dark corridor and emerge into a large airy reception hall.

Things start happening very fast. An elderly man appears. Medium height, florid-faced, with a sagging double chin and golden teeth, he is fairly dancing with excitement, blubbering phrases in Yiddish and Polish. He and Hirschhorn are hugging each other. Someone cries out, "Leiner!" My mother starts, then exclaims, "Oh! Leiner!" Hirschhorn pulls her forward and introduces them to each other. The old man looks at her, frowning. "Rosenberg?" he repeats, fumbling around in his memory. Then, suddenly, like dawn breaking: "Oh, Lutka!" he cries. They grab each other and hug, rocking back and forth, tears flowing. I blink back my own tears as I grab for my camera but miss the shot. I have no idea who he is, or what's going on. My mother is babbling excitedly to my father: "My father begged him and begged him to leave, after the war. 'What do you have to stay here for?' But he wanted to stay. He still lives here." I am amazed. I hadn't known that any Jews still lived in Żółkiew.

There are two other men waiting to greet us. One is Michael Sherman, the assistant director of the Lwów Jewish Community. (There's a Lwów Jewish Community?) The other, Vladimir Melamed, also Jewish, is to be our guide during our stay in Lwów. Both are in their thirties. Right now, it feels good to meet *"landsmen,"* fellow Jews, who will be taking care of us. My mixed feelings about Jews continuing to live on the ashes of their brethren will surface soon enough.

We board a large tourist bus that carries us through the wide streets, between row after row of the same Russian-built housing units that were visible from the air. Up close, they are even sadder-looking. Gray, concrete slabs, eight- to ten-stories tall, with balconies draped with faded laundry hanging limply in the white sunshine. Paint is peeling from the walls. Not one balcony has a potted plant or a flower. Everything looks drab, gray, dilapidated, sapped of life and vitality. Even the sky is a smudge of grayish-white above us.

The wide boulevards are almost completely devoid of traffic and people. Trolleys, rusted and peeling, almost empty, rattle along their tracks. Every now and then an olive-green military vehicle drives by, or a few old-model snub-nosed cars. Fresh from Israel's teeming congestion, we are struck by how desolate the streets are. "No traffic jams," someone wryly observes.

I write in my diary: "I have stepped back in time into former communist Lwów." This is literally true: the clock here is set one hour behind Polish time and we adjust our timepieces accordingly. But it's not just that.

On the way to the hotel, my mother explains that Leiner, who grew up in Żółkiew, had somehow survived the massacre of his entire family at the Janowska concentration camp.

"After the war," she says, her voice cracking as she delivers the staccato, almost breathless report, "he would come to the drugstore every day to talk to my father, telling him how he was helping the Russians raid the Ukrainian villages. The Ukrainians had murdered his parents. He wanted revenge. My father begged him not to risk his life, and tried to convince him to leave Żółkiew with us. He told him, 'You have no future here. You're a young guy. Come with us!' But Leiner's answer was 'No.' So he stayed, till today. I'm surprised he can still live with the Ukrainians. He married a Jewish woman, although I don't know where he found one. He had two sons. One married a Ukrainian woman, and still lives in Żółkiew, with their two children. The other son lives in Haifa."

Our bus stops. We have come to the end of the line: our hotel, the Sputnik, is located right across from the turnabout of the trolley line. The hotel is huge, ten stories tall, with several wings. As we enter the dark-paneled lobby, Barry nudges me, pointing out that not one ceiling light is on.

The woman behind the registration desk is smartly dressed, and her blond hair, cut in a short, sassy style, shows only a bit of dark root. Her manner is brisk and nonsmiling as she completes the procedure and gives us our room numbers.

The room I'm to share with my brother contains two twin beds, a free-standing closet, a desk and chair, and a small night-stand with a phone. All the furniture is finished in wood-toned Formica veneer that is chipped and peeling. Each piece of furniture has a number: five or six numerals painted unevenly in white. A carafe of water and two glasses have been prepared for us, plus two small blue plastic bottles of mineral water, Dobrá Voda (Good Water) from Czechoslovakia; we've been warned not to drink the tap water. The single wall-lamp, mounted above one of the beds, is missing the lightbulb. At our request, a hotel staff person brings us one, smiling at us through golden teeth. Barry thanks her in Polish; I stubbornly stick to "thank you."

The beds have been neatly made, with thin sheets, well-washed blankets, and huge, square pillows with clean but rough-textured cotton pillowcases. They remind me of the big pillows my grandparents used to have, but those were much softer. These barely give even when you thump vigorously on them. I am used to a very flat pillow; sleeping on these will feel almost like sitting up.

The small bathroom contains a sink, a toilet, and a small square bathtub in the corner with extraordinarily high sides, at least one and a half times the height of our tub at home. Some exposed pipes curve down the wall alongside the toilet. Two small bars of soap, pink, with straight ridges that are gray with accumulated dust, lie unwrapped on the glass shelf above the sink. We each get one towel; they are clean, but very thin and rough, probably from hanging to dry, board-flat, in the sun. One short strip of grayish toilet paper, punctuated with small irregular holes, has been folded and placed in a white plastic container screwed into the wall alongside the toilet. There is no hot water.

Barry films the room, the bathroom, and I take a few stills. We are dumbfounded by the conditions. It's livable, but so meager, so depressing. I find myself torn between sympathy for these anonymous people and the realization that we are talking about the hated Ukrainians who murdered so many members of my family, destroyed my mother's community. This discrepancy jars me over and over during the trip.

Our room looks out onto the trolley roundabout. A few people run for the trolley when it clangs its way around the tracks every few minutes, but otherwise, the streets are deserted. We've been warned not to look out the window, lest we attract attention to the fact that tourists—and their belongings—are in residence. "And don't leave anything valuable in the rooms, either, not even when you go for meals." It feels like prison.

We board our bus and begin to drive through the streets of Lwów. Our first stop is to pick up the last contingent of our group, staying at one of the remaining old-style grand hotels in Lwów. This group includes Giza Landau and her husband Sam Halpern, and Clara Schwarz and her husband Sol Kramer. As they board the bus, there's another reunion, more excitement, more cries of joy in Polish, Yiddish, and English. But this time, even our family can join in. My mother knows Giza and Clara from childhood. In fact, when she was very little, her family lived in an apartment in a building owned by Giza's family on Zwierżyniecka Street. The story of how the two little girls, Giza and Lutka, splashed together in a tin washbasin on the balcony of that building is part of family lore.

The slight age differences between my mother, Giza, and Clara made for different grades and slightly different social circles. Under normal circumstances, they might each have gone their separate ways as they grew up, but the fires of war forged the bonds between them into steel. "Giza-and-Sam-and-Clara-and-Sol" became part of the background music of my childhood. We did not see them often, but I'd hear my mother talking to them by phone (I'd hear the Polish staccato and the smile in my mother's voice). They never forgot each other's birthdays and always celebrated each other's family milestones.

Now that the whole group is together, our tour of Lwów can begin. Our guide, Vladimir Melamed, is a thin, narrow-faced man with wire-rimmed glasses and an Abraham Lincoln beard. From time to time, his lips pull back in a grimace-like smile from his teeth, set like large white Chicklets in his mouth, a careful space between each one. His fingers are long, thin, bony, with tapered nails, like skinless claws. He keeps glancing about nervously, shoving his glasses up the bridge of his nose with quick, darting gestures. He looks like he's not comfortable inside his own skin.

I look around me as we drive here and there, up and down. The city is quaint, and would be quite beautiful—if someone took better care of it. Before World War II, people flocked to Lwów from all over Europe, enjoying its cosmopolitan atmosphere, its elegance. Today, it's an old dowager, ragged and unkempt, with little to remind you that this was once the belle of the ball. The stately buildings still feature elegant filigree work and carvings, but the facades are fading, peeling, eroding. Laundry hangs everywhere, looking well-worn, dingy, poor. The entranceways to many buildings are dark, and, as we discover later when we get to walk around, as often as not, they smell of urine.

Peering at Lwów from the bus, I feel—well, not much of anything, actually. Somewhat tired, almost bored, detached and distant from the street scenes passing before my eyes. I'm not sure what I expected to feel. I just know that there's some hollow space inside me. This is just another European city, like many other European cities I have seen, either in person or in films. Big deal.

I'm worried about my reaction. I hope it's just part of the process. Maybe it'll be okay.

We crisscross the city. Unfortunately, Melamed does not give us any orientation to the city so driving around up and down the streets of Lwów leaves me confused, with no sense of direction. Like a standard tour guide, he points out buildings, historical sites. But the survivors are too excited to behave like regular tourists. Which, of course, they aren't. They were here before he was born. They knew this place as it was, he knows it as it is now. He sings out a name, they explode with a chorus. "*Tak, Tak*, yes, yes! This was _____." And: "No, that was _____." He corrects them, they override him. It's a battle of wills, of ownership, as the bus glides in seemingly random patterns up one street and down another.

Melamed is obviously discomfited by the echo chamber operating around him. I can understand his frustration, but I get irritated with his trying to swim upstream against their tide. He seems so out of touch with the drama being enacted around him, the tremendous pathos of people rediscovering their past and adjusting to its new reality. Finally, he gives up. The survivors call out what streets we are on, and what they used to be called, and he contents himself with confirming or adding pertinent information. Even when he feels compelled to correct them, he does so by first acknowledging their knowledge. He's not fighting them anymore, but is still clearly uncomfortable. His bony fingers clutch the back of his seat in a tight, white grip, and his half-smile–half-grimace is plastered across his lips.

My mother remarks that America is receding into the distance as "home." She feels as though she lives here. I want to cry as I hear that. This godforsaken piece of land had been her home until she had been torn out of it. Kicked out. An image from Shakespeare's *Macbeth* keeps coming to mind: someone ripped from his mother's womb. My mother has no home left on the face of the earth.

We visit the Jewish Cultural Center. The bulletin boards are covered with colorful murals depicting scenes of Jewish history, captioned in Ukrainian. An exhibit of photographs depicting the Holocaust hangs along the walls of the sanctuary. A pencil sketch of a soldier at the Western Wall is taped over the stage. Tacked to another wall is the last verse of the Kaddish, the memorial prayer,

141

the Hebrew words transliterated in Ukrainian characters: "*Shalom aleinu ve'al kol Yisrael.*" "Peace unto us, and unto all Israel."

We meet some of the remaining elderly Jews of the town in an *ulpan* class where they are painstakingly, devotedly learning Hebrew. Leiner, Hirschhorn, and some of the members of our group greet them in Yiddish, telling them of our mission. It is moving to touch the *She'erit Hapleita*, the last remnants of the destroyed Jewish community, the ones who "missed the boat," as Hirschhorn says. There is something very sad about these frail, gray people trying to hold on to scraps of an identity.

Only later do I realize that my response to them is based on a distortion, a time warp. I have been blurring the boundaries between past and present, responding to these people as though they are those old wartime photographs come to life. But they are not. After the war, they were in their teens and twenties, in their prime, younger than I am now. After all they had been through, how could they have stayed here, among enemies, in this huge European graveyard?

And what about Sherman and Melamed: Why are *they* here? Do they really hope to be able to develop a viable Jewish life here?

I'm curious about these issues, but not enough to pursue them directly. I'd have to dig behind the polite smiles to the real story, challenge our hosts, possibly make them—and me—uncomfortable. And through a translator, yet. I don't have the energy. I need all my energy to absorb and remember what I am seeing.

The bus zigzags up and down the streets, bumping over the cobblestones. People stare at us. Do they stare at all tourist buses like this? Do they know we are Jews? What do they think of us?

I'm trying to figure out what I think of them. I know I don't want to like them. Maybe it's projection on my part—a distinct possibility—but I don't find them at all attractive: large heads, broad foreheads, flat, wide cheekbones, thin noses and mouths. Almost everyone has at least one golden tooth. Most of the women, especially those middle-aged and older, are heavy, dumpy-looking. It's no surprise, given the heavily fried starchy diet. There are many blondes, mostly out of peroxide bottles.

Very few women wear pants. Most wear skirts or dresses, very utilitarian, with little sense of style. Here and there are exceptions. At one point, we pass a slim young woman striding purposefully down the street in a well-tailored, two-piece outfit, its dark-blue tones nicely set off by the lacy white collar of her blouse peeping out at the neckline. A belt of red patent leather and a reddish scarf thrown loosely around her neck complete the outfit with bright splashes of color. Suddenly, she quickly raises her right arm and furtively sniffs her armpit.

We pass a bridge marking the place where Jews were rounded up for extermination, stop at the memorial marker. Then we continue to the site of the concentration camp at Janowska Road.

This is where my mother's uncle Manek and his son Mietek were killed.

I remember my mother telling me about this:

"Before we went into hiding," she said, "sometime in January or February 1943, we received a note from my uncle Manek. He wrote that his wife, Zosia, and her family had been taken away on the trains in the direction of Belżec. Belżec," she explains quietly, "was one of the killing places in Poland. Like Sobibor and Chelmno. That's all they were for. Killing. Not labor, not detention. Just killing. Nothing else. He couldn't save Zosia but somehow he managed to survive and to save his son Mietek. He gave him a piece of sugar—that's all he had—and buried him in a hole. Covered the hole and left him there. When Manek went to get Mietek out two days later, he wasn't sure he would still be alive. He found him alive and pulled him out. That's what he wrote. That he and Mietek survived, but he was devastated that he couldn't save his wife."

"What happened to them after that?" I had asked, afraid to ask.

"A few weeks later they were both captured and sent to the Janowska concentration camp. I know that he did not survive there. That was the last information we got before we went into hiding. I don't know exactly how we got it. Somehow people, Poles mostly, were getting in and out of the ghetto, and somehow we got that information."

"What happened to Manek's note?"

"My mother saved that little note. She had it up until the time we went into hiding, but it didn't survive past that. It must've gotten lost."

Today, the site of the Janowska camp is surrounded by paved roads traveled by trucks and passengers cars speeding by. A large, roughly hewn stone monument attests to the massacre of countless Jews on this very spot. Beyond that, a chain-link fence encircles a stone mother and child nestling comfortably against one another amid a sea of tall green grasses and stalks of white and purple flowers swaying gently in the warm breeze. A brook burbles nearby.

But back then, the road was dirt, and the area was called *Piaski*, meaning sands, because of the large sand deposits here. Leiner was here. He starts to describe what took place here, what he saw, what he experienced. His voice breaks, his words get mixed up with huge, gulping sobs, but he keeps talking. The sand that was here, and this little river, he says, was red, full of blood, full of corpses, full of the still-dying. Men, women, and children were marched naked to this spot and mowed down on top of one another, falling on the rows of those who had been gunned down a few minutes earlier, burying one another, whether dead or still alive. His family was killed here. Somehow he managed to escape.

I can only understand parts of what he is saying, because he is speaking in Yiddish, because comprehending what he is describing is beyond my ability. I don't know how to break through that barrier. I don't know if I want to.

The group stands silent, listening. Did we then recite Kaddish, *El Moleh Rachamim?* I can't remember.

I ask my mother if she'd like to light a *yahrzeit* candle in memory of her uncle Manek. She says yes.

She strikes the match. The flame leans up toward her hand as though reaching for the skin of her thumb, then the wick bursts into fiery life within the shiny metal confines of the tin container holding the memorial candle. We place it in a tiny crack on the side of the monument.

"This is for my Uncle Manek," she says, her voice breaking.

As we board the bus, she reminds me of something I had forgotten: after the war, before leaving Poland, my grandmother came to the Janowska camp to collect some of the blood-soaked sand, all that was left of a beloved brother. I remember her showing me the canister: a small, oval-shaped tin container, about three inches high, with a tight-fitting lid, tied around with a thin, black satin ribbon whose bows had been pressed flat, like a dried flower. She kept the tin in the bottom drawer of her bedside table. It was one of her most precious possessions. Many times, she told me, as she told my mother: "Promise me. When I die, bury this with me." When my grandmother died in 1980, we kept our promise.

We return to Lwów. The sightseeing continues.

We are driving around the city again, following no particular pattern that I can discern. Suddenly, my mother jumps out of her seat, exclaiming, "This must be the street where Uncle Manek lived!" We ask Melamed, sitting right in front of us, to stop the bus for a moment so I can take a picture of Manek's building. Either Melamed doesn't understand or doesn't want to understand. It's late in the day. We are all sweaty and grimy. Maybe he's just had enough. In any case, he ignores us. We call to him, and to the bus driver, in English, in Polish, even in Ukrainian, which somehow erupts from my mother's memory. "Stop the bus! Just for a moment!"

The bus driver keeps driving. Around the corner. Down another street. Melamed finally turns around and tells us that the driver couldn't stop the bus on that corner because of traffic regulations, but that he will stop just a little farther down and we'll be able to return to it on our own. The bus continues up one street, down another, turning here, turning there. I am a prisoner on this damn bus. It keeps moving farther and farther away from the house, from that street. We will never be able to retrace our steps and find it. I am seething with frustration; Melamed is oblivious to the problem. We finally stop for a ten-minute break. We are more than a ten-minute walk away from the street. We'll never be able to find it on our own, and in so short a time. We have to forget it.

I feel betrayed by this little wimp of a *"galus yid,"* this Diaspora Jew who sided with the gentile bus driver—the two of them knowing these streets–against his own kind. What do I expect, after all, from a Jew who threw in his lot with the enemy, who lives with them, smiles at them, cozies up to them, in order to survive? My disgust for him grows by the second. I am livid. Barry tries to talk some sense into me, but I don't want to be soothed. I want blood. I want to kick him. To smash his face against the side of the bus. The exigencies of civilization not allowing for such direct gratification, I grab for some other form of revenge. I snarl that I won't contribute anything to his tip. But even that meager revenge is denied me. Barry points out, in his maddeningly rational way, that, even as we speak, Hirschhorn has just paid him for the day's work and look, he's leaving. I turn my back on him as he departs from the group.

By now, I have had it. I am thoroughly sick of this place, of its drabness, of being eyed by passersby with suspicion, curiosity, and, I imagine, hostility. The faces feel closed against me. I feel like "ŻYD," "Jew!" must be plastered, like a mark of Cain, across my forehead. In capitals.

We return to the hotel, spent after a long day. I'd love a shower but there's no hot water. I make do with a quick splash and a dab with a corner of the towel.

We make our way through the cavernous hotel hallways to the dim hotel dining room. There's not enough electricity for lighting, but the portable radio is blasting away popular Ukrainian tunes.

Dinner consists of black bread and butter, sardines and sprats, pierogi (potato-filled dumplings with bits of fried onions, swimming in little lakes of butter), boiled potatoes sprinkled with dill, and sauerkraut. I nibble at something. I want to lighten the mood; I remind my mother of her favorite winter food when she was a child: sauerkraut and potatoes. She smiles but notes that this sauerkraut is sweeter than what her grandmother used to make.

When I get into bed, I shove the enormous denseness of the pillow out of the way and try to pummel its lower-left corner into something flat and soft enough to lean my head on.

Chapter Fourteen

Wednesday, July 20, 1995

I awaken at 6:00 a.m., even before the alarm rings, too keyed up to sleep. Too much to do: have to catch up on yesterday's journal entry before today's events start to pile up.

The Hotel Sputnik reminds me of one of my favorite stories from the book *Tzedakah* by Azriel Eisenberg. The town rabbi collects alms for the poor in his community. He knocks on the door of a potential donor, very wealthy but very stingy. When the rich man opens the door, the rabbi keeps him standing in the unheated vestibule, talking of this and that, while his host turns bluer and bluer with cold. Finally, the rich man can stand it no longer, and insists on ushering his guest into his salon, near the roaring fire. When they have thawed out somewhat, the rich man turns to the rabbi and asks, "Tell me, rabbi, are you in the habit of trying to freeze your hosts to death?" The rabbi smiles and answers, "I came to collect money on behalf of people who are cold and hungry. Do you think you would have been able to really understand what that's like, had we come straight in here and had a nice glass of tea by the warm fire, instead of standing out there in the cold?" The rich man roars with appreciative laughter and gives a large donation.

Staying in this two-bit hotel (rated four-stars by local standards) with its missing lightbulbs and rationed toilet paper gives

147

me a tiny peek into the mystery I am trying to penetrate: What was it like to endure the privation, the misery? I know this pales in comparison, but had we checked into some fancy hotel with all the amenities—the hot water, the mint on the pillow—I would have even less of an idea of what my mother experienced.

There still is no hot water. But I discover that the water in the carafe, having sat out all night, is a few degrees warmer than the frigid stuff flowing out of the faucets. So I wash myself quickly—very quickly—with that. I dry the spillover with some newspapers I'd had with me on the flight that are still stuffed in my bag.

I know these tiny bits of ingenuity are nothing like the challenges of survival my mother faced. Still, I'm absurdly proud of them. Maybe I could also have survived.

At 7:30 a.m., all the members of our group emerge from their respective rooms. Dragging all our valuables with us, and sweaters, for the day has dawned gray and chilly, we troop down to the dining room for breakfast. The echoing corridors remind me of scenes from Nevil Shute's classic novel *On the Beach*, after nuclear fallout killed all the people but left the buildings intact.

We can't seem to get moving. Breakfast takes forever. Pyramids of bread and cheese have already been placed on each table. The single waitress starts bringing out servings of fried eggs, one plate per hand, to the tables. My mother and another member of the group get impatient. They jump up and start bringing teacups and small fat ceramic pots of hot water to the tables themselves, to get things rolling.

We are behind schedule. People run to complete last-minute preparations. We vacillate between impatience and understanding. Finally, at a few minutes past nine, we are on the bus.

The sun has broken through the layer of clouds and it has warmed up considerably. We won't need the sweaters.

Barry and I commandeer the right front seat, directly behind the door, in order to have a good view. We offer it to my mother, so she can have the first glimpse of her town when we get there, but she says she's fine where she is, sitting behind the driver. He handles the bus gracefully, competently, easing smoothly from gear to gear, driving carefully along a tree-lined street.

"What street are we on?" someone asks.

"Chmielnicki Street."

Bogdan Chmielnicki is a Ukrainian national hero. On his way to liberating his fellow Ukrainian countrymen, he and his followers murdered thousands of Jews in the infamous pogroms of 1648–1649.

We turn onto Żółkiewska, a two-lane highway so named because it leads to Żółkiew. City buildings give way to smaller houses, glimpses of fields. Just ahead of us rumbles a dust-covered dull blue dump truck, hauling a mound of grayish-bluish shards of broken glass, blinking in the light. I think of Kristallnacht, November 9, 1938, the Night of Broken Glass in Germany, the harbinger of horrors yet to come. The truck of broken glass lumbers on ahead of us. I look away, look back: the truck is gone.

The countryside stretches out on either side of us. Green and yellow strips of cultivated land in a delicate quilt-work pattern. Cows. Flocks of geese. Fields of corn. A horse-drawn wooden cart bears an enormous load of hay that towers over the cart like a huge muffin rising out of a baking tin.

Leiner rattles off the names of the towns and villages we are passing. The Israeli daughter of one of the survivors repeats the names into the microphone, mispronouncing them badly. The survivors correct her, in a chorus that crescendos with laughter. The atmosphere is light, giddy, almost raucous, like the bus ride to summer camp. Beneath the surface, I feel tension, tightly coiled, the ever-present sense of teetering on the edge, with tears welling up just behind the dam of my eyes and my will. No time for that. Just record. Get it all down. React later.

Many of the towns and villages we drive past had large Jewish populations. All gone. All dead.

We pass the town of Kulikow. Hirschhorn invokes the memory of the wonderful bread they used to bake here, sniffing an aroma only he can detect. He relates a true story: the town cobbler killed his wife and faced the death penalty. However, as he was the only cobbler in town, the townspeople decided that they could not get along without him. He was acquitted. This became known as "Kulikow justice."

My mother leans across the aisle: "My great-uncle Kuba lived in Kulikow," she says. He had been a doctor; he'd pierced her ears when she was a baby.

.

149

None of Kulikow's Jews were acquitted.

We pass houses painted with stenciled designs on the eaves, the walls. Fields of pale golden wheat stretch to the horizon. The stalks are only waist-high. You couldn't hide in them.

My mother points out the many *kapliczki* lining the highway. These roadside altars dedicated to Mary range from simple pedestals to elaborate stands encircled with decorative wrought-iron fences. Many are bedecked with flowers. Tall crosses stand behind some of them, festooned with brightly colored ribbons and draped with long streamers. The altars have a merry air about them, like carousels at a country fair.

Some of the statuettes of Mary are small, barely a foot tall. Others tower, life-size, over the road.

"See those?" my mother asks, pointing to one of the life-sized ones. "The one the Łozińskis had was like that."

I'd been imagining the Łozińskis' statue of Mary as a miniature statuette, the size of the figures in the crèche that my childhood friend Kathy Smith and her family used to set up every Christmas. It would have to be, to fit into the minute shack I've been constructing in my mind: a tiny structure with barely enough room to turn around, which somehow manages to house five people—two aboveground, three below—a large long-haired cat under the table, and my ghost haunting its nooks and crannies. How can another figure—life-sized, no less—possibly squeeze in there?

It reminds me of when I was five, "celebrating" my birthday in bed, fighting off yet another bout of German measles. My grandparents marched into my room, proudly bearing my birthday present: an enormous Patti Playpal doll. She had thick, glossy, dark hair, brown eyes that opened and closed, and a sweet, smiling mouth. And she was almost as tall as I was. I took one look at her and burst into tears. My parents and grandparents, taken aback by my unexpected reaction, hastily removed the doll until they could calm me down. (That doll, whom I named Debbie, became one of my favorites. I still have her.)

Now, once again, I have to make room for a new life-sized "doll."

I can't shake loose my own images so quickly.

Maybe I hadn't understood my mother correctly?

"She was big? *How* big?" I demand.

"Oh, yes. Life-size," she assures me, holding her palm out to demonstrate. "She was dressed in a white dress, with a blue robe, and stood on a pedestal covered with a cloth. The pedestal had two steps, the upper one where they'd put flowers, and the bottom one for kneeling."

No time to adjust. The bus is pulling up to a big three-dimensional structure. The bottom layer is a white high-relief sculpture depicting noble-visaged men and women gazing resolutely forward, tools and farm implements in hand, ready to labor for the greater glory of the Worker and Communism. Above the sculpture, large, brown stone letters spell out: ZULKVA. Żółkiew, in Ukrainian.

We are at the outskirts of Żółkiew. The town is not yet in sight. I try to take a photograph of my mother's face as she cranes to see but someone steps between us, cutting off the shot. I swear silently to myself.

We clamber off the bus for the photo op. Cameras whir, snap, and whine. The group re-forms, and re-forms again, as the photographers trade places with the "photographees." The combinations and permutations seem endless.

I turn for another shot, press the shutter release, wait for the film to advance. It doesn't. I press again and again. The button clicks, the eye blinks wildly, and remains open, wide open, stuck on frame 34.

Back on the bus, upset, I tell my parents and brother about the camera. My mother, surprisingly unruffled, says it's an omen: the camera didn't want to go back to Żółkiew. I decide, instead, that the camera must be keeping a wide-eyed vigil of its own for the rest of the trip.

We drive down a bumpy dirt lane, past little cottages and gardens, to the Christian cemetery, to a special section: the final resting place of the sons and daughters of the town who died fighting against the Germans in 1944. Dark tombstones rise around us, with pictures of the dead engraved above their names.

We come to a large dark-gray stone marker, engraved in Ukrainian and Yiddish. This monument was erected a few years ago by the Ukrainian government. It contains dug-up bones and dust from the execution site at the *borek*, the nearby "little forest."

Someone mutters: "They must have realized that Jews visiting cemeteries is good business."

Somewhere in this cemetery, Łoziński and his wife must be buried. I had imagined walking through a small country cemetery with several rows of headstones and finding their graves. But this is huge. We have no idea where their graves might be. Only now does it occur to me that we should have hired someone to hunt through the cemetery and find them. Now it's too late. We have only this one day.

Our group has been joined by a news crew from Lwów, one reporter taking notes and another filming. It bothers me that our private moments of grief are becoming a "Media Event," a headline: Jews Return to Żółkiew. I am uncomfortable with the notoriety.

Three elderly women appear, large printed kerchiefs knotted under their chins; they are coming to the memorial ceremony. Two of them look Jewish; the third decidedly does not, though she insists that she is.

As we reboard the bus, Barry offers his seat to one of the three, a tiny, wrinkled woman with the face of a withered walnut. She looks at me through wire-rimmed glasses and smiles, revealing three golden lower teeth. She tells us that she has lived in the town since before the war.

"Do you remember the pharmacist, *Pan* Rosenberg?" asks my mother from across the aisle.

"Oh, yes!" she nods, emphatically.

"He was my wife's father," explains my father.

"Ah!" she replies. More nodding. More smiling. She does not volunteer any more information. I feel waves of emotion, rising, cresting, inside. I want to know so much, it renders me mute. I wouldn't even know where to begin. I can't speak to her; she only speaks Polish. I doubt she'd be able to tell me much anyhow. Everyone would've come to the pharmacy at some point in their lives; maybe they would even remember the pharmacist. Those are probably not the kind of memories I am looking for.

The bus pitches and rocks down the narrow road. I am terrified that I will not absorb and remember everything. I will let the video camera do the remembering for me, although I don't like my view of the world being constricted into a little black window. I film some of the cottages and the fields, taking visual notes of the surroundings.

"Save your film," one of the reporters tells me. "There's lots more to film later in the town."

I shut the camera off, feeling foolish and unsure. I don't know how to budget the film or the battery. What if they run out? It's a particularly scary thought after the breakdown of my camera just minutes earlier.

The bus lurches farther along the rutted lane. The hubbub of conversation quiets. Along this very route, on March 25, 1943, 3,500 Jews were marched to their deaths.

From her seat across the aisle, my mother calls to Barry and me, "Do you see how long it is, how far to walk? Wait till we go back to town, you'll see how far it is to walk all that way."

In truth, I have no sense of distance, or direction, just of time passing. There is still so much to accomplish.

We pass more little houses, fields, on our way to the *borek*, the "little forest." Then we turn left, and stop. We have arrived.

But . . . the way to the *borek* is blocked by the Ukrainian Army, which now uses the area as a firing range. It's off-limits to civilians. We have to convince the officers to let us in. It probably doesn't hurt that we have the blessing of the mayor, who is apparently waiting to meet with us after the memorial service, and the presence of the newspeople. We get an hour.

We disembark and start walking. It's quiet in the forest. Crickets chirp. Birds trill in the tall trees that rise around us like canyon walls. I hear the hushed voices of people in the group as they walk ahead of me on the path. Two soldiers bring up the rear of the column of walkers. Imagine: Ukrainian soldiers are accompanying us to our memorial service to commemorate the murder that their ancestors helped commit. I go tight with rage. I loathe these young soldiers with their pinched nostrils and Ukrainian faces, slouching nonchalantly in their uniforms, stubbing out their cigarettes on "my" hallowed ground.

All day I have been walking around with tears in my eyes, right behind the lids, but I don't let them go. A reservoir is collecting in my chest, held tight by a dam right behind my breastbone.

The rutted dirt path winds to the left and opens onto an open field. The sun is shining, the sky is blue, the trees are green. Between a placid pool of water edged with bulrushes, and a small mound, stands the monument. It is a dignified, softly rounded sculpture of pure white stone. It features a Star of David, two hands outstretched in blessing, and a commemorative plaque.

We recite several psalms and memorial prayers. The Kaddish. *El Moleh Rachamim.* Oh Merciful God.

The words stick in my throat. I don't want to pray to a God who was silent. And yet, these people—including my mother—survived. Each represents a miracle. I force myself to murmur the prayers out of a sense of community, of solidarity with *them.* And as an act of defiance, of vengeance, an "in your face" gesture to the Ukrainians and the Germans. I mumble and film. I zoom in on the Star of David, the hands, the plaque, as we intone God's greatness.

"Magnified and sanctified is Your great Name."

My brother mutters, over and over: "Three thousand five hundred people *in one day?*"

I film and film. Trying to capture the pervading quiet enveloping us, the pastoral scene, the trees, the water, the ground.

I film and film. I swipe tears off my cheek with my palm, wipe them on my pants and keep filming. I have this constant sense of being outside myself, watching me experiencing this. I think: here's a "Meaningful Shot": a child of survivor recording her family's tragic history, camera to her eye and tears flooding down her face. Music should swell as a second camera zooms in for the close-up.

Speeches, speeches, speeches. Polish. Russian. Ukrainian. English. Hebrew.

"Don't forget this place."

"Come back, with your children."

"Remind the townspeople that this is their history as well as ours."

The ceremony is over. Walk back to the bus. Make nice to the Ukrainian soldiers and their commanding officer, give them a box of cigarettes. Wonder: if this were fifty years ago, what would these nice young men in khaki be doing? And I know exactly: They'd be chasing me through the woods. Chopping my head off with an ax. Or, simply, shooting me. They'd be helping the Germans force-march the entire group of 3,500 Jews over those several kilometers that we just drove, all the way from the town to the *borek*, this lovely little spot, surrounded by this same rise of trees acting as a natural screen.

Three thousand and five hundred people.

They were marched to the death-ditches that had been dug, earlier, by other Jews. Somewhere in the *borek*, they were forced to strip. To impede escape. To demoralize. To humiliate. And to save those shreds of clothing, so they could be shipped and used elsewhere. Then they were marched over planks placed over these trenches. When they reached the middle, standing right over the center of the ditch, they were shot. Just once. One bullet per Jew. No sense in wasting ammunition. Whether or not you died immediately from that shot, it didn't matter; you fell in, and lay there, with bodies around you, beneath you, on top of you. People who passed by the area reported that the earth moved for days afterward.

I cannot comprehend it. Cannot comprehend how you march to your death, how you walk, with everyone around you, everyone you know, knowing what's coming. Did you cry? Pray? Hope for a miracle? Go numb? Scream? Maybe, but the Ukrainians and Germans who propelled you forward were beating you and pushing you the whole way and screaming at you and probably would have beaten you even harder if you made too much noise. You probably tried to move to the center, to avoid the blows, trying not to fall on the way (instant death), hoping for a miracle, comforting those around you, maybe—if you had enough presence of mind, if you didn't lose your mind—lie to the children. Maybe. Maybe say nothing at all. The horror is too much to absorb, especially the bit about the children. If I allow myself—*really* allow myself—to think of having to walk that last mile with my children, I will start to scream and scream and never stop. . . . The tears start running. . . .

No time for tears now.

We reboard the bus and drive into town along Lwowska Street. My mother is on the edge of her seat.

The bus stops at the next stop on our "tour": the house where Clara Schwarz's group of eighteen people survived, hidden in an underground bunker. Many of the people on our bus, in fact.

I am torn between wanting to enter, wanting to see, and wanting to continue to my mother's part of town. What if we run out of time and can't do what *we* came for? But how can I tell these people I don't want to see where they escaped death? I feel caught in the tide of rapidly moving events.

So I follow the group. We enter the house, pouring through the living room with its dark walls hung with carpets and icons, and crowd into the bedroom. The woman of the house, who has been waiting for us, pushes aside two narrow twin beds to reveal a trap door cunningly cut into the herringbone pattern of the parquet wood floor. I stare at it. My skin prickles. I can't film. Can't move. Can't believe what I am seeing. I turn to Barry, try to call him, but only a moan crawls out of my mouth. He doesn't hear me: he's also staring, transfixed; somehow he manages to snap a few pictures.

Someone kneels down and pries at the floorboard with something sharp. The trapdoor rises from the floor. It's about four inches thick. Its uppermost level is a thin layer of shiny herringbone veneer. The layer beneath is thick, dark wood. It must be heavy; someone grunts as it's hefted and laid on one of the beds.

I fight the feeling that this isn't real. But there's the dark hole in the floor, an opening of about two by three feet, into which people start lowering themselves, disappearing into the darkness below amid soft exclamations of shock, disbelief, awe.

"Are there steps?" asks my mother, peering into the hole, awaiting her turn to climb down.

"Steps!" someone snorts. "What steps?"

I know why she's asking: because the entrance to her hiding place did have steps. And now someone does hand down a little white wooden table to someone already below so it's easier to step down into the bunker.

My turn. I lower myself carefully into the darkness, my toes searching for the surface of the rickety table and then for the uneven earthen floor. The dim electric bulb hanging from the low ceiling—too low for me to stand upright—illuminates a series of

156

roughly carved-out spaces between half walls, uneven stands of brick, wooden beams. and pilings. As our eyes adjust to the darkness, Clara serves as tour guide for this place into which she and seventeen others were crammed for eighteen months. She points to the various niches and identifies each family's "living quarters." She shows us the hollow that served as the toilet. She describes how they worked for weeks, digging out the crawl space, rigging a few light bulbs. In that dim light, she read and even kept a diary.

I remember that my mother's cellar had not been prepared at all for hiding. And that it had been too dark to read.

Back on the street. Reeling. I've just come back from another world.

I feel numb. I feel too much. There's no time. Keep moving. The bus slides into central Żółkiew. Everyone disembarks.

"Let's just get going," exclaims my mother.

My mother is bouncing all over the place. It is chaos. She's running up and down one _____ska Street after another. I'm running after her with the video camera, trying to keep it steady as I film. My brother's running after me with his 35 millimeter camera. She's exclaiming, "But this wasn't here! And this wasn't there! And this was _____'s house, and _____ lived there—" and I hope I am getting all this on film because I'll never remember it, and everything's very fuzzy and foggy; I'm observing everything only through this damn tiny viewfinder. She's like someone who's been waiting all these years to go back to one special candy store she knew as a kid. But now that she's there, everything is different. Distorted. She's been seeing things till now with her heart, now her eyes and mind have to catch up.

We turn right off the main street, and all of a sudden she starts jumping up and down.

"This is where I lived!" she cries. "This is where the drugstore was, the second drugstore!" Barry is confused; he keeps losing the thread of the story: "What drugstore? Which drugstore?" And part of the house isn't one story anymore, it's now two stories high, but she shows us the corner anyway, saying, "That part of the building wasn't there, but that's the building, and that was the cellar where we were hiding during that earlier *akcja*, and that was the outhouse across the way, and this was Turyniecka Street, and that was the wall of the ghetto." And I'm running around with the video camera and feeling tears threaten again and pushing them back because there's no time, no time, and it's already early afternoon.

We continue down the street, my mother trying to explain things to us coherently, and I keep filming, and she keeps moving out of camera range, darting here and there, talking, gesturing, and I try to keep her framed within the shot so I can capture her pointing at what she's pointing at or at least be looking at what she's pointing at, and I feel like I need ten pairs of eyes and hands and a camera crew, professionals who know how to roll a camera smoothly down the street, and how to film, who aren't blinded by tears.

Now my mother's comparing notes with another one of the survivors, what was here, what was there, what's not there anymore. And then she stops. Turns to us.

"This is not my town," she says.

And, a few minutes later, when she's out of camera range, and I have switched off the video for a moment, she looks at me and says, "Well, I have no dreams left."

Chapter Fifteen

We trot down the street and meet the others at the entrance to the Great Sobieski Synagogue of Żółkiew, a stately, imposing building. I remember my grandfather's delicately tinted photographs of the synagogue in my album back home. Before me today, the building's exterior walls are also tinted: some strange shade of faded mauve and neglect. A bronze plaque near the entranceway, in Ukrainian, identifies this as a protected historical site, labeling it simply Synagogue. A few steps lead to a small arched doorway, and through that is the synagogue. What's left of it.

Blackened walls, charred bricks, chunks of broken beams, piles of rubble. Rising to the vaulted ceiling are four central columns, of such broad diameter that it would take at least three people linking hands to circumscribe them. Fire has stripped them down to the naked bricks.

On the front wall, there are still traces of the Holy Ark, scars where carved wooden moldings were ripped from the walls. And rashlike patches: the remains of frescoes. Of the four letters of God's name, just the first three remain: Yud Hey Vav. I point the camera toward the women's section where my great-grandmother and grandmother used to sit when they came to pray. I film: a square of white light through a window. The women's section no longer exists.

The group gathers in a ragged circle and we say Kaddish. Michael Sherman opens a book, *Masterpieces of Jewish Art*, to some black-and-white photographs of what the synagogue used to look like, the elaborate chandeliers worked in copper and bronze, and the ornate filigree that once adorned the Holy Ark. From inside a worn cloth bag, he digs out a few branches of a brass candelabrum. They lie, twisted and bent almost beyond recognition, in a forlorn heap in his palm. Funds are being sought to restore the synagogue, he explains, shoving them back into the bag. As we turn to leave the synagogue, my father picks up a piece of charred brick from the floor and hands it to me.

"Take it with you," he says.

Separating from the group once again, we follow my mother as she marches us through the streets surrounding the synagogue, once a predominantly Jewish area. We pass a large stone corner building.

"That was my school," she says softly, almost as an aside. "Not the nuns' school where I went till fourth or fifth grade, but the one I went to afterward."

Barry and I approach the door. We expect it to be locked—it's summer, after all—but it isn't. My mother doesn't seem all that interested, but she follows us in. She finds her classroom, but it's locked. The room next door is unlocked, however, and my brother and I enter and film it, figuring that the rooms must look pretty much the same.

We call to my mother to come look but she has left the building and doesn't turn around, just plows ahead. We run after her.

"What have they done to my town!"

"They" means everyone: the Germans, the Russians, the Ukrainians. It also means time, fifty years' worth of occupation, of destruction, of neglect. She can't get over it. As she darts here and there, she mutters little comments about each place, and who lived there, and her relationship to it. She's oblivious to us, to our puny attempts to make some order out of all of this chaos. The impressions are hitting her fast and furious, and she is moving fast and furious with them. It's all we can do to keep up with her.

It's almost two o'clock. We are due to meet the group for the midday meal. I'm not hungry. I'd keep going. But maybe my parents need a rest, a break. We make our way to the main street and join the group for lunch at the Żółkiew Social Club.

Over lunch, Clara Schwarz comes over to chat with my brother and me. We have many questions about her experiences in hiding, although it feels strange to be discussing that while chomping away on sardine and tomato sandwiches. Barry asks her, "But what did you do down there?" I am relieved to hear the question come out of someone else's mouth after it has been echoing in my own head for so long.

The look on her face is of—surprise? Impatience? The answer is so clear to her, apparently, how could we not know? But then she answers, "Not much. You just sat there. What could you do?" And then she adds, "We did have electric light, because we had prepared it a little bit. So we could read a little. Mostly, we did nothing."

The old, familiar answer. I already know it. I could have told him myself. In fact, I almost answered for her. I'd heard it so many times from my mother it has almost ceased to shock, even to disturb. "You just sit."

After lunch, we mill around outside the building, revving our motors, gathering momentum for the final push. My mother and Giza tick off their memories of the stores on this main street: the leather goods store across the way, the *cukiernia*, the sweet shop, a bit farther down. "Ah, what wonderful cakes!" They break into broad smiles, remembering.

My family leaves the others and walks quickly down the street to where my grandfather's pharmacy stood. There still is a pharmacy there. But it bears no resemblance to what used to be. Where my grandfather's store was narrow and long, this is wide and shallow. It is all white Formica surfaces and drawers, with nothing particularly interesting about it except the leeches floating in a big glass jar on the counter near the cash register. This place has none of the character of the old store to which the one remaining photograph attests: no elegant dark wood paneling, no old-fashioned implements. There is no glass jar of honeyed throat lozenges. And of course, no debonair, gently-smiling grandfather, leaning on the wood counter at a jaunty angle, balanced on one elbow. The woman behind the counter is polite, but distant. Yes, she confirms, the old pharmacy had been renovated. We remain inside only briefly.

I feel cheated. Hirschhorn had told me that my grandfather's pharmacy was still standing. It's not.

My mother suddenly says that she'd had a question about something, and she had thought to herself, "Well, when I get home, I'll ask my mother." I know what she means. These last few days, I've also been feeling that my grandparents are very close. And then, I remember: they're not.

We walk through the area of the *rynek*, the main town square. The square is still there but many of the original houses were partially destroyed. The municipality is now excavating the cellars of the Jewish houses that had surrounded the square, and there are plans to renovate the area.

Suddenly we are on the street where my mother was born. Small two-story houses on both sides, with small gardens bordered by chain-link fences. All built after the war. The street itself is narrow, unpaved and bumpy, with practically no sidewalk. Chickens everywhere. My mother can't get over the chickens clucking and pecking in the middle of the street. What had been a thriving, elegant cosmopolitan town has regressed back into a primitive little village with unpaved streets and chickens cackling in every direction.

All of a sudden, she stops.

"That's where I was born," she announces.

What used to be a two-story house is now three stories tall. We enter slowly; the vestibule is dark, the floors and walls are peeling and in disrepair. We climb the stairs carefully, because many of them are cracked and one is completely broken through in the middle. On the second-floor landing, my mother pauses for a moment to get her bearings. Yes, it was the apartment on the right. The door is ajar, and we step inside, into a hallway. The interior has been completely redone, subdivided into several small apartments off the central hall. It is nothing like what she remembers.

Back on the street, we circle the building. The balcony where she remembers playing with Giza, two little girls splashing away in a big tin washbasin one summer, still perches on the side of the building. But the garden that used to surround the house has been paved over with concrete, and Ukrainians now live in the house.

We pass the house of my mother's piano teacher, Clara Apfel. "This is where I had my lessons, and that's where I played, in that garden, and that's the kitchen." She doesn't want to knock on the door and ask to look around.

"And there was the *cukiernia*, the sweet shop."

We pass the *zamek*, the medieval castle. Several Jews tried to hide from the Germans in its tower; they were caught and shot. Behind its wall was my mother's high school, with the big yard where the students did twenty minutes of calisthenics each day before class. And somewhere nearby, beyond the enormous park sprawled in front of us with its luxuriant grassy expanses well-shaded by tall trees, is where she went ice-skating. We don't have time for a closer look.

The locals gawk at us. Some approach us, asking us suspiciously who we are, what we want. Maybe they're afraid we want to reclaim lost property. My father greets them all with his usual warmth, soothing them with his open manner. He explains that we have come to visit my mother's hometown in honor of her birthday.

One old woman in a faded housecoat comes forward, greeting my mother warmly with a hug and kiss and a blessing. I am embarrassed, even irritated, but my mother takes it in stride and returns the greeting in kind. Maybe this feels to her like some kind of homecoming. I remember her telling me that relations with the Christian townspeople before the war had been cordial. The woman tells her that a Jewish family still lives in town and insists that my mother call them from her apartment. We wait in the street below.

I am impatient. I know that my mother had no choice but to be polite, but we still have so much to cover and so little time. As the minutes tick away, I get edgy. What if this woman secretly hates Jews and has taken my mother up to her apartment to slaughter her with a huge kitchen knife? I try to shake such thoughts out of my head, but am about to ask my father to go up there after her just in case, when, to my immense relief, she reappears. She had had a brief, pleasant though ultimately irrelevant conversation with the Jewish family. My mother was aware that time was passing but she felt she couldn't refuse, not after this woman had gone out of her way to be helpful.

My mother can't get over how tall the trees are. I remember how many times she'd wondered how big they would be by now.

We reach her street. She lived at Mickiewicza 21, named after a renowned Polish Romantic writer. The street has been renamed Bandera, "after a Ukrainian bandit," says my mother. We move down the street, with me photographing, photographing.

"This house is where my dentist lived, the one I hated, and here was the waiting room and where she had her office. . . ."

I'm walking behind her, trying to keep the camera level and steady, trying not to fall over the low curb—

". . . and this was the house of Rubinfeld, the head of the Judenrat."

I take in the house, and the blue-shirted guy in a big, flat round hat who's standing on the front steps, watching me, and now he's waving at me, but I don't pay much attention to that because I am concentrating on what I am doing and a lot of people have been waving and nodding at us all day; and we realize that he's not waving at me at all but calling me over to find out what I'm doing filming a security area.

It turns out that Rubinfeld's house is now the headquarters of the local militia, considered a security installation. The policeman demands to see my permit to film it, which, of course, I don't have. A couple of officers appear in the periphery of my vision.

We all start talking at once, explaining who we are, that we had no idea this area was off-limits. Although it's hard for me to believe, it starts to dawn on me that I could really be in trouble: they could confiscate the camera, the film, or both; or hold us for questioning and waste our precious time. I am angry about being in this situation, in their control. I hate the placating tone that has crept into my mother's voice.

Then my father takes over. With a hint of a bow (I can almost hear him clicking his heels together), he turns to them.

"*Witam, Panów!* Greetings, Sirs!" His smile reaches out to enfold them.

"*Dzień dobry!* Good day!"

He introduces himself, using the full majesty of his name. Mieczysław Wyszogród. From Warszawa. There's no mistaking the pedigree. He repeats once again the story of our visit. His speech, his accent, his intonation are pure Polish. The officers are impressed; such command of the language even after living in "Amerika" all these years.

"*Dziękuję za komplement!*" he replies, thanking them for the compliment, his tone, his eyebrows, the tilt of his head, of his whole body conveying: But of course. How could there be any doubt? Of his background, or his intentions. And we are so happy to be able to be here, now that the era of "Big Brother Russia" is over.

The heads are nodding now, the faces relaxing, smiles appearing. They appreciate the empathy and snort sarcastically about those days under communism.

"But now," declares my father, "it's a new era. *Swaboda!*" He uses the Russian word for freedom, then, continues in Polish: "*Dzień wolności.* A day of freedom! *Demokracja!* Democracy!"

Laughter all around.

"Do you want me to take your picture?" he asks the officer who'd first waved us over. Before you know it, he's done just that, and is jotting down the man's name and address so he can send him a copy (which he later does.)

The officers wave us on our way, wishing us well on our quest.

We continue down the street. I don't allow myself to think about what might have been until much later that night—there's still too much to do.

My mother is talking to herself as she draws near the next house.

"What happened to the roses and the bushes in the garden? And the trees got so big!"

And I'm filming and only half paying attention so I almost miss it when she turns to us suddenly.

"This is my house!" she declares, with a big smile. Barry and I snap to attention.

"What!"

Raspberry and currant bushes still luxuriantly hug the fence in front of the building, although the garden behind the house is now a square of cement.

Guarding the path to the front steps is a mother goose and her three goslings, balls of yellow and tan fluff. The mother opens her beak menacingly and honks at us. My mother edges by her carefully, saying, "Sorry, goose, but this is my house and I am going in." The goose and goslings waddle off in the opposite direction, their tail feathers twitching like windshield wipers.

"These are the steps I used to ride my tricycle down," she announces proudly, bounding up the six or so steps leading to the building's front door. My brother and I exchange glances; it's almost as though we are now the bemused parents of this irrepressible little girl.

As we enter the building, a young woman carrying a pail of water comes down the stairs and greets us, smiling. When my mother explains the purpose of our visit, the woman tells us that she lives upstairs, in my mother's old apartment, and offers to show it to us once she has finished her chores. We thank her and proceed to the first-floor apartment where my mother lived when she was between five and ten years old.

The door is opened by an elderly lady, her white hair gathered into a bun at the back of her head from which wisps of hair are softly escaping. She smiles uncertainly. My mother shyly tells her that she used to live in this apartment, fifty years ago, before the war, and could she please come in and look around. The old lady agrees. Her daughter, hard-faced, emerges from the depths of the apartment. She doesn't smile. Three times, she asks, "What do you want?" and "Did this apartment belong to you?"

"No," my mother repeats politely, patiently, "I just lived here, we rented it. It was not ours."

"Then whose house was it?" she demands.

"Templesman," replies my mother. She stops short of saying anything more. She knows that Anna Templesman survived the war.

We walk in. The layout is as my mother remembers it: the kitchen to the left of the hallway, the living room with its ceiling-height tile-covered stove to the right, a stove that served for heating the room, not cooking. The decor is different: the walls of the salon are hung with carpets, painted with stencils, and decorated with numerous icons and statues of Mary bedecked with wreaths of paper or plastic flowers. But in the kitchen, just as in my mother's time, berries are bubbling on the stove, and the delicious, sweet-tart smell of currant jelly washes over us. We are not allowed into the back room down the hall where my mother slept. Only later

166

does my mother wonder whether she might have found some of her old furniture there.

I'm filming like crazy, hampered by the cramped quarters and the long narrow hallway, trying to counterbalance against the weight of my backpack dragging off one shoulder so I don't knock anything over. Meanwhile, my father is explaining to the two women that we are here on the occasion of my mother's birthday. Then I hear him say that she and her parents were saved during the war by a Christian in the town, *Pan* Łoziński. My stomach clenches as he reveals this long-buried secret. Although Łoziński is far beyond the reach of any possible mortal reprisal now, I'm not sure he would have appreciated being exposed like this, even after all these years. But it's too late to stop my father.

We bow out of the apartment, thanking the two women gratefully. My mother says she's had enough, she doesn't need to see the upstairs apartment. But at that moment the smiling young woman appears, her pail empty now, and invites us to come upstairs. We can't say no.

Here, we are allowed full access to the entire apartment, even the back room that was my mother's bedroom. She shows us how she shared the room with her grandmother: the two beds were perpendicular to each other, hers on the left, her grandmother's on the right.

My mother wanders about the apartment, very excited, uttering little exclamations. Barry and I move around slowly, careful not to bump into anything, taking in the large brown-glazed tiled stove in its now-familiar place in the living room, the big-bellied glass jars of conserves and pickles in the kitchen, backlit by the sun and glowing like red and green jewels. The little balcony off the bedroom affords a sweeping view of the park across the street. The park in which my mother took refuge, with her mother, grandmother and her dog, when the bombs started falling.

The apartment is lovely, full of light and sunshine. It may need plastering and painting, but its elegance is evident. I am happy that my mother enjoyed a gracious life here.

As we are leaving the building, the door of the first apartment opens again. The old lady presents my mother with two *pisanki*, elaborately decorated wooden Easter eggs, and wishes us well.

We leave the building in good spirits, hardly believing the miracle that we were able to see all of my mother's homes from before the war.

Now it's time to find Łoziński's house. After the good fortune we have enjoyed so far, we are hyped, sure that we will find it too.

Chapter Sixteen

July 20, 1995:
We cross what's left of the *rynek*, the town square, half-walking, half-trotting. My mother keeps up a running commentary.

March 25, 1943:
"We split up. My mother and I left first, and my father left after us. It was March, so by 6:00 p.m. it was already dark, though it was still before curfew. We wore kerchiefs on our heads, carried nothing in our hands.

"We each took a different route to Łoziński's house. My mother and I walked through the center of town. That was the shortest way. The center of the town was the open square, the *rynek*, with buildings on all four sides. Two sides of the square had covered walkways, with arches supported on old columns, in front of the buildings and stores.

I guess you'd call them arcades. On market days, people used to spread their wares along these arcades because they were protected from the weather. Before the war, many of these stores and buildings had been Jewish. Now this was the border of the ghetto.

"I didn't want to walk right under the edge of the ghetto. I didn't know what the situation was in the ghetto and I didn't want to get too close to it. And I didn't want to walk in the shadow .of the buildings. I wanted to walk openly, like two people normally walk. So we walked diagonally across the center of that square. I had to drag my mother—she was so scared.

"And we were walking through the center of town. It was empty. Nobody was on the streets. Not Poles, nobody. And then we saw a German soldier— not Gestapo—coming toward us, from across the square. And my mother froze. And I said, 'You can't stop, you have to keep moving,' and I kept pulling her, and we kept walking, and he looked at us, he didn't get too close to us, he never called out, he never stopped, and we just walked, and he just walked. We passed him on an angle and then we turned right, past the Ukrainian church, the Cerkiew Church, and then down the few steps next to the church. Once we passed that soldier, we walked faster."

July 20, 1995:
We reach the great Ukrainian church, rising majestically in gray stone over the area. There, to its right, is the short set of steps, a half-dozen or so, just as my mother remembered. We clatter down them, my mother muttering to herself: "Is this right? Did we walk this way, or around in the other direction?"

March 25, 1943:
"We went down the steps and then to the right. We walked pretty fast, trying not to look like we are scared, and not to look like we were running, but as if to say: 'After all, curfew is coming and we want to be home.'"

July 20, 1995:
We are trotting along narrow streets and tiny lanes, all hard-packed dirt. Small houses rise around us to our left and right in tumbled confusion. These are one- and two-story houses, brick mostly, with pointed, tiled roofs. Though the streets are almost completely empty, once in a while we notice people sitting at their windows, silently watching our movements on the streets below them. We are too intent

on our search to pay attention to them paying attention to us. My mother moves in the lead, excited, agitated, tense. I follow, trying to hold the video camera steady against my eye, intent on preserving every moment, terrified that I'll never remember it all otherwise. My brother lopes along, now next to me, now behind me, snapping away with his 35 millimeter camera. He photographs me filming her. My father brings up the rear, not quite able to keep up.

Our pace slows. My mother is confused, upset. Things are not as they had been. Too many houses. Too many gardens. Chickens scratch and cackle as we trot along, and each time we pass them, my mother swears anew at the desecration of her lovely town by peasants and their poultry. My brother and I tell her to calm down, forget what's there now, close her eyes and try to get her bearings, revive her old images. We keep moving, more uncertainly now, down one alley after another. Suddenly, an old dusty, red brick wall rises in front of us. Can this be the wall of the Jewish cemetery? Is this, finally, a marker?

March 25, 1943:
"It was a corner house on a very narrow street. Across that street

172

stood the wall of the Jewish cemetery."

July 20, 1995:
The wall is about six feet high, dipping lower in some places where it has fallen into disrepair. We peer over one of the broken places, but there is no cemetery. Just a large dirt field, with some low shacks, deserted now, in this late afternoon. There is no one to ask. We halt. Could we be mistaken? No. This is an old wall, red brick and gray dust and plaster, obviously laid by hand. This has to be it, no matter what they have done to the cemetery. The house has to be nearby. We start walking and pick up the pace.

March 25, 1943:
"We walked pretty fast . . . trying not to look scared . . . or like we are running . . ."

July 20, 1995:
We turn right and move quickly up the street, alongside the wall. We reach a house on a corner lot, across from the wall, just before it curves off to the left. My mother stops again. Could this be it?

March 25, 1943:
"It was a corner house. There was a small street to its left that ran perpendicular to the cemetery wall and up toward the town center and the church. The back wall of the house was solid,

173

with no windows, and it came right up to the street. That wall *was* the fence. And there were very few houses around it."

July 20, 1995:
But *this* house stands back from the road, surrounded by a chain-link fence encircling a lush, green garden. There is no little street adjacent to it, just a tiny lane, one person wide. And there are houses all around, built close to one another. This can't be it.

March 25, 1943:
"In front of the house, they had a nice-sized garden, probably bigger than the whole house. Some potatoes were growing, and some fruit trees. But it was very neglected. A garden requires a lot of work."

July 20, 1995:
All the houses have gardens growing heavy with the summer harvest: tomatoes, beans, vines curling wildly on fences and poles, flowers. The air is warm, redolent with lushness and fresh, green country smells. We turn up the lane and walk up the row of houses. There are very few people about, and the ones we see are too young to know what we are looking for. A man disappears under the hood of his car, working on the engine. A voice floats out of somewhere. Feeling

lost, tired, sweaty, desperate, the clock ticking away, we retrace our steps and come around again. This has to be it.

March 25, 1943:
"So we got to the house. I don't remember who got there first. But the door was locked and we were outside, and it was dark, after curfew."

March 25, 1943:
"And Łoziński was not there."

July 20, 1995:
And the house is not there.

We stand on the corner. To our right is the old cemetery wall. To our left is the tiny lane leading back toward the town center. At the intersection stands a house. But it's not *the* house.

"This can't be it," says my mother, over and over.

"Remember, I told you that it had no windows in the back, that the wall was right on the road?" she repeats.

I film. Stop filming. We shuffle around, don't know what to do. This has to be the place. It *has* to be. But Łoziński's house is gone. Now what?

A young woman emerges from the front door. My father steps up to the gate. Bobbing his head slightly in a courtly nod, he recites, yet again, the litany explaining our trip. But this time he adds that my mother's father had been a good friend of a man who had lived around here. Perhaps *Pani* knows if someone by the name of Łoziński once lived here?

She smiles, showing the dark spot of a cavity between her upper-two front teeth. She herself has only lived in the house for several years and doesn't know. However, her grandmother, who's in the house, sick, might be able to help. She'll be happy to ask her. She disappears inside. We wait. A few minutes later, she reappears. Yes, she tells us, her grandmother remembers a *Pan* Łoziński who lived here after the war, but at some point he and his wife moved to another house a few blocks away. The original house, which was very old even then, was subsequently demolished and this new one built. She proudly points to a recent renovation: the added-on section is clearly visible in the two-toned plaster on the side of the house.

She takes us to the house to which the Łozińskis had apparently moved. The current tenant refers us to yet another place, and we are joined by yet another helpful townswoman, dressed in a faded housecoat and sucking on several missing teeth. Despite all the consultations, we learn nothing more about what happened to the Łozińskis after that. Nobody knows exactly where—or even if—they are buried in the local Christian cemetery. "You just have to walk through the cemetery and look."

Dead end.

No house, no tombstone, no nothing.

I am defeated.

It's late, almost six o'clock. We stumble through the streets toward the rendezvous point. My bags and cameras slam into my back and bang into my shins. On the bus, everyone is waiting. We apologize profusely for the delay, explain what we've been doing, how we tried to find the house, and didn't. Whatever people may be feeling, no one criticizes. They just nod. It has been a very long day.

I am wiped. I don't remember much about the ride back to the hotel in Lwów.

At the end of the day, all I can write in my journal is:

"We did not find Łoziński's house."

I force myself into bed and fall asleep.

Chapter Seventeen

Thursday, July 21, 1995, 6:00 a.m.

Had a fitful night's sleep. Wake up feeling hollow. Like I have lost something. Our frantic footsteps through Żółkiew still clatter through my brain. I can still hear my mother crying, "This is not my town!" and then: "I have no dreams anymore."

A wave of sadness sweeps over me. We do not belong here. My parents do not belong here. Everything was ripped away from them: their families, their homes, their culture, their past, their present. It's no accident that for the last few days, one line of music has been playing over and over in my head: "Sometimes I feel like a motherless child."

I'm all packed. Can't wait to leave.

I'm tired of being in a strange place, in this strange place, where I am part tourist, part avenging recording angel.

I'm tired of feeling exposed. Is it my imagination or are people really looking us over, trying to figure us out? It's a strain trying to be invisible.

I'm tired of constantly girding myself against potential danger. Driving through the countryside, I calculate where someone could hide. That hay is too short. Those woods are not very deep, and they're too close to the farmhouses.

And those pedestrians on the sidewalks of Lwów, would they really have turned me in to the Germans? Or killed me with their own hands? Are they still a threat?

I'm tired of being on guard against letting down my guard, against the erosion of memory. Sometimes I almost forget, am swept up by a pretty vista, by the excitement of being on a trip, by a glimpse of a cute souvenir. Then I remember.

I want to go home.

On the bus heading back to the airport, the mood is somber. We quietly autograph each other's copies of the book, *Masterpieces of Jewish Art*, which everyone bought yesterday from Michael Sherman. It's the one purchase I have made—will make—on this trip.

The driver maneuvers smoothly through Lwów's early morning traffic. I look at the houses we are passing. I keep asking my mother, "Can't you just show me something? Something similar to Łoziński's. A similar house. I can't visualize it. . . ."

I point at a house.

She shakes her head.

"No, no, nothing like that."

"What about that one?" I point at something darker. Gray.

"Maybe theirs was lighter, some light gray."

"Or that one?"

"Their roof may have had a less steep slope. And maybe there were dark window shades, probably brown."

Then she shakes her head again.

"This is not at all like it was. . . ."

Back at the airport, the ornate cupola gleams whitely in the morning sunshine, but the room into which we are ushered is as dark as I feel. Above us, stylized figures of Soviet Realism flex their powerful muscles in flat shades of brown and gray, a gentle reminder that you are entirely at the mercy of the system, could easily be crushed under its fist.

Burly baggage handlers loiter about, leaning against doorjambs and walls. They could use a good, hot shower, and strong deodorant. So early in the day, and one already reeks of whiskey.

We fill out more of the same customs declarations, carefully, to avoid any unpleasantness with customs personnel, known for their sour suspiciousness. It's frightening: we've done nothing wrong, yet I feel as though I'm one step away from prison. I almost begin to check myself for contraband.

Ukrainian Air Flight 453 to Warsaw. The airplane is small, flimsy, practically held together by spit and rubber bands and— I could swear—a twist-tie. As we lift off, a few members of the group, laughing a bit hysterically at themselves, frantically mumble the prayer for a safe journey.

My body throbs with the intense reverberation of the plane's engines. As we vibrate over the green countryside, I hear comments: "How rich that farmland is! If only Israel had such resources."

We're back at Okęcie, Warsaw's airport. People bustle to and fro, darting through sleek, well-lit corridors. Illuminated signs in red and white, Poland's national colors, point the way. The large complex hums with well-orchestrated activity. Warsaw is one hour, and light years, ahead of the Ukraine. Ceremonially, almost symbolically, we reset our watches.

Our group splinters. Some are off to brief vacations in Europe. Barry and I are returning to Israel. My parents head off to New York, but not before asking Hirschhorn, traveling with us, to keep an eye on us. It reminds me of a story my mother told me:

After the liberation, she had traveled with a group of high school classmates to a neighboring town for a track meet; she was running in the one-hundred-meter dash. My grandfather, apprehensive about allowing his attractive teenage daughter away from home for the event, asked the coach of the team, a few years older than she was, to keep an eye on her. That coach was Yosef Hirschhorn.

When I remind him about this, Hirschhorn laughs.

"You know," he says, "I didn't want to tell this to your grandfather, but it was a bit like telling the fox to watch the chickens!"

I doze through most of the flight and wake up only when the lights of Israel's coastline are already winking up at us. I am so excited I can barely sit still. Everyone around me is sitting quietly, status quo normal. Does anyone else feel that their heart is close to bursting from their chests? That they want to laugh and cry and do wheelies down the aisle?

The plane dips, the lights rise to greet us, and we touch down. The passengers break into their usual "Thank God we made it" round of applause, and proceed to disregard the attempts of the flight crew to keep them seated until the plane comes to a complete stop at the gate.

To the heavy-lidded, yawning young woman at Passport Control, I am just another traveler passing through. To me, she is the embodiment of my Motherland. I want to hug her—actually, I want *her* to hug *me* and welcome me home. One quick stamp slapped on the passport. Out into the night. Back in a cab. Speeding through the black velvet darkness. Heading home.

4:00 a.m. Everyone is sound asleep. I tiptoe through the house, kissing everyone hello. They hug me, kiss me back through a rumpled, sleepy haze. Yehoshua has a strange lisp; he lost his first tooth while I was away. The house slides back into slumber.

A few minutes later I drop into bed. My head is pounding with the staccato cadences of Polish and Hebrew. I feel so keyed up and overtired that I toy vaguely with the idea of staying awake already to greet the sun. But I fall asleep within minutes.

At 6:30 in the morning, the kids tumble in to greet me again, fully awake this time. They fill me in on all their doings, ask how the trip was. Chaim and I catch each other up; I sketch out the basics. The rest will come later.

By 8:00 a.m. the house is still once more. Everyone's gone to their respective activities. I feel vulnerable about being all alone with so much emotional baggage weighing on me. I stay in bed, trying to catch up on sleep. I wake up several times, remembering dream fragments: huge rolling expanses of land. Trotting after my mother, showering her with questions. And walls of stones, with small crumpled notes shoved between the cracks or tacked with colored push-pins into the mortar between them.

Chapter Eighteen

We blew it.

It's late at night. Everyone's asleep but me. Crouching in bed and feeling the words thud into me like a sledgehammer.

We blew it.

How could we have thought one day in Żółkiew would be enough?

"Oh, there's not that much to see there," my mother had stated confidently. "It's such a small town; one day should be plenty."

I was totally unprepared for how big Żółkiew and its surrounding area were. I had imagined meandering around the fields, the woods, through a little village. I had pictured finding the Łozińskis' graves in one of those tiny, rural cemeteries like the ones I've driven by in Upstate New York, a small green hillside with a few slanting tombstones, a flag here, a wreath of flowers there. I never expected an enormous sprawling area, bristling with gravestones.

We didn't figure on getting off to such a late start, that we'd spend so much time photographing one another at the entrance to the town. We didn't take into account how long the commemoration at the *borek* would last, or lunch.

And mostly, we hadn't taken into account the effect of the shock of simply returning. That my mother would need time to

181

readjust to being back, to absorb all the changes, simply to get her bearings.

Now each of us is left with regret.

"I would have liked to show you my first school," she writes me in a fax. "All the places I used to walk with my friends, where I went skiing. And the place I worked during the war."

I would also have liked to see those places. And what haunts me in addition is not having seen Łoziński's house, especially the cellar. Maybe if we'd spent more time looking at the property, at the garden, I could have calculated how close the neighboring houses had been to theirs and to the cemetery, could have understood how clearly you could hear what was going on in there, particularly the sharp popping sounds of shots. Maybe there still is a cellar under the house. Maybe traces of the original one remain. Maybe we could have seen it.

How could we have missed so much?

I cringe.

We blew it.

My stomach lurches.

Tears stream down my face. I taste them. My nose is running and I mop my face with the bedsheet.

I had wanted to see it, to climb down into it, to sit there, just like she did.

I wanted to hold my mother and make it all better.

I wanted to tell her that I'd never let anything hurt her like that again:

No more darkness

No more holes in the ground.

But I couldn't even protect her

from being disappointed in this trip

from being shocked by the changes

from the loss of the fantasy that you can go home again.

I will never be able to make things right.

I'm locked in this great darkness of my own: my not-knowing, not understanding.

There's no way in.

Because there's nothing there.

No house.

No cellar.
And no way out.
I'm locked in—and out—forever.

Re-entry.

I move through those first days back in a haze. It feels as though my insides have been scraped raw. They are as fragile as a soap bubble and could shatter at the slightest touch. I need time, to crawl into a corner and lick my wounds, to heal.

Some clone of me is doing the shopping, arranging playdates for the kids, making appointments with clients. I'm functioning, but I'm functioning through gauze. I'm not really here. The medieval poet and philosopher Yehuda Halevi once wrote: "My heart is in the East, but I am at the end of the West." Me, I'm in the East, but my consciousness is west of here, in Żółkiew. I feel rootless. Displaced. Just what my mother says about herself: that she has no home anymore.

I am choking on myself, on too many thoughts and feelings. I spend hours writing them down, filling in the gaps in my journal from the trip, recording every detail I can remember. And trying to calm the anguish, the disappointment. Now that it's too late, my expectations have suddenly crystallized into shards—sharp and clear—that score my insides:

We would find the house—it never ever occurred to me that we wouldn't. And we'd make some small talk with the Ukrainian peasant living there now, chatting politely about this and that, waiting for the appropriate time to ask, if we could perhaps, if it's not too much trouble, take a quick look in the cellar. After all, such an important family trip . . . my mother's birthday . . . showing the children . . . such a historic moment . . .

We watch, barely breathing, as he pries the trapdoor up and swings it over to rest on the floor. One by one, we turn around and step gingerly down in the gloom, climbing slowly and carefully backwards, with the Ukrainian peasant warning us, apologetically, that the ladder is old and rickety, and we should be careful, we should duck slightly just before entering or we'll bang our heads. In the semi-gloom we crouch and look around, and notice the slightly raised earthen border running around the sides, and how tight a fit it is for four of us, an area that had once sheltered three of them.

I keep an eye on my mother. She keeps shaking her head, muttering to herself, then to us:

"Sixteen months! Sixteen months!" she repeats, like a mantra. And: "I don't know—how did we manage?" and "See, the light comes in from the shed above us." And "You see how dark it is. Too dark to do anything. Now you know why my eyes are the way they are."

I angle for a position to take a picture, knowing there's no way to take it all in, even with a wide-angle lens, and anyway, I am seeking to capture an experience and not just a dark hole. Barry is trying to shift around me with the video camera and find something to focus on.

My father, then my brother make their way back up the ladder, up to the light, up to where the old peasant stands, nodding his head and waiting, politely, anxiously, for his guests to reappear. I hang back, to be the last one in the cellar after everyone else has left. My mother reaches the ladder, looks questioningly at me. My cheeks flame with the idiocy, the audacity of the request I'm about to make—if I have the guts. I quaver out my question: "Can I stay here for a few minutes, by myself?" My mother shrugs. To her, on this crazy day, nothing is crazy. "Why?" she starts to ask, but she doesn't wait for an answer, just climbs up the ladder.

I wish they'd move away from the trapdoor already so I can pull it closed. I don't want them to see, I don't want them to know what I have in mind.

I hear feet shuffling slowly across the wooden planks as my parents and brother follow their bowing, obsequious host away from the trapdoor and into the small salon. I hear them murmuring somewhere above me. If I concentrated, I could probably make out the words, but right now all I can hear is my breathing, jagged and harsh. I try to calm my pounding pulse. I lower myself to the floor and try to focus on being there, in that spot, in that very spot. But there are so many voices in my head clamoring for attention that the space is anything but silent.

"What's the matter with you? What are you trying to prove?"

"Leave me alone. This is where they sat. I want to get a sense of what that was like."

"You can't get a sense of what it was like. They were trapped. You're not. You can get up and leave any time you please. In a minute, you're

184

going to go join them upstairs, have some tea, and probably some cook-ies, just to be polite. You're just play-acting down here. This is ridiculous. You are ridiculous. Hurry up. They're not going to wait forever, up there."
"I need more time."
"How much time, sixteen months?"
"Oh, shut up. . . . This is no good. This isn't what I wanted."
"Well, this is all you're going to get."

"Di—?"

My brother's voice reaches me through the floor. A sudden slit of light cuts my face. I scramble to my feet, the camera hanging around my neck banging into my ribs.

"We have to go."

Dammit.

God damn it.

This isn't what I had in mind. Try again. Cellar Fantasy, Take 2:

The trapdoor slides into place above me. Daylight is snuffed out. Dark-ness envelops me. I sit in it. It slithers into me.

The shuffle of feet, the rustle of fabric, the thrumble of bodies overhead fades away.

Stillness pounds at my eardrums, then fades in a long pianissimo.

The air currents eddy around me—are they the feathery frosti-ness of my breath, or the walls' musty exhalation? The cold of the floor seeps into my legs, into my butt—or is the warmth of muscle and tissue slowly draining away into the floor?

I sit. I sit. For a long time. Time is long. Time is dark. I feel time slowing down. I slow down in it. We become one. Time and the cellar and me. I become my mother. I feel her mouth movements in mine as she purses her lips. Her eyebrows furrow above my eyes. As my eyes adjust, the monolithic black blanketing me unfurls slowly into thick folds of dark gray shadings. I sense other shapes nearby: My grandmother. My grandfather. I could talk to them now, if I wanted to, but it's not wise to talk now. The walls are so thin, and the world outside so close. The walls surrounding us are as thin as the translucent membrane embracing an egg yolk. So easily punctured. So easy to spill its guts all over, gooey and gluey, life spurting, then congealing, making a mess for someone to clean, face contorted in disgust, scraping up the crusting rims and still-soft center. Better to sit still, absolutely still. And not move. And not speak. Just breathe. Softly, silently. Like a sigh without the sibilance, without the softest hiss, that leaves no trace but the presence of a breath. Becomes just: *I*.

I just sit.

I sit.

I

The silence pours through me. Maybe I could even enter that stillness. But how will I ever penetrate the fear? The heart-banging terror? The listening for footsteps, for foot-*stamps*, for violent cries, even in sleep? Could that be why I hated games of hide-and-seek as a child, why I still hate suspense? Or is that too glib an explanation?

What is it like to know that you can never go back? That your world has been destroyed behind you, and is no more? That the flames, flicking their searing breath at your heels as you fled, cremated your world. Accent on *your*. They didn't destroy everyone else's. They scorched selectively: *your* home, *your* family, *your* friends. *Your* youth, *your* dreams, *your* plans. Only the chosen ones. Only those branded and marked. Like Cain. But very unlike Cain: He *deserved* his mark of shame. He committed murder. In this rewrite, the ones with the brand are the victims. Their marks betray them to their killers. How can one live in a world turned upside down?

I sit in the silence, in the dark, and questions fly around me like a flock of restless vultures, circling, squawking, wheeling, and darting. Will they ever settle, ever quiet, ever roost? Will they ever stop pecking at me with bloody bills, gouging flesh, tearing pieces of soul? Will they ever leave me in peace?

This is what I came to see—and I'm as blind as ever.

I feel—but it's only what *I* feel, not what *she* felt.

I have reached the Source—and am no nearer to it than before. Nor am I likely to get closer. There is no way.

I pull myself to my feet, knees unfolding stiffly, limbs straightening slowly, creakily, from their cold-encrusted stance. I reach up, over my head, fumble for the handle, push the trapdoor up and open. A ray of gray light slashes across my eyes and I blink. I grasp the sides of the ladder and climb back into the world.

Take 2 isn't any better.
No resolution here.
No comfort.

Chapter Nineteen

The weeks pass. The raw, acid feeling that burned my insides on returning is fading. My reactions are muting as I get farther away from the trip. That's good, I suppose. Certainly more comfortable. But how will I be able to convey the pain and anguish I felt if it's sealing over inside?

Anyway, I wonder: What *is* the point of writing this? What will it mean to anyone besides me and my family? Does anyone really care, in a world so full of people hiding and dying?

But this has to mean something. You can't just put people in a hole, hiding for their lives, praying not to die, and have it not mean anything to anyone afterward.

Maybe this is one answer: these single solitary voices, each telling its individual tale. Of suffering. Of bravery. Of doom. Of courage. Tiny flickers of light in a dark universe.

A month after the trip, my mother writes me:

> I am still under the influence of our trip and can't stop thinking about it. Even though I was very disappointed in the conditions of my hometown, I'm glad I made the trip and visited the sights of my childhood.

She may be reconciling herself to the trip, but I still feel awful. Guilty. We missed so many things. And I couldn't protect her from being hurt yet again by the town. The first hurt was the war. The second was the shock of seeing the changes fifty years had wrought, and the pain of returning, only to find that you can never return.

I'm haunted by those deadly words: *if only*. If only I'd thought it out more in advance. If only I'd have arranged to spend more time there, maybe the shock could have eased, and she could have reconnected with more good memories.

If only we could do it again, do it better this time, make things right.

"Could we?" I ask my mother. "Maybe we could go back . . . ?"

She's quite definite.

"That's it," she says.

"It's finished. Over." she says.

I guess it's over.

I dream:

I'm on the platform of an old-style New York elevated train station, only it's in Poland, in winter, and the station is covered with snow. A train is pulling in. People are hurrying to and fro. Some enter the train, some exit it. My mother is walking in one direction, and my father in the opposite direction. They pass each other without knowing each other, but I know this is okay because they're not destined to meet yet.

One of the entrances of the trains is marked "Jews" in old-fashioned black Hebrew letters. My mother doesn't go to that entrance; she heads for another one and sits down. She is sitting next to me, to my left, next to the window, and I am on her right, on the aisle. I look around and notice that there are other people on the train, clearly Christians. They don't look hostile or unfriendly, but I am very aware of the potential threat. I turn to look at my mother, and suddenly see several images superimposed in her profile: I see myself; I see her as she is today, gray-haired; and I see her as a young woman.

She turns to me and says, "See? Here are the papers that can save me." She pulls out from somewhere a bunch of folded white papers, a little dog-eared from being shoved into a small space such as a bag. And her gesture—bright, saucy—is full of trust, in me, and in the future. The gesture of a teenager who's got the whole world ahead of her.

I wake up with a warm tingle, feeling good. It's as though I got in touch with my mother as she was before "Everything" happened: bouncing around her streets, full of life and sparkle, and feeling sure of herself. I really liked this person sitting next to me on the train. I didn't feel older, or younger, than her, just that we were allies, and could trust each other.

It reminds me of my imaginary meeting with my mother as she packed to go into hiding. It's as though I keep trying to meet her, somehow maybe even take care of her. Maybe she's telling me not to worry about her, that she's all right.

Laura Majblum, Helen's maternal grandmother, pre-World War I.

(Left to right) Agatha (Helen's mother), Laura (née Majblum), Leopold (Poldzio), Mozes Schenker, and Emanuel (Manek).

Agatha Schenker, about age 13.

ATELIER *Bermann* WIEN II.
Franzensbrückenstrasse 24

Josef (Joseph) Rosenberg. This photograph was taken in March 1919, in Vienna,
upon his discharge from the army.

Majblum-Schenker family portrait. Potok, Poland. Photo taken around 1912.

(Top row, standing, left to right): Rozia Majblum, Saul (Cioylo) Majblum (Rozia's husband), Leon Majblum (standing slightly behind Saul), Frederika (Frycia) Majblum Eckhaus, Jacob (Kuba) Majblum, Isidore Eckhaus (Frederika's husband), Zygmunt Majblum, Sala Hammer Majblum, Bernard Majblum (Sala's husband)

(Middle row, sitting, left to right): Laura Majblum (Helen's grandmother), Mozes Schenker (Laura's husband, Helen's grandfather), Amalia Lempert Majblum (Helen's great-grandmother), Marcus Wolf Majblum (Helen's great-grandfather), the little boy standing between Amalia and Marcus is Konrad (Kuncio) Eckhaus (Frederika/Frycia and Isidore's son), the little girl standing between them is Lola Majblum (Sala and Bernard's daughter), Regina Majblum, David Nagler (Regina's husband)

(Bottom row, sitting on ground, left to right): Leopold (Poldzio) Schenker (the older of Agatha's brothers), Shimon (Szymek) Majblum (Son of Rozia and Cioylo), Emanuel (Manek) Schenker (Agatha's youngest brother), Joseph (Jozek) Majblum (Rozia and Cioylo's son), Otto (Otek) Nagler (Regina and David's son), Benedikt (Benio) Nagler (another son of Regina and David's)

Agatha Schenker. Photo taken pre-World War I.

Żółkiew – *rynek* (central town square). Photo taken and developed by Josef Rosenberg.

(Left to right) Sophia (Zosia) Bardach, Manek's wife, their son Mietek, Emanuel (Manek) Schenker.

Zosia Bardach and her son from her first marriage, Richard (Ryszek).

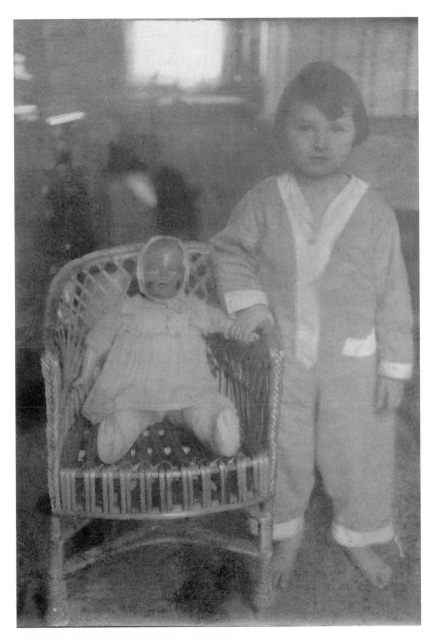

Helen (Lutka) Rosenberg with her favorite doll, Zosia, named after her beloved aunt.

Helen on her tricycle in front of the steps to her house.

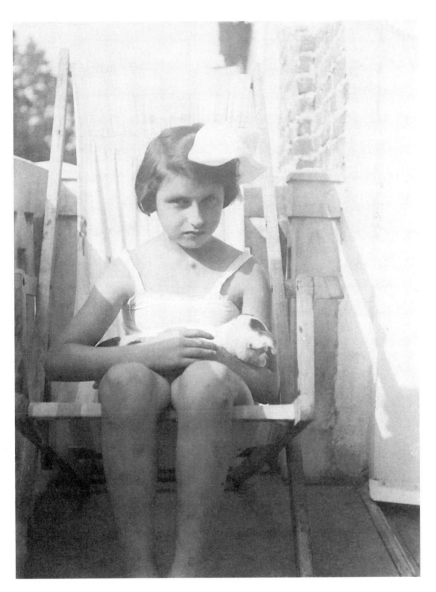

Helen with her dog Joker (Jock).

Helen, age 9, ready for her Cousin Shimon (Szymek) Majblum's wedding to Elizabeth (Etka) Mandel, in a dress sewed by her grandmother Laura Majblum Schenker.

Helen and her mother Agatha Rosenberg near Muszyna, Poland, 1935.

In front of the pharmacy, October 1933. Left to right: unnamed policeman, Emil Łoziński, Mr. Berger, Josef Rosenberg, and Mr. Zipper.

Josef Rosenberg in his pharmacy. May 26, 1937. (Note glass jars of hard candies on the right!)

Жовківчани на обласній спартакіаді

В честь роковини визволення Львівщини від німецько-фашистських загарбників, Жовківчани прийняли активну участь в I-й Обласній Спартакіаді — огляді спортивних сил Львівщини. Перший день обласної спартакіади перетворився у велику масову демонстрацію сили і гарту молоді.

В цей день стадіон «Динамо» (Львів) був прикрашений прапорами, а перед глядачами на протилежному боці трибуни встановлено великий портрет любимого вождя і вчителя, творця великої Перемоги товариша Сталіна, який врятував міліони радянських людей з фашистської неволі.

Спортсмени Жовківщини на обласній спартакіаді по II-й групі показали великі досягнення в змаганнях. Спортсменка Розємберг зайняла по області перше місце по бігу на 100 м., друге місце по стрибках у висоту і довжину.

Спортсменка Андреєва зайняла по області перше місце по стрибках у висоту і перше місце по метанню гранати.

Спортсмен Кінаш Яник зайняв по області перше місце по бігу на 100 м. і перше місце по бігу на 1000 м.

Спортсмен Заремба зайняв перше місце по стрибках у висоту.

Футбольна зустріч між командами м. Бібрська і Жовкви вели напружену боротьбу. Жовківчани уміло, тактично проводили гру на протязі I-го і половини II-го тайму і мали перевагу в грі 2:1, але в II-й половині II-го тайму Бібрська команда напружила сили і виграла матч у Жовківчан з рахунком 3:2.

Футбольна команда Жовківчан на осінньому змаганні повинна взяти першість по області. На це можливості всі є, тільки необхідно більше тренировок і приділення належної уваги з боку Райвиконкому в питанні забезпечення формою.

Не дивлячись на цілий ряд недоліків у підготовці до спартакіади, команда Жовкви вийшла в передові ряди, занявши III-те місце по області і одержала грамоту від Обласного Комітету фізкультури й спорту.

I. Роженко
учасник обласної спартакіади

Clipping from local newspaper recounting standings of the *Spartakiada*. Paragraph 3, lines 4-8 reports: "Sportswoman Rosenberg took first place in the 100 meter dash and second place in the high jump (115 cm) and the long jump (3 meters 79 cm)."

Nusia Ringler.

Helen after World War II.

Friends in Katowice, 1946. Eulalia (Wiesia) Jedrzejowska is in the middle.

Eulalia (Wiesia) Jedrzejowska about to do a backflip, Katowice, 1946.

Helen at Gabersee DP camp, 1946.

Helen skiing behind Gabersee DP camp, 1946.

Classmates at ORT School in Munich. Helen is fifth from the left. 1949.

Helen with Morris Wyszogrod, Jones Beach, New York, 1952.

Helen and Morris Wyszogrod, Wedding, June 8, 1952.

Helen sharing her love of animals with Diane. Spring Glen, New York, 1958.

Uncle Poldzio and Ciocia (Aunt) Jadzia in Caracas, Venezuela.

Agatha and Joseph Rosenberg, celebrating Joseph's birthday, Nov. 15, 1953.

(Left to right) Diane, Helen, Morris, and Barry at the entrance to Żółkiew, now called Zulkva, Ukraine. July 1995.

Helen in front of her house, Żółkiew/Zulkva. July 1995.

Entrance to the Garden of the Righteous among the Nations, Yad Vashem Holocaust Memorial Authority.

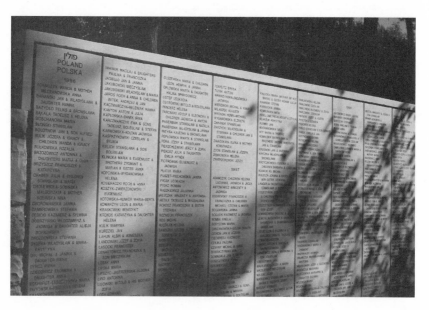

Memorial honoring Righteous Gentiles from Poland.

Names added in 1999. Emil and Maria Łoziński are midway down the right column

Łoziński, Emil and Maria.

David, Morris, Helen, Diane, Yehoshua, and Yonatan. 2004.

Helen, Diane, and Morris. 2004.

Chapter Twenty

Several months have elapsed since I returned from Żółkiew. I'm back to my routine: Shopping and cooking, hosting Shabbat meals for family and friends. Shuttling the kids between school and after-school activities. Bath time, reading stories, singing along to tapes and CDs, doing homework together. Meeting with my clients, listening to their stories, helping them make sense of their narratives, helping them climb out of the darkness of their pasts to find solid ground and peace in the present.

Trying to do the same in my own life.

I finally take the rolls of film from the trip to be developed. Picking them up a couple of hours later at Photo Doron on Emek Refaim, the main business thoroughfare near our house, I leaf through the snapshots and am shocked: I could have *sworn* that just about everything in Lwów was some shade of gray. I hadn't realized the extent to which my emotional turmoil had bleached the color out of almost everything I saw. I had reduced the landscape to a black-and-white documentary. The camera captured colors I don't consciously remember seeing: Tan housing blocks. The red siding of a trolley. A woman's purple blouse. The blue-and-green plaid button-down shirt on a passing man.

More distortion: running after my mother through Żółkiew that day, I could have sworn that we documented every move, every step. And yet, looking at the small stack of photographs now in my hands, I berate myself again: I should have taken still more. I should have documented every moment, every corner. There are still so many gaps. Even after all these hours spent interviewing my mother, even after having been to Żółkiew.

An ache persists, a sense of loss.

I will have to come to terms with that, I realize.

I will probably never get any closer to that cellar than I already have. Whatever I had hoped to find under the Łozińskis' house will remain unfound. Whatever truth I have not yet uncovered will remain covered. I have to let it go.

I focus my attention inward, checking how that "sits" inside me.

Something settles inside, but it isn't complete.

Unease . . .

What is that about? What else am I seeking?

Eventually, it begins to become clearer.

I realize: I've been so tightly focused on what it was like to be *in* that cellar that I neglected life *above* the cellar. I've been so fixed on my mother's family; now it's time to pay attention to the *other* family, time to shift my attention from the sanctuary under their house to the source of the sanctuary in their hearts.

Ahhh. My restive soul settles down. Yes. That's it. I need to learn more about Emil and Maria Łoziński, to understand them better.

Time to get back to work.

"Whenever you talk about the Łozińskis," I say to my mother during our next session together several months later, "you talk about him. You rarely talk about *her.*"

"*Both* of them saved us," she declares. "We knew him better, because of my father, but the decision to let us hide there he discussed with her. They both decided, they both agreed."

"What was she like?" I ask.

"Well, I told you that she was younger than he was, probably in her sixties. She came from my parents' hometown, Brzeżany. She apparently knew my grandfather, because it was a small town, and he was a well-known lawyer there. She also remembered my uncle. My father vaguely remembered her maiden

192

name, but I don't. I don't even know when she came to Żółkiew."

"Did you like him more than her?"

"Yes," my mother answers. "I *trusted* her, I just didn't *like* her that much. She was not always very pleasant. He was. She could be very pleasant, but sometimes if she got in a bad mood, then she would just, not abuse you, but sort of—talk out. Snap at you. One time she talked about my mother's family back in Brzeżany, and she brought up an incident. This was in the evening, after we had come up from the cellar, and she was sitting and talking, talking about her life in Brzeżany. I don't know why, but she suddenly mentioned that my mother had always been very well dressed. She mentioned that once she had wanted to buy something she saw in a store window, some clothing, and her mother said they could not afford it right then, but that they would try to save the money and buy it for Christmas. And when she finally saved the money and came to buy it, she was told that it was sold. And then she saw my mother wearing it. And she remembered this so many years later."

It's like an explosion going off in my head: ". . . came to buy it . . . it was sold . . . and then she saw my mother wearing it." Heat, like an electric current, shoots up my arms. The nape of my neck contracts as though someone splashed ice water on it. I am riveted by the awful symmetry of this story, which I have never heard before. My mind reels, trying to absorb it. I think: Oh my God. What a coincidence. What a story. Like a movie. Then: what the hell's wrong with you? What movie? This is real! Then: How am I going to convey this properly?

And all the while the conversation continues, unwinding quietly, matter-of-factly, across the tabletop.

I ask, "How old was she then, a little girl?"

My mother answers, "I don't know. I don't know when the incident took place, if it was right after the war, meaning World War I, or before then. And I don't know what she wanted to buy. We did not want to ask too many questions or get into arguments. Whatever she said, we just let her talk. But there was definitely some jealousy. Although otherwise, she was nice. She tried to help us, she felt sorry for us."

Suddenly, there's an edge in her voice.

"She felt sorry for *herself.*"

Then she pauses, and when she continues, her tone is softer.

"I mean, they were scared. It was very hard for them. The whole situation was very difficult."

I feel as though I am swimming in a dark aquarium, submerged amid murky layers of meaning, coincidence, significance, like some fish trapped between dense growths of seaweed. I have to get out, to pull my thoughts together, to react somehow to this revelation.

"Hard to imagine," my words emerge slowly, ponderously, "that the girl you were jealous of because she got the clothing you wanted, ends up in hiding in your cellar with her husband and daughter, and you have to share your food and your clothing with them . . ."

This is coming out so wrong. I sound so phony, so stilted. I'm forcing the words out of stiff lips. Underneath, my guts are quaking in hot and cold spasms. I'm shocked at what I've learned. Maria wanted something, and instead my grandmother got it. . . . She was upset, and disappointed, and jealous . . . and then my grandmother ends up in her cellar, at her mercy, in her power, so many years later . . . And she saves her! . . .

"Strange twist of fate, don't you think?" I hear myself finishing lamely.

And my mother's quiet reply, "Very. It is. That was the only time she mentioned it."

I try to imagine this scenario and realize how much more I want to know. When did this incident take place? How old were Agatha and Maria at the time? My mother and I explore this over and over and the best we can come up with is her very hesitant guess that there might have been at least a ten-year age difference between a young adolescent Agatha and a twenty-something Maria. If so, what item of clothing could they both have coveted? My mother has no idea.

I mull it over. A dress? Probably not, I decide. Gloves? A muff? A hat? Not likely to cause such a fuss, or be so hard to replace. Maybe: a coat.

And another question: Would the mother of a twenty-something Maria have been as involved in this purchase as she reports? That I can believe: my mother always shopped with my grandmother, and later, with me.

I have a photograph of my mother and grandmother striding arm-in-arm down some lane in the Polish prewar countryside and it's this image that I see when I imagine Maria and her mother setting out to make that special purchase.

. . . It's a beautiful day, bitter cold, as is usual for Poland in midwinter. The air is brittle as glass and as crystal clear. The hard-packed snow crackles and crunches underfoot as Maria and her mother walk quickly toward the center of town. They've had to get up early to catch a ride on the next-door neighbor's wooden wagon from their little house on the edge of town, but it was worth it. Maria has been waiting for this moment for months. Today, she is going to buy it, to make it her own.

She can still remember the thrill that had rushed through her when she'd first seen the coat. She'd been with her mother then too, the two of them walking, arm in arm, their shopping done, waiting for the hay wagon to drive them home. Even now, so many replays of the memory later, she can still feel the prickles of delight that rippled through her then, feel her breath sucked into an involuntary "Oooh!" of pure pleasure. Her mother, no less smitten, had kept her head while she kept gabbing, "Oh, it's glorious! Oh, Mother, I must have it!"

Her mother's smile of pleasure had faded into a sigh, as reality set in. "I wish you could, Maria dear. But, the price . . ." Maria had felt her world crumble, the sun setting right in the middle of the day. How had she overlooked that? The "Oooh!" deflated, became an "Oh," sagging and sorry. "But, wait, Maria," her mother had said, "there's time till Christmas. Maybe we can save enough till then."

She had worked hard since that day, carefully setting money aside. And now Christmas is here, in all its glittery splendor, and she is on her way back to the tailor's shop, her purse with its precious store of *złotych* tightly clutched in one hand. She tucks her other arm firmly into the crook of her mother's, and the two of them walk quickly across the town square to the row of shops on the opposite side. The arcade shielding the stores is full of people heading to and from the market, calling cheerful holiday greetings to one another.

Maria almost drags her mother the last few feet and bursts into the shop, breathless from the cold, the pace, and mostly, from the excitement.

Slight, stooped, the tailor appears from behind the curtain at the back of the store and approaches them, bowing politely.

"Yes, what can I do for the ladies?"

"Oh, *proszę Pana*, please, Sir, we're here to buy the coat you had on display in the window. Black, with shiny buttons, and a little fur trim at the neck."

"Ah, yes," he replies, smiling gently, "I know the coat."

"Oh, good," cries Maria happily, bouncing a bit in her eagerness.

"But, *Pani*," he says slowly, "Miss, I'm afraid I don't have it anymore. It's been sold."

"Sold!" she gasps in dismay, and clutches at her mother. Her mouth goes dry. She opens it, but no sound comes out. Her mother tries to help.

"Are you sure?" she asks. "Maybe it's just in the back."

"Oh, no, *Pani*. I know the coat, Madame. It was a lovely one. *Pani* has good taste. But I'm afraid it really is gone. Such a pity. Perhaps the ladies would like to look at something else. I have some other ones, very nice—" But Maria is already outside the shop, fighting back the tears that are beginning to freeze at the tips of her eyelashes. Her nose runs and she jabs at it with a mittened hand. Her mother comes up behind her softly and gives her a quick squeeze.

"Oh, *moja droga*, my dear, I am so sorry," she says. "I know how hard you worked." She sighs. "Come, Maria. We must be getting back. *Pan* _____ski will be waiting."

They trudge through the streets. Maria keeps slipping on the hardening snow, but she doesn't care. Keeping her eyes pointed stonily ahead, she plods on.

They stop at the corner to let a heavy wagon lumber by. As it creaks past, she prepares to step out over the snowdrift, and stops short. Stops so suddenly that she almost falls, and her mother grabs at her to steady her. On the opposite corner, stands *her* coat. Black, sleek, with a little fur trim, buttons twinkling in the sharp light. On someone else's body.

There is a strange roaring in her ears. She blinks to force her vision to clear. She recognizes the young woman in the coat.

196

She's seen her around. Her father's a lawyer, well-known in town. *Żydówka.* One of the Jewish girls. She's wearing a dark muff, soft and sleek and perfect against the dark fabric. She is always so well-dressed. Just as she is today: in the coat that was supposed to be *Maria's.*

I try to put myself in Maria's shoes. How did it feel to have wanted something so desperately, to have saved for it, penny by penny, only to see it walk off on someone else's body? Was she disappointed? Resigned? Jealous? And by the time she revealed the incident to my grandmother, what had the passage of years done to the memory and the feelings? Was the hurt still there, smoldering, seeking an accounting? Or had she developed a more philosophical view of the turn of events?

What must that conversation between my grandmother and Mrs. Łozińska have been like? . . .

They sit in the small living room, around the rickety old table. The windows are shuttered and draped with curtains and old blankets, the light dimmed to save precious fuel and money, and to comply with wartime blackout regulations. It also protects them from possible prying eyes of neighbors and passersby. Not that there are likely to be any at this hour. It's past curfew, and the night is bitterly cold. Still, you never know.

Agatha wraps her hands around the chipped cup and sips slowly. "Oh, for a real cup of coffee," she sighs to herself, not for the first time. "This is brown water. But at least it's warm."

She shivers slightly in her worn coat. The room is chilly but it's better than sitting on the earthen floor of the cellar, with the cold eating into your bones. She's tired. Those hours of sitting in the hole underground make you tired, even if you are doing nothing. Sitting, staring, whispering from time to time to her husband, her daughter, thinking and not thinking, trying not to think. She feels her eyes growing heavier and forces them open. Josef and Lutka look just as tired as she feels, but Maria is in a talkative mood. She has an audience. Who can blame her? For her, it's a break after the long monotony of her day, scrounging for a few scrawny vegetables in the rock-hard garden, struggling to turn them into something edible and to stretch it to feed five souls. Agatha knows how difficult it is for her: she's not young, her eyes are bad, there's no money, and she's cooped up with them. *Ach,* this terrible, terrible war.

Maria's reminiscing again, saying something about Brzeżany, about how funny it is that she should come from the same town as both Agatha and Josef, although they didn't know her then. And after all, why would they? Different religions, different social circles. And anyway, she was older than they were. Agatha stirs, forcing herself to perk up and pay attention.

". . . a lovely town, *nie tak,* isn't it so, *Pani* Rosenbergowa?"

Agatha nods tiredly, forcing her lips into what she hopes is a pleasant, social smile. She's not really listening, just letting the words wash over her. Some phrases stand out, borne on the waves of Maria's rising inflection.

". . . *Pani's* father . . . dis*tin*guished . . . I remember . . . *isn't* it so, *Pani?*"

Agatha keeps her head bobbing, struggling to focus.

". . . and *Pani* too! Oh yes. *Pani* may not remember me, but I remember you."

Something has shifted in the way she is talking now. Agatha is not sure what, but something about the words slices through the fog of her fatigue.

"I used to see you walking in the street sometimes, with your parents, or your friends. I always liked to see you; you were always so well dressed, isn't it so? So elegant . . ."

Agatha gives a tiny shrug, a weak laugh, feeling self-conscious, not sure what to say, how to respond. Sitting here in much-mended clothes, it seems worlds away: well-dressed? Why is she bringing that up?

"I remember it like it was yesterday," Maria continues. "I loved the shops with the pretty things in the window . . . I would walk with my mother, and once I saw such a lovely coat. And it's funny, to think of this now. . . . it was in the tailor's window. It was dark, with shiny buttons, and fur, some kind of fur trim around the neck. . . . I wanted it so much. But, there was no money. . . . My mother said, 'Soon it will be Christmas. Maybe you can save enough till then. Your father and I were going to give you something anyway, so we will give you some money toward the coat.'"

"So I waited. You know how it is to wait for something you want. . . . So, I saved and saved, and then came Christmas, and I did get some money from my parents, and from some others, and it was enough. And I went to the tailor shop to buy the coat. But it was gone."

She pauses to take a sip of coffee. Agatha waits. Maria swallows, puts the cup down on the table.

"Ah, yes." She presses her lips together in a rueful kind of smile, nodding sadly. "It was gone. Someone else had bought it in the meantime."

Agatha feels her head nodding in rhythm with Maria. Poor thing. What a disappointment.

"I was so unhappy . . ." Maria sighs, drinks again, sets down the cup. "And do you know, later I saw you walking in the street, and *you* were wearing that same coat! Imagine . . ."

Agatha freezes. Her stomach contracts sharply, painfully, with the intake of breath. She sits absolutely still, gripping the cup.

What? Thoughts fly like frantic birds. *What did she say? I bought her coat? What coat? I don't remember. I never saw her. Oh, Boże mój, My God. What will happen now?*

Agatha forces herself to keep her head moving, in that slow and stately tempo, nodding up and down, the two heads rising and dipping in tandem across the scarred tabletop. She says nothing, keeps her eyes locked on the other's face.

"No, *tak jest*," murmurs Maria. "That's life . . . can you imagine? . . . Funny, no?"

She stands up abruptly and collects the cups, to wash them in the sink.

And later: Do they discuss it, Agatha and Josef and Lutka? Briefly, in hurried, abbreviated whispers, in their life-space that allows no privacy? Do they decide: "Don't say anything, just act normal. It happened a long time ago. Maybe she still bears a grudge, but she agreed to take us in, so it can't be that bad. Anyway, there's nothing we can do about it now." Does it simply fade away?

And Agatha, racking her brains, tries to remember the coat, but it was so long ago, who can remember? Better not tell *her* that, though;

it was so important to her. It seems to Agatha that she did have a coat with a fur collar, but she just doesn't remember. . . .

As I try to puzzle out this story, I realize: When I first heard it, first heard that my mother and her parents had been in the hands of someone with a potentially lethal grudge, I was frozen by the sense of threat. But I realize that my mother didn't report it that way. There's no cataclysmic ending to the incident. Just Maria's telling the story, them receiving it in silence, and then moving onto something else. All the rest lives on in my head. All the drama lives in *my* head.

My mother, too, keeps coming back to this incident, picking at it like at a scab. The unsettled questions nag at us both: *When? What? Why?* Both of us burrow in vain into layers of reluctant memory; there are no other sources of information. There is no one else to ask. My mother is the only witness left. To her credit, she never gets angry at me for all this poking and prodding, she just gets exasperated—with *herself.* Her desperate litany continues: "I don't know, I don't know. I can't answer these questions because I don't know. It's hard to remember all the details after all those years. Especially when I wanted to forget them anyhow."

She gives up.

I give up.

And bring it up yet again, over a year later.

"I want to go back to that incident with Łozińska," I begin. "You told me that she'd wanted something she'd seen in a store, and then your mother ended up with it. And you have no idea what that object of clothing was?"

"I think some coat," she says, frowning. Then, her face clearing, she repeats, "It was a coat."

"*Real*-ly!"

My voice rises in a squeak, then cracks. It was a coat! Oh my God. I hadn't known that. I'd simply settled on it being a coat by following the process of imagination and association to fill in the gaps in the story. Realizing that these processes had unexpectedly, ultimately led me to the truth—to her truth—sends heat flooding up and down my arms. A tremor passes through me. I feel like

I've just made contact with the Beyond, that I've been given a Sign.

It's a good thing the tape recorder is running. I don't hear a word of what my mother's saying over the roaring in my head.

Chapter Twenty-One

"Were you worried about the Łozińskis when they left the house?" I ask, because *I* suddenly am—retroactively, foolishly. "Or was it relatively safe for a Pole to leave the house and be outside?"

"Well, you never knew," my mother says. "If something happened to a German soldier, for example, they would round up whoever was on the street. Or they could·just surround an entire area, and say, 'Everybody out!' and set the houses on fire. You never knew. It could happen at any time. But, for the most part, Poles wouldn't be in terrible danger if they just minded their own business and weren't in the wrong place at the wrong time. And mostly, the Łozińskis did stay home. They only went out to do some shopping and to go to church."

The scene in my mind's eye is split horizontally.

Below are three shadows, motionless, only a shade's difference from the darkness that envelops them in silent folds of gray-black and black-gray.

Above: earth and sky and sun and shadows, black and crisp. Bricks and flowers and stones, birdsong and breezes. And Łoziński, walking slowly along a narrow lane, walking to church . . .

He didn't go to church every day, like Maria. Once a week, usually. On Sunday. He loved the radiance of the stained glass windows, sparkling like a jeweled brooch in the shadowed setting of the surrounding walls. And the music: there were fewer voices in the choir now, and the organ bleated rustily, but when the music soared he felt his soul dancing with the angels.

In winter, it was warm in the church, the dark fruitiness of the incense mingling with smoking tallow and the faintly sour smell of bodies pressed closely together amid the pews. The wooden grain benches were pockmarked with scratches and nicks that had been worn smooth by the fervent fumblings of fingers grasping them for support as old knees were creakily raised and lowered in prayer.

The deep voice of the priest rolled like waves over their heads and echoed between the arches. He was a decent man. He preached simple, basic, cautious sermons: passages from Scripture that would not antagonize the authorities, extolling the old, good values of hard work, patience, and trust in God—good messages, things you needed to hear, over and over, especially these days. He kept the community informed about births and illnesses and deaths and who needed a helping hand (among the Christians). Łoziński wondered, not for the first time: What about the nonbaptized? Many times he tried to imagine what the priest would say if he knew Łoziński was harboring three Jews right under his own house, in his cellar.

Not that he would ever ask him, or even hint at it. He'd never bring it up in confession. Maybe that was why he didn't come to church so often; maybe he felt uncomfortable about the fact that, after all had been said and done and rationalized, he was still hiding something from the good Father, before whom he was supposed to be an open book. *Was that a sin?* he wondered. He had no answer, couldn't get one. Surely it could not be a sin to hide these Jews, any more than it had been sinful to offer shelter to the Holy Mary and her newborn babe, back in Bethlehem. Were Jesus alive now, he might also need to hide!

The thought startled him. He drew in his breath so sharply it twisted into a cough.

"*Nic, nic,* it's nothing." He shrugged apologetically at his neighbor who glanced over at him, concerned, annoyed at the interruption in the priest's smooth flow. You had to be careful, so careful. Had to watch every glance, everything you said. Be on guard, always. It was so hard, so hard. *Ach,* what a bad business this was.

203

He remembered the shock he'd felt when *Pan* Rosenberg had first approached him, so pale, so tremulous, that he, Łoziński, had worried that he was sick. With typhus, God forbid. When he'd heard the request, he was flabbergasted. It was impossible. How could he possibly . . . ? And at his age? Playing hide-and-seek games like a schoolboy? He'd never liked those games. Even as a child, he'd hated being flushed out of his hiding place by his chums yelling "*Boo!*" He could feel the same clutch of fear even now, squeezing his bowels. But *Pan* Rosenberg kept insisting, pleading, in that quiet, dignified way of his. Just to get through the next *akcja*. These things never lasted very long; the Germans were very efficient. Just a few days. Please . . .

What a crazy idea. Still, how could he say no? *Pan* Rosenberg was his friend. Keeping his face absolutely still, he smiled inwardly, remembering all those hours he used to spend at Rosenberg's pharmacy. The chats with Berger. Oh, how Łoziński missed those days, and those conversations, and the sense that no problem existed that reasonable men and rational discussion could not solve.

All that felt so long ago. Nothing was reasonable anymore. Everything was upside down, topsy-turvy. It was preposterous that anyone would want to kill this gentle, good man. Yet, there it was. He still couldn't believe it, any more than he could believe that he had agreed to this crazy idea.

He hadn't known what to do. He said he had to talk it over with Maria. Of course, of course, agreed Rosenberg.

They had talked and talked that night, almost all night long. She kept wrapping her rosary around her fingers and rocking back and forth, crossing herself over and over.

By morning, they had decided. Maria was scared but determined; he could see it in the set of her jaw. She knelt longer than usual at her morning prayers, he noticed, and kept silent. He knew much of the day-to-day burden would fall on her. Of the two of them, he was the talker, the dreamer. She was the practical one, molded by life into a tough, no-nonsense woman who knew how to manage on very little. She could be kind, he knew, having felt the tenderness of her caress, having watched her stroking the big cat she loved so well. Yet those very fingers could tighten mercilessly around the feather-soft necks of that same cat's newborn kittens and hold them underwater in the battered old pail until the bubbles stopped rising to the surface. Once she decided to do something, she did it. She's a strong woman, he thought admiringly, strong and determined.

They'd needed that strength. Who would have thought that it would turn out like this? Days turning into weeks, into months. No end in sight. Always hungry. Always afraid. Always on guard.

It was strange having three people hiding in your house, under your very feet. He tried not to think about it. It was easier that way. Not to think. Not to plan too far ahead. Just do what needs to be done, from day to day, and leave the rest to God. Mary will take care of her children. Somehow, even in his deepest despair, when he was so sick and tired of the whole thing, he still believed that "his" Jews would survive, though why he felt that way, he couldn't really say. He just did.

The velvety shadows inside the church were soothing; you could burrow into the darkness like the thick comforter he'd had as a boy. Although sometimes he'd catch himself thinking about "Them," buried for hours in a different kind of darkness, cold and unforgiving. Then he'd be grateful to be able to step out into the open air, into the sharp burst of white-gray brightness that made his eyes water.

In the old days, he and his neighbors used to gather on the well-worn steps in front of the church, trading gossip, discussing politics. These days, no one lingered long. Time, and the right to do with it what you will, is not yours unless you are free. There were other masters here now, and you were better off moving along quickly, not attracting unnecessary attention. A few nods, a quick low-voiced exchange. That was all.

"Did you hear who 'They' got last week?"
                                    "So-and-so was caught!".
          "Caught!"
                            "Caught! Sent to Janowska Road."
                "Shot."
                                    "Shot."
      "Shot."

His stomach would lurch, his heart skip a beat. But he'd keep his face neutral, impassive.

"You don't say. You don't say." He'd receive the news gravely, somberly, presenting the right balance of reactions: curiosity—morbid, at times. Some sympathy—tempered, of course. He collected the few precious tidbits of information like a beggar gathering crumbs after a feast, carefully wrapping each morsel in layers of memory and tucking it away for slow, meticulous retelling later on.

Once he heard:

"They caught the Rosenbergs. The whole family. The father, the mother, and the daughter. They were all shot."

"Ahhh! Who saw? Does *Pan* know where, or when . . . ?"

He tried to get more information but that was all. He felt strange, as though his mind were a great distance away, looking down at his body standing there, watching his head nodding sagely at this news. His limbs felt heavy, terribly heavy, but his thoughts raced. Could it be? How could it? He had left them not long ago in the cellar. Was it possible? Could something have happened? He was confused. He must go back and check. His mind settled back into his body. He bowed politely to his companion, wished him a good day, and turned homeward. What could this mean?

His mind was flooded with scenarios of brigades of storm troopers deployed about his house, the trapdoor wrenched open, the three fugitives torn from the enfolding darkness like a yanked tooth, he and his wife disgraced, dishonored, facing humiliation, torture, or—Oh, Mary preserve us, I can't even think about it. Heart in his mouth, he urged his ancient legs homeward, his breath coming in little puffs and wheezes until he rounded the last corner and saw the hut, nestled in quiet meagerness at the end of the tiny lane, just across from the old Jewish cemetery, and everything was, mercifully, silent.

They were where he had left them, sitting in silence, in the gloom. They looked up quickly, in alarm, as he raised the trapdoor and squinted into the darkness at them.

"*Co się stało?* What happened?"

Relief flowed through him like a warm stream. He mopped his forehead with his sleeve.

"Oh-ho!" he chortled, "You will live! You will live!"

Over their soft, startled cries, he continued, his words shooting out into the darkness in harsh, intense whispers. "I just heard it from _____. You were shot! They think you are dead! So you see, no one will be looking for you now! You will survive! Oh, yes, you will live!"

It took several repetitions to make them understand. There wasn't much information to go on. The tiny bit they had would be discussed and dissected over and over, and quietly. Through it all, his eyes shining, Łoziński felt again the nearness of Mary, hovering over them all, cloaking them in her divine protection and love. He would say a special prayer to her tonight.

Chapter Twenty-Two

The Talmud teaches that a person's true nature is revealed under three conditions: when drunk, when broke, and when angry. I would add at least one more: when under extreme duress, such as in wartime. What might you do if you saw your neighbors and friends unjustly discriminated against, deported, murdered?

"People say that not enough Poles helped Jews during the war," says my mother. "I sometimes ask myself what we would have done if we had been in the reverse situation. If we would have been willing to risk our lives for someone else. It's hard to judge. I could understand if someone didn't want to help you, didn't want to take you into their house, because that was a big risk, and you had to be very, very courageous and devoted to do that. To me, not actively saving Jews wasn't their biggest crime. It's that some of them were happy to do the Germans' work for them. For instance, they killed Jews who came begging for a piece of bread. They could just have let the person go. That was pure sadism.

"And they also turned Jews in to the Germans. The Germans themselves were not always able to tell who was Jewish. The Poles could. For example, the Germans rounded up many Poles and ·sent them to Germany to work in factories and on farms. Some Jews who spoke Polish well and had a 'good look'—meaning, they didn't look Jewish—pretended they were Poles to get sent to Germany. They thought that their chances of survival were better there because the Germans couldn't distinguish that easily whether you were Polish or Jewish. But the local people could tell. And that's who you had to be afraid of. Because *they'd* often denounce you.

"That happened to a friend of mine, Nusia Ringler. She was heavy-set, with an excellent look: a dark face like a Ukrainian peasant, a clear, healthy complexion. But someone in her transport to Germany—a Pole? A Ukrainian?—denounced her and she was killed. That's what you had to be afraid of."

Then there was Janina Dennenfeld, a Polish girl who was my mother's best friend in high school. Everyone called her Janka.

"Dennenfeld is a German name, but they considered themselves Polish patriots. She lived near me, one minute away, just across the Swinia River, and we became close friends," says my mother.

"She couldn't be without me one single day. We walked to school together, we walked back home together, we were together after school, we went for walks, she with her dog, me with mine. We were always at each other's houses. They'd invite me for the holidays. I was like a second daughter to them.

"When the Russians occupied us, her family moved away. But we kept writing to each other. Then the Germans came and we lost contact. Someone told me they became great German patriots, claimed German origin, declared themselves Volksdeutsche.

"One day, in the summer of 1942, she came back to Żółkiew for a visit. I was at the window of our apartment, and I saw her walking across the street with some friends. I called to her from the window. She turned around, she saw me, and didn't say anything. Just turned and walked away. She pretended she didn't see me. She didn't want to know me. I didn't exist. I was very disappointed. Very hurt."

I ponder the range of possibilities. My mind comes up with a "Grid of Altruism" with two major dimensions: passive to active, negative to positive.

	PASSIVE	**ACTIVE**
NEGATIVE	• Anti-Semitic opinions, no action taken	• Turn away from friend ↓ • Denounce Jew to local authorities or Germans ↓ • Kill Jew outright
POSITIVE	• Sympathy, no overt action ↓ • Recognize a Jew, but don't denounce	• Providing food/ provisions secretly ↓ • Spontaneously save someone ↓ • Deliberately shelter someone ("Righteous Gentile")

The negative dimension runs the gamut from Janka, who turned her back on a friend, to someone who denounced Nusia Ringler on a train, to someone who killed, whether with their own hands or by orchestrating the killing, like the Łozińskis' gauleiter brother-in-law.

Along the positive dimension, some were sympathetic and silent, while others acted spontaneously and protectively. I think of Kasia, volunteering to spirit Lutka away to her village, and the Ukrainian pharmacist who lied to the Gestapo about my mother and grand-parents' whereabouts on the day of the final akcja.

And then there were the Łozińskis, Maria and Emil, who actively put themselves at risk to save a Jewish family. Why? What propelled them into that most special, most select category of Righ-teous Gentiles?

What might Łoziński say if I could ask him? . . .

Łoziński sits, waiting. The hubbub of a city in the middle of its workday flows and eddies around him.

He sits still. His eyes are aimed at the opposite corner of the square, but are focused on other scenes, other times.

He hasn't thought about them for years. Well, that isn't exactly true. Every once in a while, he'd see, in an article here, a news report there, something about Jews, or Israel. Or he'd overhear a neighbor's casual anti-Semitic remark. Then he'd remember.

He is happy enough to forget those times. He never wanted anyone to know about it, that's for sure, especially not his nosy neigh-bors. That's all he needed. He darts a glance around him, scanning the square. There isn't much chance of anyone seeing him here, or making any connection with back then, but it's still a reflex action, so many years later. That's why he had suggested meeting here, in the central city square, kilometers away from his hometown where it had all happened.

As he glances around the square again, his gaze falls on a figure standing at the opposite corner. His breath catches in his throat. A woman of medium height, with short, slightly wavy, light brown hair and a bag dangling off one shoulder. The pants she wears, and the modern sneakers, jar with his memories. But that is the style nowadays, and he is almost used to it. The face, though—that's the same, the long nose with the small bump at the bridge, the frown of concentration as she turns in his direction. Her searching gaze meets his, rearranges itself into something more purposeful. She glances quickly left and right, checking traffic, and strides across the square. He remembers her quick movements. She hasn't changed.

He leans heavily on his cane and stands up, unfurling slowly, straightening his shoulders. He reaches up and doffs his cap, clutching it in one wrinkled hand.

She stands in front of him.

"*Pan* Łoziński?"

Her voice shakes a little, hesitates over the words.

"Lutka!" he cries at the same time.

211

"What? Oh, no," she blurts, coloring a little, "Lutka's my mother! I'm Diane, her daughter."

Her Polish sounds very rusty, very uncertain, very American. For a moment, he is confused.

"You look just like your mother!" he says, shaking his head as if to rearrange the kaleidoscope of images into their rightful places.

"I know," she tells him. "Everyone says so."

They are still standing, ill at ease. He still holds his cap in one hand, leans heavily on the cane with the other.

"*Noh!*" he exhales. "*Proszę usiąść.* Please sit down."

They sit facing each other, the glass-topped table between them, slightly off to the side. He studies her for several minutes. Images, past and present, swim together in his mind's eye. The girl then, the woman now. She waits, breathing rapidly, bright spots of color in her cheeks, eyes flitting around, now looking at him, now glancing quickly away.

The waitress appears and takes their order. Just some tea, please. Perhaps some cakes? No? Nothing else, thank you, just tea.

The young woman rummages through her bag.

"I brought some photographs," she says, taking out an envelope and rifling through it. She lays them on the table. He reaches out and picks them up slowly, holding them close to his eyes.

"Ah, *tak*," he murmurs. "Your grandpa, your grandma. *Tacy kulturalni ludzie.* Such refined people." He leans over a photograph, then peers up at her. He nods his head gently, a slight smile on his face. "Just like your mother!"

He places the photographs carefully back on the table.

"I remember your mother coming into your grandfather's *apteka*. She would stop in on the way from school, to say hello, get some candy. She was such a lively little thing, always running. Running in, running out."

She collects the photographs so the waitress can place the tea things on the table. She feels him looking at her.

"What else do you remember?" she asks.

He sighs.

"Ah, it was so long ago," he says. "And who even wants to remember? First the war, and then afterward. The communists. My wife was not well. She had problems with her eyes. Cataracts. She needed treatments. They helped a little, not much. She died a few

212

years ago, God rest her soul. . . . *Tak, tak jest,* yes, that's how it is," he says, acknowledging her murmured sympathies.

He leans forward, raises the cup carefully, hand trembling slightly, sips slowly through lips reaching for the liquid. Then he sets it down again, carefully, in the center of the saucer. It makes a quiet sound.

He looks up. She sits, not moving, waiting.

"Yes, my dear. What is it? What do you want to know?"

"*Pan* Łoziński, you hid my mother and grandparents in your home for sixteen months. Please tell me: What made you do this?"

He sits silent a while longer, eyes focused off in the distance. He shrugs, more with his eyebrows than any other part of him.

"I don't know myself, really. Who can say? Those were strange times. No one understood what was happening. The whole world was upside down. Who would have believed that one man, one mad man, could almost defeat the whole world!"

Just talking about it, he can feel them stirring: the old feelings.

"And this business with the Jews . . . an ugly business. We lived a little outside the center of town. So I did not see all the terrible things that the Germans did to the Jewish people in the town, but we heard. The neighbors were always talking. They were terrible gossips."

Their faces suddenly rise up before him. Especially his neighbor, what was his name? The army guy. Hated Hitler but was still proud of him for getting rid of the Jews. He would have been horrified had he only known—horrified and enraged. Łoziński shivers slightly; both he and Maria would have been killed had this neighbor found out.

He brings his gaze back to the present, to her. He shakes his head.

"I don't know how to explain. . . ."

"You see," he tries again, "I used to spend time in your grandfather's *apteka.* I liked sitting there. It was so orderly and pleasant. Like your grandfather. He was such a gentleman. A man of his word. That's how it should be. Anyway, I used to sit there with another man—oh, what was his name?"

"*Pan* Berger?"

"Ah yes. Berger. That's right. Also a nice man. We used to meet there every day, to discuss. Politics. 'Will there be war?' 'Won't there be war?'" He snorts. "As if it made a difference, all that talking.

213

"Your grandfather never got involved in these discussions. He was busy working. Sometimes we got a little on his nerves." He smiles, a little mischievously, at the memory.

She takes a deep, ragged breath.

"And then?" she prompts.

His smile fades. "And then . . . then things got worse. There were *akcje*. We knew more were coming. Your grandpa asked if they could hide during the next one in our cellar. . . ."

His voice trails off. This is hard. It is bringing things back: The fear. The terrible helplessness. How can people do such things?

"And maybe we were naïve. Stupid. We knew it was dangerous, but somehow, I thought, a few days . . . and where we lived, who passes by anyhow?

"And then the Germans killed everybody. No more Jews. Poof. Just like that."

It comes back to him: the shock. The disbelief. The horror. *All the Jews in town, gone? All* of them? His friend, Berger? And all the others?

And then the terrifying realization: *Swięta Maria*, Holy Mary, what was he going to do with the three of them now? They could not come out anymore. They—and he—were trapped. Thinking about it, he shudders.

He looks at the young woman across the table, so like her mother. He sees her fidgeting with the handle of the cup, tracing its outline with her fingertips. Waiting. He can feel how important this is to her. How can he explain?

"We could not send them out. They had nowhere to go. The Germans would catch them and shoot them. They were still finding Jews and shooting them right up to the very end of the war. They'd have shot us, too. So we were stuck. We with them, them with us.

"It was very hard. For all of us. At first it was strange for me, to have them down there, right under my feet. After a while, I got used to it. People can get used to everything. Sometimes I think that it's not good, to get used to everything.

"The worst thing was the fear. We were always scared. Of the Germans. Of our neighbors. Even after the war, I did not want anyone to know that we had hidden them. It was still not safe. For us."

He wonders if she could understand. He doubts it; he hardly does, himself. In some strange way, it had seemed obvious, the only possible decision. His friend asked him to save his life. He couldn't say no. He just couldn't. How would he live with that?

He must have been mad, taking a chance like that. Deluding himself: "Only a few days." "Who'd ever know . . . away from the center of town . . . two old people?" He must have been crazy. That's the only possible explanation.

Later? Later was different. Later they were all stuck.

Or maybe it was fate. God's plan. That's the only other possible explanation.

He hears her speaking and pulls himself back to pay attention.

"What's that? Oh, our being religious? I don't know. We prayed all the time that the war should end. I told your grandparents that the Holy Mary would protect them, and, you see, She did."

She nods. "And *you*." Her cheeks are very red, he notices, and he sees tears. She leans over, fumbling in her bag for a tissue; he hands her a napkin and she crushes it in her hand.

"*Pan* Łoziński," she starts to say. "I came to say . . . I don't know how . . . you and your wife—"

He reaches across the table and pats her hand, still clutching the napkin.

"*Tak, tak,*" he says, "Yes, yes. Everything is fine. '*Oh-kay*' as you Americans say, no?" And is relieved to see a watery half-smile struggling to her lips. She dabs at her eyes.

"And now, you drink your tea, and I will finish mine. All this talk has made my mouth very dry."

He drains the tea from his cup and sits back.

"It's strange to be speaking of this after all these years. It has been a secret for such a long time. Almost like it happened to someone else, like in the cinema. A film with a happy ending, no?"

He watches her finishing her tea and replacing the cup in the saucer.

He signals for the check. She reaches into her bag for her wallet but he wags his finger, gnarled as an old branch, at her.

"No, no!" he chides playfully. "It's not often I get to drink tea with a young lady. This is my pleasure."

He counts several brightly colored bills out carefully and places them neatly under the edge of the saucer. He settles his cap back onto his head, adjusting it slightly. Grasping the cane firmly with one hand, he reaches for her arm with the other.

"Come," he says, hoisting himself to his feet. "You can do me the honor of walking me back to my trolley."

Chapter Twenty-Three

For the first time in a long while, my guts are quieter. The cellar is quieter inside me. The Łozińskis sit more quietly inside me. Time to move on, as my mother would say.
Time to resume the chronology.

Several months later, I am back in New York, in my parents' apartment at 522 West End Avenue. I'm on my way to a conference, and as I often do, I've tacked on a few extra days to be with my parents.

I look around the living room, the tall west-facing windows flanked by ceiling-high Dieffenbachia and rubber trees—my mother has a green thumb and everything flourishes under her devoted care. The morning light illuminates the simple, familiar furnishings: the plant-filled coffee table around which my brother and I used to march to the rousing tunes of John Philip Souza blaring from the phonograph, the long off-white couch we all still love to fall asleep on, and the two gold-toned armchairs wide enough to cozy into cross-legged.

My parents' life is reflected in the cheerful display of artwork around the room. There's the original *Happy Mother's Day* embroidery prepared by my father for a fund-raising card used one year by Women's American ORT (Organization for Rehabilitation through Training). A framed array of photographs of the grandchildren. My pastel drawing of a sunshiny little girl carrying a basket of berries, drawn at my father's art table when I was almost six. He says it reminds him of a Matisse. My brother's rendering of a train bearing down on the viewer, a colorful experiment in perspective. The creations of artist-friends: Ilya Schor. Tadeusz Lipski, my father's art teacher in prewar Warsaw, later a mentor and friend. And one of my favorites, done when I was a child: my father's portrait of my mother. I remember standing at his elbow, watching, as he captured forever, in lightning-fast brushstrokes, a moment of brooding intensity.

My mother and I sit at our usual places at the rectangular Danish teak dining table. She always stations herself in the seat nearest the kitchen so she can jump up and run back and forth from oven to refrigerator to table, serving and clearing and taking care of everyone. I sit diagonally to her right.

She absently runs her long fingers through the silky white fringes on the red-and-yellow table runner as I set up the tape recorder and align my notebook and pens. From the street ten stories below, sounds of traffic float up: A car horn bleats. Tires squeal, protesting, as a driver takes a turn too fast, trying to make the light. Otherwise, a quiet peace fills the apartment; my father has gone out on an errand, leaving us alone, giving us privacy.

"So you left Żółkiew, in the summer of 1945," I prompt.

"We left that summer, when the Russians announced that former Polish citizens could repatriate to Poland. We went to live with my mother's brother, my uncle Poldzio and his wife Jadzia, who had survived, and were living in Katowice."

"Where did you live in Katowice?"

"My uncle lived in a big, old apartment which some Germans had vacated; the area around Katowice had had a big German population. It had a big living room and a few bedrooms, with some furniture. It had silverware and linen, and some bottles of old wine. There was even an old German woman, some sort of maid, who'd worked for the former occupants. My aunt Jadzia let her stay there, in a small room off the kitchen, in exchange for doing the cooking. She was glad of it; it was very hard to make a living right after the war.

"The apartment was like a big hotel. People were always showing up, and my uncle was always collecting strays. Another lost soul. And another. My aunt's niece and nephew, whom my uncle had somehow helped survive, though I don't know how. A friend's daughter and her husband. Another friend's son. A young guy named Tolek, who had survived with the AK, the Armia Kra-jowa, the Polish underground army, posing as a Christian. He was rough; he had to be, to have survived with the AK. They were *very* patriotic Poles but they hated Jews as much as they hated the Germans. He was the only survivor in his family.

"And we had even brought someone with us—a woman named Żenia, a few years older than me. She had been saved by my dentist, Gryznowa. Remember the dentist who would sing and drill on my teeth at the same time? She'd scared me as a dentist but she was a very nice person. Anyway, she hid Żenia and saved her life. After the war, when Gryznowa heard we were leaving Żółkiew, she begged us to take Żenia along with us. She said, 'There is no future here for her under the Russians. Take her along with you.' So we did, and for a while she stayed with us in my uncle's apartment as well. There were sometimes a dozen or more people in that apartment. Some stayed a week, some a month, some longer, like us, until each one left for the West."

"How did all these people support themselves?"

"It was very hard to find work. Żenia found some office work, but most people were involved in some sort of '*bus*iness.'"

Her tone highlights the first syllable, her eyes widen, eyebrows perking upward. At my questioning frown, she hastens to explain.

"Black market. People were crossing the borders back and forth between the various zones of occupation, smuggling any-thing they could put their hands on: salt, sugar, penicillin, and of course, people. The smuggling was unbelievable. That's how people survived.

"One couple in my uncle's apartment was involved in smug-gling liquor. They did everything: buying the bottles, filling them with liquor, making labels and putting them on the bottles, and putting in the corks. I helped with the labels. All this was illegal, of course. You needed a government license to sell wine or whiskey. It was a state-owned monopoly.

"It's because of them that I was almost arrested by the militia. Me and my mother."

"You and Grandma?"

My straight-as-an-arrow mother and grandmother?

"Yes. One day they needed someone to deliver some of the bottles and they decided that my mother and I looked innocent enough. They gave us a couple of valises and sent us out. We'd gone barely two blocks when we were stopped by two members of the militia who opened our suitcases and wanted to know where we'd come from. I froze. I couldn't think of any lies so they made us take them back home with us.

"Uncle Poldzio opened the door and almost had a heart attack when he saw us. He immediately realized the danger, so he walked these two guys into the front room and kept them busy there while these friends somehow managed to get rid of all the evidence in the back of the apartment. My uncle bribed the militia and they left. The two big smugglers, my mother and me."

We laugh. It's funny—now.

"What about the three of you? How did you manage?"

"My father didn't want my uncle to support us, so he tried to get work, even though he wasn't feeling well. He looked for work in Wrocław, which was formerly in Germany, but found nothing. Once he even went to Warsaw by train looking for work. By the way, this was when he also tried to locate those Polish forgers who had promised to supply us with false papers while we were in hiding.

"When my uncle Poldzio heard that my father had made the trip, he was horrified. 'What, you traveled by train between Katowice and Warsaw? The Poles can pull you off the train and kill you!' Because there was still a lot of anti-Semitism in Poland. Many Poles were sorry that Hitler hadn't gotten rid of all the Jews, and some tried to finish the job for him. There were several pogroms after the war in which Jews were killed. Like in Kielce, in 1946.

"Even if they didn't kill you, they certainly didn't want to hire you. Nobody told my father directly that they didn't want to hire him because he was Jewish, but he sensed it. So when he couldn't find work, and with all the anti-Semitism around, my father decided we should leave Poland. He told me, 'I don't see a future here, not for me, not for you. Let's try to get out.'"

"Did your mother work?" I ask.

"Actually, she did, a little. She was a very good baker, and she and my aunt Jadzia sold homemade baked goods. She'd done something similar before the war, with my uncle Manek's wife, my aunt Zosia."

"Besides smuggling liquor," I tease, "what did you do in Katowice?"

"I went to school. We arrived in Katowice in time for me to register for my senior year of high school, which started on September first. I had to meet with the principal, who asked me some questions about what I had studied and agreed to admit me. I didn't tell him I was Jewish and he didn't ask."

"Would that have been a problem?" I wonder.

"My father felt there could be. My uncle Poldzio was not registered as a Jew. He had survived by pretending to be a Christian Pole, and he was still living on his Christian papers, so we couldn't suddenly show up as Jews."

"What about your name?"

"We continued to use our name, but Rosenberg could also be a German name."

"Did you come across any anti-Semitism in school?"

"No. I didn't come across any Jews either, officially. I suspected that a few of my classmates were Jewish, based on looks, and some words. But nobody said anything openly. Everybody had his own war experiences and tragedies and problems but nobody asked too many personal questions. I didn't want to ask them questions, I didn't want them to ask me questions.

"Tolek, the young guy living in my uncle's apartment, ended up in the same class as me. He was very unhappy about that. He insisted that we pretend we didn't know each other, because he said I looked Jewish and he didn't, and he didn't want anyone to know there was any connection between us. We never walked to school together; we would come and go at different times."

"So you were still in hiding," I conclude.

"Yup," she nods.

"What was that period like for you?"

"It was a very good time. It was like a normal life. School. Having fun. Being with other kids. There were students of all ages. I was not the only one who had lost all those years. There were Poles who had lost time because of the war. Some had fought in the underground; they were seventeen, eighteen, nineteen years old. And there were students even older than me. Don't forget that in 1946, I was twenty-one. I should have finished school a long time ago. Had it not been for the war, I would have gotten my high school degree in 1943. Everyone worked hard to blend in and catch up, to fill in all those gaps that we were missing. And it was a very good education, for a change. Finally.

"It was the best time." Her voice starts to shake, to crack. "Because I didn't think. I didn't think about what had happened. I had friends, and a lot of fun. Going to the theater, to the movies, for walks. I had fun."

She's crying now.

"And then it started again. On the move. From place to place. Without having a place of our own. I was on the go again."

This is the only time my mother cries—really cries—during all those hours of taping, of talking, of remembering. She hadn't cried when talking about the time in the cellar, or about the loss of her friends, her family, her grandmother, her dog. And suddenly now? It catches me completely off guard. I hadn't realized what those few months in Katowice had meant to her. I had expected her to be chafing at the bit, eager to flee Poland the first chance she got. I never expected her to have found happiness, friends, a new life in postwar Poland, of all places. I had never realized that her experience during the war was only one trauma. Leaving Katowice was another.

Watching her, I feel my control slipping, tears rising to my own eyes, my vision getting blurry and stuff catching in my throat. Hidden under the tabletop, my hands are clenched so tightly I can feel my nails etching half-moons into my palms. The pain helps—it gives me something else to focus on as I struggle to keep my cool.

Thinking about it later, I am angry at myself, and full of regret. I wish I had jumped up and hugged her, and we could have cried together. I do remember how hard I struggled to sit still, not wanting to move, to intrude, to intervene. Afraid that she would feel worse if I did. She was the type to dry her tears quickly and get on with life. And I was a kid once again, having a hard time watching a parent cry.

"When did you actually leave Katowice?"

Her tears begin to subside. I gradually stop slicing my palms with my nails.

"In April. We had to leave before the end of the school year. I would have finished school in May. One more month, and I would have gotten my diploma. I was very upset. I told my father that I wanted to finish the year. I mean, I had had such an interrupted education, it was unbelievable! The education I was receiving now was really good for a change. But my father didn't want to wait any longer. He didn't want to take any chances of not being able to get out."

"When did you get permission to leave Poland?"

"You didn't get permission to leave. It was the Russian system: you didn't leave. You had to get false documents, false visas. I had no idea how my father got the papers and I wasn't interested. I was interested only in going to school. That's all I wanted. But one day my father came home and announced, 'I have the papers, we are leaving on this-and-this day, and that's it.' So that was it.

"He told me not to say anything to anyone, because leaving Poland was illegal. In school, I only told them I was moving. One of the guys in my class, who I suspected was Jewish, came over and said to me, quietly, 'I know why you're leaving; you're doing the right thing.'"

"My principal gave me a paper certifying that I had finished all my course work. But this wasn't an official high school diploma."

"What were your plans at that time?"

"We wanted to go to America. Each of my parents had a cousin there, something I found out only after the war. My father's first cousin Pauline (Pepka—you remember her!) was already there, and my mother's cousin, Ludy—that's short for Ludwig—had moved there already in the 1920s. Remember I told you that my mother had stayed with his family in Vienna before World War I, when she'd gone to have her birthmark treated?"

I nod.

"Ludy and his wife Ethel were willing to sponsor us to come to the U.S., and even sent us the papers. But we were advised to go through the JDC, the Joint Distribution Committee, and UNRRA, the United Nations Relief and Rehabilitation Administration, because that process was supposedly faster, and once you got to the U.S., these agencies would help you find an apartment and a job, so you wouldn't be a burden to your relatives, something my father did not want. That meant going through the DP—Displaced Persons—camps in Germany. So that's what we did. But first we had to get out of Poland."

"What was it like, leaving Poland?"

"My uncle Poldzio came to the train station to see us off. It was very hard for my mother to leave her only surviving brother, especially when we didn't know when we would see him again. We hoped he would follow us soon."

"When did they leave?"

"A year after we did. But they went to Venezuela, via Paris and Cuba. They chose Venezuela because Poldzio knew someone there, there were supposedly good business opportunities there, and Venezuela allowed people in more freely than the United States. But not as Jews. Venezuela did not accept Jews at that time. So my aunt and uncle went there as Christians, and established themselves well in Caracas. They built a business with some partners, making fancy lingerie. Your father even designed some of their boxes for them at one time. We saw them only a few times after that, when they'd come to New York to visit. After many years, they left Venezuela and eventually settled in Vienna. That's where they are buried."

"Tell me about leaving Poland."

"We took a train from Katowice to Prague, a regular passenger train, not a refugee train. The train was crowded. For all we knew, there were many other refugees like us on board, smuggling themselves across the border. The Polish and Czech police checked our papers at the border. They probably knew that these papers weren't one hundred percent legal, but they let us pass. They must have been bribed.

"As soon as we crossed the border from Poland to Czechoslovakia, we were no longer Polish citizens; we were officially displaced persons. DPs. We were put up in Prague for a few days and then were moved to Bratislava.

"All of this was arranged by the Bricha, an organization that handled the illegal immigration of Jews from Eastern Europe. They handled everything: our papers, the transports, where we stayed in Prague and in Bratislava. The idea was to get all these Jews across Europe, across all the zones of occupation, to Italy where they would board ships to Palestine. Not everyone ended up in Palestine, of course. There were many transit stops along the way, and people went all over.

"From Bratislava, we had to walk across the border. They divided us into small groups, told us to be ready to leave at five a.m., warned us not to take much, only what we could carry. I think they allowed us each two valises and a knapsack, but my mother couldn't carry two valises, and my father certainly couldn't. He had never recovered from the beating he'd gotten from the Germans at the beginning of the occupation, and now he had emphysema. And my mother had already been sick in Katowice; she had a heart condition and high blood pressure. If I remember correctly, the Bricha provided some kind of cart or wagon for the elderly, the sick, those who couldn't walk.

"Once we were across the border, they put us on an all-night train to Vienna. They gave us papers saying that we were Greeks returning home from the camps. In the middle of the night, the Russians boarded the train to inspect our papers. The Bricha had warned us not to say anything, not a word, in any language. So we shut up and didn't answer anything they asked us. I remember one Russian saying to another, 'They are so stupid; they are even worse than the Jews.'

"Austria was then Russian territory and the idea was to get out of the Eastern bloc and go to the Allied zones. Vienna, or at least the American Zone in Vienna, was a transit stop for refugees from all over—Poland, Hungary, Czechoslovakia, Romania, Yugoslavia, Austria. Everyone waited to be moved. There were so many refugees there that they couldn't move them all at one time.

"In Vienna, we stayed in the Rothschild Hospital, which had been converted for refugees. I remember big rooms, twenty to thirty people in each, sleeping on cots, on beds, on the floor. We had to stay there about three months, just killing time, supported by the JDC and UNRRA."

"What did you do there during that time?"

"I walked around the city, and my parents took me around; they had each lived there, remember? So they showed me around. It was a big city, very old, very beautiful.

"And the rest, we just waited until they were ready to move us. We were just told: 'You're taking this-and-this transport,' and we went. We didn't even know where we were going. You went wherever they sent you."

Chapter Twenty-Four

Sometimes it feels as though I am in some dark space, me and this story, the two of us frozen in another time. Sometimes I wish I could crawl into such a space, could hunker down there with my family, until life is safe and secure once again. But time is not standing still, and the world around me is very present, very turbulent, and very dangerous.

It's March 4, 1996, a Monday evening in Jerusalem. It's hard to believe that, only a few short years ago, we expected a peace agreement with the Palestinians "any day now." Now I fear we will never see one. It reminds me of my mother, her parents, and the Łozińskis waiting desperately for the end of the war. Any day now. Tomorrow. Maybe tomorrow. And each day meaning more fear, more risk, more death.

Each of our days also means more fear, more bombings, more suffering, more deaths, and less of a way out.

Over the past two weeks, Palestinian suicide bombers have set themselves off again and again in public spaces in Jerusalem and Tel Aviv. The latest attack was only hours ago, ripping apart a major shopping center in the heart of Tel Aviv that was teeming with children savoring the carnival atmosphere of the Purim holiday.

I'm trying to write but the Angel of Death is in the room, breathing foully over my shoulder, dragging down my pen. The tension is palpable. I feel drained. Exhausted. Don't know what to write. Don't want to write.

Against the backdrop of endless scenes of carnage replayed on TV, my chorus of self-doubting voices has been unusually strong: All this writing and revising and editing, what's it all for? What difference could it make? Even if you believe that you must remember the past, do you really believe that memory will serve as your bulletproof vest, or prevent you from floating, headless, into oblivion if you're in the wrong place at the wrong time? What is the point?

Still, there must be a connection between my reactions to the events of the past few weeks and my odyssey through my mother's story. I can sense it, can feel something shifting inside, like an animal beginning to stretch itself out of slumber. I just don't know what it is, yet.

Conversations with friends reveal that their lives, like mine, are just as splintered into attempts to cope with life between news bulletins. I'm not alone in frenetically cleaning my house, straightening out my desk. I'd even sorted through my computer files, trying to bring order to the raw material of this book, scattered through various files. Just in case. What if something happened to me? How would anyone find all the pieces, let alone understand what I was doing?

I ask my dear friend, Hannah Levinsky-Koevary, "If something happens to me, would you please explain this to my kids? Tell them what I was trying to do." I talk quickly, before the words are choked by the thickening in my throat.

"Of course," she responds immediately. She, too, is a child of survivors. Some things you don't need to explain.

Saturday night, March 9, 1996

The late night news comes on: "Hamas has declared an end to their cease-fire."

I hadn't actually believed their self-declared cease-fire. But how I had clung to that illusion! Now, suddenly, that illusion is ripped apart, like kriya, *the sudden violent tearing of the mourner's lapel following a death. I wonder—really wonder—whether I will survive. Whether my luck will continue to hold. Fear slams into my chest like a sledgehammer.*

I write to a good friend in America. I want to tell her honestly how I feel, coping with the threat of death. I don't want to sound melodramatic, I hate to upset her, long-distance no less. But I also don't want to cover things up with hearty assurances that all is "b'seder," A-OK. Because, if it's not, if I were killed, all she'd have left is what I write of my feelings, my thoughts. Let me be as honest as possible.

"Right now," I write, "what scares me most about dying is the thought that my kids would never grow to know me, all of me, beyond what children usually know of their parents. There's more to me than the person who alternates hugs and stories with nagging about unmade beds, neglected toothbrushes, and sock balls that missed the laundry hamper. What about the rest of me: the hopes, the fears, the ambitions, the worries, the pride, the struggles, the successes, the failures, the wants, the wishes, the everything? I'd hate to think that, if my life were ended now, all of that would die with me. They'd never know me. So, if anything did happen, please find some way to be in touch with them, to tell them about the person you knew."

I hope I'm not asking too much. I hope she's not too freaked out.

Writing this letter calms me down. As does the knowledge that at least some of this project has been completed. I'd be dead, but at least not all of me would vanish. There'd be some trace left, and someone to bear witness.

I flash on my high school yearbook, senior year. My selected quote, by William James, still speaks to me: "The greatest use of life is to spend it on something that will outlast it." Whatever grandiose fantasies I had when I chose the quote as a teenager, what I want to know, need to know, now, is that I'll outlast me.

Remember me.

Remember.

The refrain echoes inside me like a muffled cry in the fog. Where have I heard this before? The voice becomes more distinct. I know where I've heard it before. It's the refrain of the dead, repeated six million times over. It's the mantra of the survivors. Tell the world. Tell them what happened to us.

Until now, I always thought I understood all those exhortations. Santayana warning the world: "Those who do not remember the past are condemned to repeat it." Or the Baal Shem Tov: "Remembrance is the way to salvation." It seems to me now that I have never really understood these messages before. Not down in the gut. Now I hear: Remember me. Tell them what happened to me. Tell them about me. Don't let me just disappear. Without a trace. As if I never existed.

I remember my mother's voice:

". . . Being in the cellar, that was the worst time. When we were still in the ghetto, you still had hope. As tough and as hard and as dangerous as it was, you could still go out, you still existed, you were still there. Once you ran away, you were like a hunted animal, you had no place to hide, you were not supposed to hide, you were not supposed to live, you were worthless. You hit that point when you knew you didn't exist anymore."

Now I feel the plea, the desperation, in my own body, my skin crawling with tension, my breath torn into ragged scraps by dread.

Now I understand the connection.

Chapter Twenty-Five

I prepare to continue exploring with my mother her experiences after the war, and specifically, the time she and my grandparents spent in the DP camp. All I know about that, I realize, is a vague mishmash of fact and unease: that my mother and grandparents "sat there"—her words—for three-and-a-half years, waiting for permission to come to America (while Nazi scientists were being whisked straight through Immigration into the waiting arms of the U.S. Army and the space program).

I discover that my mother and grandparents had been in the dark about this new phase of their lives: no idea what to expect, no choice about where they were going.

"You went wherever they sent you," she recalls.

"Wherever they sent you" was Gabersee.

Gabersee, pronounced Gah-ber-zay, a displaced persons (DP) camp under UNRRA auspices in the Munich district of Germany, a rural area near the towns of Wasserburg and Rosenheim, in the American zone of occupation. Before the war, Gabersee had been an institution for the mentally retarded. Through his infamous euthanasia program, Hitler killed the residents; the Master Race had to be unblemished. After the war, with so many refugees flooding Europe, the Allies pressed every available space into service, and Gabersee's emptied halls were once again filled with clamor, echoing this time with the anxious, eager babble of the displaced.

As DP camps went, Gabersee was on the smaller side. The largest camps in the American Zone, Pocking and Landsberg, housed

6,300 and 5,000 Jewish residents each, respectively. By comparison, the Jewish population of Gabersee averaged 1,750 between 1946 and 1949, when my mother and grandparents were there.

The camp consisted of a long line of buildings on both sides of a narrow road, labeled simply, most uncreatively, A, B, C, and so on. These dormitories with their communal dining rooms housed a hodgepodge of humanity flung together here from all over Europe. Many of the young women were from the area known as Zakarpacka Ukraina, between Czechoslovakia and Hungary. They had survived Auschwitz and were the last remnants of their families, of their entire communities. Orphans. All alone.

At the end of the long line of dormitories were three small two-story administration buildings—X, Y, and Z—housing the few remaining intact families in small, three-room apartments, sparsely furnished and equipped. One family per room. A shared kitchen in which the families could eat if they did not want to join the others in the communal dining room.

My mother and grandparents shared one of the apartments in Building Z with two families: the Apfelbaums, about whom she remembers little, and the Guttmans, an observant family from Munkatsch, Hungary. My mother especially remembers their daughter, Leah, whom everyone called Laicia, "a cute little girl with blond curls like Shirley Temple." Some hip problem made it difficult for her to walk. She adored my mother and called her "Luluka." Smiling, my mother recalls that whenever Laicia would see her leaving the apartment, she would sing out: "*Zei matzliach begegne mashiach.*" Be successful, and meet the Messiah.

Relationships between these families were cordial, but contact with many others in the camp was strained, even hostile, despite the shared experience of loss and pain. A hierarchy of suffering existed with regard to language and expression. Hungarian, Czech, and of course, Yiddish, were acceptable. *Polish*, however, was not. Its syllables reverberated as a hated curse, a death-cry in the ears of the young women survivors of Auschwitz. When they heard my mother speaking Polish with her parents, they reacted in fury.

"How can you speak that ugly language?" they screamed at her. "Speak Yiddish, not *that*!"

"But this is *my* language!" she protested. *They* had *their* languages, didn't they? And Yiddish was foreign to her. She gradually picked up enough Yiddish to manage—"*sher'l* is a pair of scissors," she learned in the dressmaking course she later took—but those initial attacks still rankle. I can hear it still, all these years later, as she talks to me.

Gabersee was only supposed to be a temporary way-station on the road to America. The DPs registered at the consulate in Munich, were interviewed by staff, once, and then a second time, to catch any discrepancies signaling that they were "undesirable." They then waited for word that they had passed inspection and would be allowed into the United States. With *waiting* the operative word.

I ask my mother what they did there, what *she* did there, in Gabersee, for three-and-a-half years.

"Not much," she tells me.

In some spooky replay of the experience in Łoziński's cellar, it turns out that Gabersee also had not been prepared for its role in this vast human drama. Just as before, the expectation was that once the storm blew over, people would simply go back home. Except that—just as before—once the cataclysm ceased, whether that was the final *akcja* on March 25, 1943, or the final destruction of the Third Reich, there was no way back, no home to go back to. Not for Lutka and her parents. Not for the tattered remnants of Jewish Europe, uprooted and traumatized. In each case, there was no choice but to take care of them, right here and now.

And, as before, nobody ever expected it to take this long.

So besides cobbling together the basics—simple accommodations, food allowances, and cigarette rations, for example—Gabersee offered very little to relieve the endless, endless boredom. Organized activities were few: An occasional movie screening (or you could go to the movies in the nearby town of Wasserburg). A few sightseeing excursions to the highlights of Bavaria: Linderhof Palace, Walchensee, even Berchtesgaden, including the infamous Eagle's Nest. A soccer team for the men, to compete against teams from other DP camps.

"What about for the women?" I ask, remembering my mother's love for—and proficiency in—sports.

Her answer comes back, flat.

"Nothing for the women."

"What about Zionist activities in the camp?" I'm pulling questions from scenes remembered from Leon Uris's *Exodus* and various documentaries, having very little other frame of reference for this period.

There were some Zionist rallies and activities, she recalls. She remembers representatives from the Jewish leadership in Palestine coming to speak, trying to convince the DPs to immigrate there, despite the British blockade of Palestine and the risk of ending up in British detention camps on Cyprus. A sardonic note creeps into her voice as she reports that many of these great Zionists had no problem sending people to Palestine to fight for the Jewish State while they themselves ended up living in the United States.

I ask about the United Nations vote on the partition of Palestine in 1947. Her eyes sparkle. Oh yes, she remembers that. There were no radios, she tells me, so the UN vote was broadcast to the camp over loudspeakers. "Everyone was waiting, counting each vote . . . counting . . . counting . . . still short . . . still short . . . and then they announced: 'the resolution passed!' and the people went *wild*," she says, her voice rising triumphantly, her cheeks flushed with the memory.

My grandfather wanted to go to Palestine, but my grandmother preferred to be reunited with their only remaining cousins in the United States. My mother sided with her mother; she'd heard so much about America. "After all," she smiles, "you find gold in the streets!" And there was something about having been cooped up with her fellow survivors for these three-plus long years that scared her when she considered living once again in a potential pressure-cooker of a Jewish state surrounded by enemies.

"What about school?" I ask, knowing how upset she had been at having to leave Katowice just before completing high school.

"No school."

She did take some private English lessons from a German man in the .DP camp who claimed he had studied at Oxford.

"He taught me the Queen's English: 'I *cahn't*' and other expressions like that. I still '*cahn't*' speak English well with all those lessons," she tells me, laughing.

Eventually, the Organization for Rehabilitation through Training set up vocational training programs in the camp; most of the young people had never finished even elementary school and now needed to learn a trade. My mother studied sewing and pattern-making, and later, at the ORT school in Munich, pocketbook making. There was nothing else to do, and maybe it would come in handy in America. Besides, "the authorities kept reassuring us, 'Any day now, any day, you'll be out of here.' So we waited."

Again waiting.

And again, my old restless question: *What did you do there?*

My grandmother managed the home, did the laundry and the cooking, bartering with the local farmers for fresh fruits and vegetables.

My grandfather worked in the pharmacy of the camp's small infirmary.

And my mother—?

"I wasted my time," she says.

She had one chance at a real education.

In 1947, the university in Munich decided to accept qualified refugees as students. My mother had her certificate from the high school in Katowice stating that she had finished the courses there, so she could apply.

There was one catch. She had to pass the entrance exam. And it was in German, a language she had always feared. But her father insisted that she take the test anyway, so she went.

As she tells it: "On the day of the test, a big group of us came to the university. Some lived in the DP camp with me, others already lived in Munich, where they survived by dealing on the black market. I was sitting in the waiting room, waiting for my turn. Some of the students who took the test before me came out and reported that they had been asked questions in chemistry, in math, and that the exam had been quite difficult. And of course it was all in German.

"I was sitting in that waiting room, waiting and waiting for my turn, and the longer I waited the more nervous I became. Had I been one of the first, I would have gone in, and whatever happened, happened. But the longer I waited, the more scared and nervous I became. Finally I decided: no, this is not for me. I expected to leave the DP camp and Germany very soon anyway;

I didn't want to get stuck in a German university for several years. I decided to forget about the university and to concentrate instead on learning English. So I walked out of the examination hall and went back home. I didn't take the test."

"What was your father's reaction when you returned home that day?" I ask.

"He was *furious*. 'How could you do it?'"

"How did the other students do?"

"All of them passed. The examiners had been very lenient. They understood that people had lost all those years in school, and they really tried to help. I would've been accepted, I'm sure."

"Couldn't you take the test again?" I ask.

"No, it was only given that one time. I blew it."

Silence.

"I didn't expect that I would be sitting in that DP camp that long," she says, after a pause. "This was only 1947. We ended up staying there for three-and-a-half years, until the end of 1949. But all along they kept telling us, 'Oh, it'll just be a few months, maybe half a year, and then you'll be out of here.' Had I gone to the university, I'd have had to stay on even after we got permission to leave, in order to finish the degree. And I didn't want to do that. I wanted to be out.

"But later, when time was dragging and dragging and dragging and you sit there in that DP camp, wasting your time, doing the same thing over and over again, and there's no future, nothing, and you just drift, and you don't know what to do with yourself, while the others are studying in the meantime, and getting their degrees. And when they came to United States, they all had professions. *My* profession was sewing and pocketbook making."

Three-and-a-half years. Almost 1,300 days. Sitting and waiting. Sitting and waiting. That was the experience during the war, and that was the experience once again after the war, in the DP camp. Sitting and waiting. This refrain, from so much of my mother's adolescence and early adulthood, gives me the chills. I begin to understand how the darkness of war continued to cast its shadow-tentacles way beyond the actual date of liberation. How, despite the tremendous wish to shake off the war like old dust, to leave it behind, to forge ahead and build anew, the past with all its fears still wound itself silently, like

236

an invisible creeping vine, around her ankles, preventing her from dancing quite as freely as she would have liked.

Her split-second decision. That fateful choice. Was it a mistake? Who knows. Who will ever know?

Only—I wish she'd stop giving herself such a hard time about it. About all the time lost, about all the time spent, once again, sitting and waiting, sitting and waiting. . . .

"If you were only supposed to be in the DP camp a short time, why were you stuck there for three-and-a-half years?"

"Because the American officials in Munich made a mistake. They had gotten our papers mixed up with some Hungarian, also named Rosenberg, whom they were investigating. They did not want to allow him into the U.S. Once this confusion was cleared up, our process moved much faster."

"When did you finally leave Gabersee?"

"We left the camp in November 1949, and arrived in New York on December 2, 1949. UNRRA paid for the trip. They gave us tickets for the train to Hamburg, and put us up in a hotel for a few days until we boarded the ship. It was a small military transport ship, a Liberty Ship, carrying about two thousand people, and it brought us to America."

"Do you remember the name of the ship?"

"Oh yes. The *General Muir*."

Sometime later, not expecting to find anything—I am still not entirely clued in to the ubiquitous reach of the Internet—I nevertheless do a search on Google and am shocked and delighted to find an entry about the ship.

The USS GENERAL C. H. MUIR 1945:

One of a class of 30 ships designated C4-S-A. Built as a U.S. Navy transport ship by Kaiser Shipyard, Richmond, Calif. 10,654 gross tons, length 523ft x beam 71.2ft, one funnel, engines aft, single screw, speed 17 knots. Accommodation for 3,000 troops. Launched on 24th Nov. 1944.

Commissioned AP-142 on 12th April 1945.
Maiden voyage: 13th May 1945, San Francisco to Pearl Harbor.
18th June 1946: taken over by the US Army.
Used for carrying displaced persons from Europe to the USA.

I even find a photograph of the ship, as well as several first-person accounts of people crossing the ocean on the General Muir. I start reading these, but quickly realize that the only story I am interested in is my mother's.

Chapter Twenty-Six

Spring 1997. The next time I interview my mother, it's in the new home that Chaim and I have bought in the Baka neighborhood of Jerusalem, a few blocks away from the apartment we had rented until now.

Baka takes its name from the Arabic word meaning valley. For years, from the establishment of Israel in 1948 until the Six Day War in 1967, the neighborhood's status was as low as its topography: it was a dangerous border area, all too near the fighting and the enemy. Undesirable real estate. As a result, anyone who was poor, who had no choice, was dumped into the old houses on this side of town. In recent years, however, the area has been undergoing gentrification, a process received with mixed feelings by its longtime residents.

For a while, as naïve newcomers ourselves, we are blissfully unaware of the undercurrents of envy and anger that pulse beneath the surface in this part of town, with its current checkerboard of fancy housing and tenements, privilege and poverty. We still very much believe the old maxim that *kol Yisrael areivim zeh la-zeh*, all of Israel is responsible for one another. We still consider everyone we meet a potential long-lost brother or sister. It takes a few unpleasant experiences—neighborhood kids picking on our kids in the playground and their parents subsequently taunting us to go back where we came from—to teach us that our idealized Zionist family, like all families, has its strains and tensions. With all due respect to the obvious differences, the friction we experience with our grouchy, grudge-bearing neighbors nevertheless reminds me of my mother's report of life with some of her fellow Jews in the DP camp.

Our lives are also marked by another major change: since last year, our family has expanded by not one but two dogs—the fulfillment of one of my childhood dreams twice over. Both dogs were tiny, barely two fistfuls in size, when Yonatan, a dog magnet like his grandmother, found them. First came Lucky, a silky black mostly Belgian Shepherd puppy with a snowy patch on her breast and the sweetest disposition in canine-dom. Yonatan rescued her on his way home from karate class.

Simba, a fuzzy brown furball with black ears and nose, was discovered quivering under the wheels of a parked bus outside the hall in which we were celebrating Yonatan's bar mitzvah. "It's a sign!" Yonatan declared, insisting that we keep the pup until we could find him a good home. We did—ours.

And so my parents' love has expanded to include the dogs. It's uncanny to see how crazy both Lucky and Simba are about them. Recognizing my father's distinctive four-note whistle from down the street, they rush into the front hallway, prancing back and forth and pawing eagerly at the door, Lucky whimpering with excitement. My mother is just as delighted to see them. She exclaims at how big they've grown since she last saw them, when they were still wobbling around unsteadily on great, outsized paws. Now when they throw themselves at her, they practically bowl her over. Bracing herself against the onslaught—she's an old hand at this—she playfully swats their insistent noses away from her legs, bending down to kiss them, talking to them and laughing at their antics all the while. It takes several minutes before she can make her way past this panting, pawing reception committee into the rest of the house.

When my mother and I eventually sit down at the dining table to work, the dogs sniff and circle around her until they are ready to settle down. Simba curls himself into a ball under the table, leaning against her foot, and Lucky plops herself down right next to her chair.

We can begin.

"Okay, so now you're finally on your way to America. On the boat. Were you excited?"

"Very. Until we got to the boat. Because once we were on the boat, we were separated—men from women. The best quarters of the boat, the center, where it was less rocky, were given to the men. The younger men, in their twenties and thirties, were put to work cleaning the decks and the lifeboats, fixing things, painting the ship. Older men like my father did not work.

"The women and children were useless, so they put us at the very tip of the boat, where the ship was going up and down, up and down. My mother got a bottom bunk, because she was older, and I slept in the bunk above her.

"The day we started out was fine. The weather was nice. I saw Dover on the English Channel with its white cliffs. I even ate supper in the dining room that first day, and then breakfast the next morning. It was the first time in my life I ate Corn Flakes. And that was the end of my eating for the rest of the trip. I never set foot in the dining room again. Because the second day, when we crossed the Channel and were out on the Atlantic, on the open ocean, I got seasick. Almost everyone did. It was late November and the water was very choppy. We were lucky that we didn't have a major storm. The trip took ten days. Ten miserable days.

"The first night, I still slept in my bunk. The second night, my mother and I couldn't take it anymore, so I took our blankets and pillows, found some spot in some corner of the corridor where it was more stable, made some sort of bed for my mother, got myself next to her, and we stayed there for the rest of the trip. I didn't move because I was afraid that somebody else would take our places. Others did that too, or slept on deck, in the fresh air, anywhere you felt a bit better. The crew didn't like it and kept trying to chase us back to our rooms. Because if you threw up, they had to clean it up."

She shudders, remembering. "U-u-up and down," she sings, her voice following the words, sliding up, and then dropping. She shakes her head. "It was no picnic."

This is the only "wartime" story my mother ever told me, growing up. The way her voice rose and fell, mimicking the pitch of

241

the vessel—"U-up and down, u-u-up and down"—always made me laugh. I'd never taken it seriously.

But now I remember the time I went whale watching off the coast of Half Moon Bay in northern California. It was 1981, and Chaim and I were living in Palo Alto. Knowing we would be there for only two years, we were determined to experience as many California highlights as we could, and this adventure was particularly recommended. We entreated my parents, visiting us from New York, to join us, despite my mother's apprehension about being back on a boat.

"Come on, Mom," I cajoled. "This isn't like when you came to America. You're not on the ocean. You can take Dramamine." She finally agreed.

Early on the appointed morning, we ate the hearty breakfast the boat crew had recommended. Half an hour before boarding, as prescribed, my mother gulped two Dramamine tablets. She offered me the package. I laughed and said, "No, thanks." I'd been on boats before: Joszi's fishing boat along the coast of Long Island. The Staten Island Ferry. I didn't get seasick.

We boarded the small vessel with the other eager nature lovers. My mother stationed herself in the very center of the boat, its most stable point, and didn't budge. The boat churned out into the bay. It was windy and the boat began to sway and pitch in the choppy waters. Suddenly I began to feel—the only word for it is green. My stomach started lurching inside me, rolling and rising with the movement of the boat. I dashed for the side and made my contribution to the ocean.

A crew member's metallic voice blared from the loudspeakers and spouted cheery little tidbits about whales into the chill. In the meantime, the horizon tilted. Uuuup. Then dowwwwn. Everything inside me was spinning. I had already puked up most of breakfast. Whatever was left went over the side.

I kept heaving. And praying. That the ocean would stop. That the boat would stop. But we had at least two hours to go until we returned to the dock.

I tried everything I could think of. I watched the horizon. I didn't watch the horizon. I breathed deeply, trying to push down the rising tide from within by sucking in sea air. Nothing worked.

Through it all, my mother, sympathetic to my misery but unable to help, sat glued to her perch for dear life. Despite her apprehension, the Dramamine worked and she was fine throughout the voyage.

At long, long last, we disembarked, without having seen one single whale. My legs trembled. My stomach was sore. I almost kissed the dock.

The very next day, there was an article about seasickness in the local paper. "First you're afraid you're going to die," the headline ran. "And then you're afraid you won't." They got that right.

Thinking about it now, I am embarrassed at how completely I had missed the boat—pun intended—on how awful my mother's trans-Atlantic passage had been. I had certainly never empathized with the depth of her misery until I remembered my whale watching experience.

"The only thing that helped us feel a little better was fruit—oranges—which they served in the dining room. But they didn't allow those who could go to the dining room to bring food back to those who were too sick to get there on their own. I still don't understand their reasons for this.

"My father managed to get us one or two oranges, and I knew someone who worked in the kitchen who managed to sneak us a few more during those ten days. Otherwise we wouldn't have had anything but water for the entire trip."

"Did they take care of you? Was there a doctor on board?"

"There was a doctor on board, because I remember one woman was so sick that she nearly died, and the doctor came and gave her something. But otherwise you were on your own."

"Do you remember coming into New York Harbor?"

"We got pretty close to New York. We could see land, and the Statue of Liberty from far."

"What did you feel?"

"Here I am!" She sings it out. "Mostly, I remember the relief that the boat wasn't shaking anymore. And then they said, 'No, we're not docking here, we're going to Boston instead.' So they rerouted us, and a few hours later, we arrived in Boston. There was no Statue of Liberty there. It was very disappointing.

"You know, when we arrived at the port in Boston, the crew threw crates and crates of rotten food and fruit overboard. So many people had been sick on the trip over that much of the food had spoiled. They hadn't allowed anyone to take it from the dining room and bring it to those who were sick. And now they just threw it all overboard. I remember thousands of oranges floating in the water, and the seagulls diving and eating all that wasted food."

It is this memory that gets triggered, I now realize, whenever she hears on the news that American farmers were destroying surplus crops to keep market prices up.

And it reminds me of her recounting how my grandfather's precious Philips shortwave radio, confiscated by the Germans, had been thrown out the window of the municipal building, smashed with all the others, never even used.

All that waste.

"So you landed in Boston and from there you came to New York?"

"No. In Boston, the Jewish representatives who met us suddenly informed us that they were shipping us right out to Seattle, Washington. Without asking us what we wanted, where we wanted to go, without even giving us time to recover from the trip. That same day, when we had just gotten off the boat, after being sick and not able to eat for ten days, they wanted to put us right on a train and send us to Seattle!"

Her outrage is palpable, even after all these years. Her voice rises, the color is high in her cheeks.

"My mother was so sick, she could hardly walk. I was weak, too, but I was younger, so it was easier for me. It was like being hit over the head," she declares in ringing, angry tones.

"My father was upset. He told them, 'If someone wants to go to Seattle, fine. But we have nobody there; the only family we have left in the world is in New York. We want to be with them, after all these years and everything we went through.'"

"'Oh, *that's* okay,' they said." And her voice slides around like oil, placating, condescending. "'The Jewish community in Seattle is waiting for you, with apartments.' They told us that each city had a quota, that New York couldn't accept everybody, the social organizations were overwhelmed, so they had to divide us up."

"How did you feel about all this?"

"I was very, very disappointed, and scared! It seemed like these people had no compassion. None. They were rough. Here you come to a new country, and you're stuck. They're the bosses, you have nothing to say; they don't ask you, they just tell you what to do. You have no choice. That's the reception you get after waiting for three-and-a-half years. This was our introduction to Jewish America."

"How was this problem resolved?"

"First, somebody said to my father—that's how I remember that we arrived on a Friday—'Tell them you don't travel on Shabbat.' That way they'd have to let us stay in Boston over the weekend. Then my father managed to contact his cousin Jules Roth in New York. Julek—that's what we called him—had arrived years earlier, had established a clothing business, and even had some connections with a congressman. He was able to convince the Jewish representatives to release us from the shipment to Seattle and reroute us to New York.

"That first Sunday, my father gave me some money and said, 'Go buy a copy of the *New York Times*, that's the best paper.' We couldn't read much English, even with my English lessons, but my father wanted us to get that.

"So I take the money, find the newsstand, and there's the *New York Times*, and it's a pile this high." She holds her hand out in the air, several feet off the floor. The gesture recalls for me the great stacks of the Sunday *Times* lying by corner newsstands in Manhattan. "After all, it was the Sunday *Times*, with all the sections. But how did I know that the Sunday *Times* had all those sections? I tell the man at the newsstand that I only want one paper. He says, 'This is the paper.' I say, 'I only want one. *Only one!*' He looks at me and repeats, 'This *is* the paper.' Finally I only took one section and ran. I was afraid I would have to pay for each part and I didn't have the money. He probably thought I was crazy. A stupid refugee."

It's a funny story, and yet I cringe at the confusion and fear of this young woman, facing such unknowns, and at the self-deprecation. It dredges up the memory of being sent, as a young child, to buy a loaf of bread or a container of milk at the corner grocery behind our house. I remember clutching the hard-earned money, the painful, breathless shyness in the face of the huge adult towering miles over me behind the tall, slanted glass counter, and the sense of relief when I had done what I was sent to do and could beat a hasty retreat back to the safety of home.

"So after the weekend," my mother continues, "many people were sent to Seattle, and we were put on a train for New York.

"We arrived at Grand Central Station. My mother's cousins, Ludy Schenker and his wife Ethel, were waiting for us. It was a wonderful greeting. They hugged us and kissed us. Everyone was crying.

"They had a car and drove us around Manhattan, showing us the United Nations, the East River, telling us that Manhattan was an island—*that*, I knew! They took us to their apartment in the Bronx, introduced us to their three children, Dick, Fred, and Diane, and we stayed with them the first couple of days."

"What was it like, being with them?"

"We knew a little about them before we arrived. They wrote to us in the DP camp. I remember Diane wrote to me about her Sweet Sixteen party. I didn't know what that was.

"We couldn't understand each other much. They didn't speak German, and there's me, with my English! And they laughed at my accent, at my '*cahn't*'s. But they were nice. Dick, the oldest—he was also a pharmacist and worked with his father—took me downtown the next day to show me around the city. He took me to Times Square."

Her eyes widen and her tone gets so big you can practically see her capitalize the words. Her remembered excitement is palpable and my own words tumble out a bit breathlessly.

"What did you think of it?"

"It was overwhelming! Vienna was big, but this! It was so big, I felt so lost. I was wondering how I was ever going to find my way around."

I wish I could have been there to see her wonderment.

"And then?" I prompt.

"A few days later, we went to register with HIAS, the Hebrew Immigrant Aid Society, the organization that supported refugees until they were settled and self-sufficient. But when the caseworkers found out that we had stayed with our cousins for those first few days, they didn't want to support us. 'Oh, you can stay with them! You don't need us to put you up!' And of course we couldn't stay with these cousins; we had only gone to them for a short visit. We had to fight with HIAS to take us back and support us. Finally they agreed and put us up in the Hotel Marseilles. That was on Broadway and 104th Street."

"Did you have any money?"

"UNRRA had paid my father a small salary in exchange for working in the infirmary in the DP camp. German money. Before we left, we had exchanged whatever we had for American dollars. But this was not enough to live on our own. We had to depend on the organizations."

"How did that work?"

"You had to report every week to a caseworker. The caseworkers made all the decisions about your life. They gave you a weekly allowance, about six dollars a week per person, which had to cover all your expenses. They figured everything out down to the penny. You were allowed to buy a newspaper every day because you needed that to find a job. That was five cents. And you got enough money for two rides a day on the subway—I think the subway cost ten cents in 1949—so you could look for work. We ate at the Automat, across from us. You could have a roll and a juice and a tea for breakfast—that came to about thirty cents—and for lunch you could have a main dish and two vegetables. If you decided to spend two dollars on one meal, you went hungry the rest of the week. You got your money for the week and that was it.

"All our caseworkers were Jewish women, and they were all mean. Once, when I was already working, I saw a blouse I liked in a store window. It cost seventy-five cents. Today it seems like nothing, but back then it was a lot of money. I bought it. When I reported it to the caseworker, she started yelling at me, 'you had no right to buy anything on your own! You have to tell me when you want to buy something, because we have to calculate how much money you get!' I was furious. I told her, 'I need something to wear to work; I need a change of clothing!'"

"Did she allow it in the end?"

"She did. But first she gave me a hard time."

"Did your parents work?"

"The caseworker said my father had to work even though he was sick, and no youngster. In 1950, he was already fifty-six years old. He wasn't allowed to work as a pharmacist because he didn't have an American license. He would have had to go back to school to get relicensed. He would have loved to study, but his health was poor, and he figured that by the time he finished, nobody would hire him anyway because of his age. And it wasn't clear that HIAS would have paid for his education.

"My father suggested that he could work in a pharmacy, selling all those things that aren't medical: candy, film, postcards, toys. Or that he could dispense medications in a hospital pharmacy, where everything is already prepared. They said no."

"Wait a minute," I say. "Cousin Ludy was a pharmacist. He even owned his own drugstore. Couldn't he have given Grandpa a job?"

"He knew that Grandpa was having a hard time finding a job. Maybe he would have felt bad hiring my father for menial labor. Or maybe he didn't need anyone else because he already employed a few other workers. All I know is, he said he couldn't use my father."

"What happened then?"

"The caseworker got my father a job as an orderly in the Hospital for Joint Diseases on 125th Street and Madison Avenue. It was very physical, which was hard for him because he was sick and weak. He did that for a while and had to stop. So they found him a job with the Cerebral Palsy Foundation, in the mail room, sorting the mail. That was better, because it wasn't such a physical job. It was still hard for him to travel there by subway, climbing all the steps. But he held that job until he reached the age of sixty-two, when he could retire and get some sort of pension. That was in 1957. That's why you don't remember Grandpa working. You were too young."

"Was his income enough to support the three of you?"

"No."

"What about Grandma?"

"She wasn't healthy, either, with a weak heart and high blood pressure, so she didn't work. I had to support us."

"Could you have gone back to school?"

"No. When I told the caseworker that I wanted to go to school, she started screaming, 'No! No! No! You can go to school at night! You go to work! We'll find you a job!'"

"What kind of job did you get?"

"First, she sent me to some factory in the East Bronx, where they made skirts. It was a very cheap line of skirts. I think a whole skirt cost about two dollars. They paid by piecework. I had no idea what piecework was. He paid, I think, two or three cents apiece. I come into the factory, and all I hear is *brzzh, brzzh, brzzh,* you know, the machines going—"

As she talks, she lines her hands up side by side, the fingers aligned, and pushes them forward, together, mimicking the motion of guiding fabric through the sewing machine. It reminds me of her showing me how she sewed little yellow useless gas masks before the start of the war.

"—and everyone working on something else. One doing hems, someone else doing seams. He told me to sew seams, because he decided those were the simplest. They were adjusted so they'd be more or less straight, but you know me—I couldn't just do it *brzzh brzzh.* I had to make sure they were perfect. So when everyone else did twenty, I think I did five. At the end of the day, he told me I was too slow. I lost my job."

Too slow. They called me that too, back in first grade, Class 1-1 at PS 73, the public school up the hill behind my house, on Anderson Avenue. My teacher, Miss Murphy, was a tall young Irish woman whose glossy brown hair was gathered behind her head with a big oval silver clip. She handed out mimeographed sheets with circles, triangles, and squares on them and told us to color them in. Everyone else started scribbling. I shook my brand new Crayola crayons out of their box and laid them out carefully on my desk: the red one, the yellow one, the blue one, in a precise neat row, like soldiers. Then I started filling in the shapes, one at a time, working very carefully, staying within the lines, the way I'd been taught by my grandmother. By this time, everyone had already finished and was on to something else. A few more experiences like this, and Miss Murphy decided I was "slow," and transferred me to Miss Adams's "slower" 1-2 class.

"I finally got a job through someone we knew in a pocket-book factory on 125th Street and Fifth Avenue."

"Your skills from the ORT School in the DP camp came in handy!"

I'm almost giddy at the chance to jump at this bit of information and prove that she hadn't wasted her time.

She nods. "Yes. It was run by a German, of all people, not a Jew, who employed many German-speakers there, mostly Christian, some Jewish survivors. The foreman in charge of the cuttings was a very nice man, a German Jew. I was earning seventy cents an hour, forty hours a week. Twenty-eight dollars a week."

"Was that enough to live on?"

"No. We still had to report to the caseworker. She calculated how much I was earning, how much we still needed to live on, and HIAS made up the difference. That went on for about a year, until I got a raise at work of five cents an hour, so that I was earning thirty dollars a week. That's when HIAS stopped supporting us and we were on our own."

"What do you mean, on your own?"

"Since I was earning some more money, HIAS wouldn't pay for us to stay in the hotel anymore. We had to find our own place to live. We rented a series of rooms in people's houses in the Bronx. One was a rabbi who rented rooms to three or four families. That was off Fordham Road. The next was a German Jew, a Mr. Berger, who lived at 221 East 168th Street, off the Grand Concourse. He was an elderly widower, and his niece did not want him living alone. So he rented us some space in his apartment. That was a good arrangement. He had one bedroom, my parents had the other, and I slept on the couch in the living room. He was a lovely man. Before he died, he even arranged with his niece to let us continue living in the apartment as long as we needed it. My parents continued to live there even after I got married and moved into Daddy's apartment."

"Where was that?"

"On 74th Street between First and Second Avenues in Manhattan."

"Wow, the Upper East Side!" I laugh. I've always preferred the funkier Upper West Side.

"Well, in those days, it wasn't like it is today, fancy and rich. It was a small studio apartment. And don't forget, the subway still ran above the streets. The Third Avenue El."

"When did you leave Manhattan and move into our apartment in the Bronx?"

"A few months before you were born. We wanted to be closer to Grandma and Grandpa, who still lived in the Bronx, in Berger's place. In those days, it was very hard to find apartments. You had to know someone, and often had to bribe the superintendent. Some friends had a cousin—that was Dora Kettler, Roanna's grandmother—who lived at 941 Jerome Avenue. Mrs. Kettler tipped the super and he rented us an apartment. He and his wife were German, an older couple, very nice people. The Wiests. Later they rented another apartment to my parents so we could all live in the same building."

"What was your social life like when you first came to New York?"

"Mostly other people from Poland. Groups of Polish Jews would gather in Riverside Park, or Fort Tryon Park, on Sundays, so my parents would go and meet them. And here and there, someone from home: the brother of the Strichs, a family from our home town. A pharmacist, Weinfeld, whom my grandfather remembered from before the war. You remember his daughter."

I nod. I remember the names clearly, have some vague image of some of the faces. I do remember going with my parents and grandparents to Fort Tryon Park in Upper Manhattan on the occasional Sunday, and the sense that these were "formal outings" rather than chances to romp around in the park. Now it makes sense.

"What about people your age? Going out on dates?"

"I met some young people, a group that would get together. I went out with some of the young men I met through friends, or at dances. Survivors, mostly. Some had been in the DP camps."

"Any Americans?"

"No, I didn't have any American friends at the time. You stuck to your own. You felt more comfortable with them. And actually, after the DP camp, and then in New York, I wasn't too close with too many people. Years later, after you were born, Geula became my good friend and we've stayed close all these years," she says, referring to the mother of Roanna, my best friend growing up.

"Tell me about meeting Daddy," I prompt.

"Mutual friends of my parents introduced us, relatives of people we had met in the DP camp whose sons had studied at the university in Munich. I don't remember their names."

"Okay, but tell me about your first date."

I'm hoping for some juicy little tidbits—how she primped, how he looked, what he said, what she thought—but my mother's recollection, typically enough, is simple and unadorned.

He was "nice," she tells me.

"What does that mean?" I push.

"He behaved nicely." For her this is enough of an elaboration. Not for me. When I press a bit more, I hear that he was "polite" and "respectful" to her parents.

I try once again.

"What did *you* think about him?"

"I liked him." A soft pink tinge rises to her cheeks.

"You're blushing, Mom!" I tease, and she ducks her head slightly.

"*Ohhff,* stop it," she laughs, motioning slightly with her hand as if to bat me away gently.

"Okay, okay." I surrender. "Just tell me when you met."

"We met in January 1952. And we got married five months later, in June."

June 8, 1952, a date chosen to coincide with my grandmother's birthday. My mother was twenty-seven, my father, thirty-two.

"What about the wedding? Who performed the ceremony?"

"A Rabbi Philip Blackman, whom I met for the first and last time that day. A Rabbi Avraham Weiss read the *ketuba,* the marriage certificate. I also didn't know him. He came from Warsaw, but he'd been lucky: he'd been smuggled out by some prominent Jewish leaders before the war started. He'd had such a narrow escape from Warsaw—maybe he felt a little guilty—that he wanted to hear about it from someone who had been there. One of Daddy's friends, Ilya Schor, the artist, introduced him to Daddy, so Daddy could tell him what had happened in the ghetto. Somehow he ended up reading the *ketuba* at our wedding. These were the men who married us. And Ilya Schor designed our wedding rings."

"Where did you get married?"

"At the Hotel Bolivar, on Central Park West."

To this day, every time I walk past that building, recently upgraded to a New York City co-op and designated The Bolivar, I feel a frisson of surprise that it really exists. I wish I could reach back in time, I wish I could hear, floating faintly within the building's girders, some echo of the ceremony that took place that day in which the foundations of a new bayit b'Yisrael, *a new House in Israel, were laid. And not just a house, but a safe haven in which each could finally find—and give—shelter.*

In their wedding photos, my mother is radiant in a dress and veil borrowed from a friend of her cousin Diane. And although my father has never stopped complaining about how he hated being dressed "like a monkey!" in a tuxedo, you'd never know it from his proud bearing. I imagine their joy and relief at finding each other: someone who shared devotion to parents and commitment to family, who spoke a common language and understood what could not be expressed in words, who would honor the ghosts at the table but who would also lovingly set places for all the new guests, all the new members of the family in formation.

My mother smiles suddenly.

"You know," she says, "After we were married, I sort of adopted Daddy's friends, the three guys, all single, all alone. Daddy had met them when they were all living in the student dorms at the 92nd Street Y. Your father was the first of the four to marry and I got four husbands. That's what the neighbors said."

I crack up.

"It's true!" she protests, also laughing. "They would drop in every weekend, eat with us, hang around until late at night, even when I was falling asleep at the table. And later, even after they got married and had children and moved away, they stayed close with us. They were like your uncles, the ones you never had."

Uncle Larry, Uncle Joel, and Uncle Jack. They each seemed totally American to me, although, as it turned out, only Larry Samuelson was the true Yankee, born in America to American parents. Joel Julie had been born in Poland but came to the U.S. as a young man before World War II. Jack Pinsen was from Warsaw and had survived the concentration camps, including one, Budzyń, where my father had also been incarcerated. At liberation, Jack was rescued by a young American Jewish GI who sent him home to his family in Brooklyn; they even helped put him through school.

At Uncle Jack's wedding, I was nine, feeling very grown-up in a pink dress and black patent-leather shoes, tasting my first champagne (a disappointment—not at all like Ginger Ale, as I'd been promised). A young man, one of Jack's friends, asked me how we were related. I still remember the flurry of internal confusion: something I'd always taken for granted was suddenly being called into question. Because the truth was: my father had no brothers; they'd both been killed. There were no uncles. We weren't related. But— this is "my Uncle Jack"! That was another truth, and one that also needed—deserved—to be honored. How to convey all this, and not drag in the war and the deaths, and get it over with as quickly as possible? I replied that we weren't really related, but that Uncle Jack was like my father's brother. I believe he nodded and the conversation ended.

"What was your life like after you got married?"

"We worked hard. Daddy was a freelance artist, just starting out, and he worked seven days a week, and late every night. I continued to work, until a few months before you were born. But I had a new job. I had left the pocketbook factory and, since about the end of 1951, worked for a drafting company. Mrs. Kettler's son Louis, Roanna's father, was an engineer there and he hired me to do technical drawing. Drafting. I made seventy-five dollars a week. That was a good salary. And I enjoyed the work. I was good at it. It reminded me a little of what I had wanted to do when I grew up, to be an engineer and build bridges. I worked there until shortly before you were born."

She still has the letter from the personnel director, who wrote: ". . . Her work has been excellent and her personality exemplary. We regret that due to lack of work we are forced to lose her services and would rehire her at any time."

"The truth is," says my mother, "that they fired me once they knew I was pregnant. They were trying to reduce their staff anyway, so it was easy to fire me. That was in September 1954, and you were born in January."

"What about school?" I backtrack, wanting to understand what had happened to this particular dream.

"I studied English in night school, first at Roosevelt High School on Fordham Road, and then at Taft High School. Then, when we got married and I moved to Manhattan, I stopped going. And then your father started complaining that talking Polish with me was killing his English. And I also wanted to improve my English; I needed it for work. So we started speaking English to each other and then to you. I spoke Polish only with my parents, and if I didn't want you to understand something. But then you started to understand Polish anyway."

"What about your dream of going back to school, to study something besides English?"

"I wanted to go back to school, but—I don't know. Grandpa was always ailing. He had emphysema, and a heart condition, and his back had never healed properly from that beating from the Germans, back in 1941, so he was in constant pain, especially when he walked. Then Grandma had her first heart attack a few months after we were married, in 1952. That's why we all moved into the same building, to make it easier for me to take care of everybody. It was very hard for me. I always had to be ready, in case I got that call in the middle of the night: my father telling me that he wasn't feeling good. I couldn't think of going to school in the evening and concentrating on studies, because I never knew when that would happen. And that happened a lot. He was in and out of the hospital. So I said, 'Forget it. I won't have a career. I'll just work.' Then when you and Barry were born, Daddy didn't want some stranger taking care of you so I could work. So I stayed home."

"Wait a minute," I say. "I want to ask you about that. Why did you wait three years to have children?"

"Well, at first, Daddy didn't want to have children. After what he went through, after what he saw, he wasn't sure it was right to bring children into such a world."

"Did you agree with him?"

"I was also a little afraid. I also knew what it meant, not being wanted in the world, not knowing whether people would accept you or if they wanted to harm you. But I was less afraid than he was."

"But in the end, you obviously decided to have kids."

"Yes."

255

"And then Daddy didn't want to leave us with a babysitter?"

"That's right. Even just to go out in the evening. He said, 'You never know who the person is. How can you trust them?'"

"Were Grandma and Grandpa able to help?"

"Well, the fact that they lived so close was a big help. They were not healthy enough to do the more physical things, like diapering you, picking you up, but they were always happy to sit with you, read to you, tell you stories, watch TV with you. Especially the programs we didn't let you watch!"

We smile at that, and it's as if the years melt away, remembering how I used to sneak off to "see my grandparents" and watch *The Wild Wild West* and *The Man from U.N.C.L.E.* with my grandfather, thinking I was getting away with murder. How shocked I was to discover, much later, that my parents had known all along what was going on "behind their backs."

"Did Grandma and Grandpa also worry about leaving us with a babysitter so you could work?"

"They agreed with Daddy about that. Even though my father was never happy that I didn't go back to school, that I hadn't made something more out of my life. But they were also worried: 'Who would watch the children?' So I went along with them. I didn't feel I could oppose them on this issue. I couldn't fight all of them."

After a brief pause, she continues.

"When you two were a little older, I wanted to call them at my old drafting job and see if they would take me back. But your father insisted, 'No, the kids need you.' Did you? Well, yes, you did. You'd come home from school and wanted me to help you with your homework. And I had to look after my parents. I did their shopping, their washing. I was busy, full-time."

"Could you have gone back to work part-time?"

"No, because they only wanted someone full-time. Part-time, I could have probably made it."

"But eventually you did go back to school, right?"

"Yes. You two were already in college and graduate school by then. And Grandma and Grandpa were no longer alive. I first had to get my GED, the Graduate Equivalency Diploma. Remember that I never officially graduated high school, even though I had that letter from the principal in Katowice saying that I had finished all the courses. But that wasn't enough to go to college with. So

I finally enrolled in the GED program at Stuyvesant High School and received my high school diploma. That was in 1980."

She was fifty-five.

"I remember how hard you worked and how excited we all were when you finished."

"Yes. It wasn't easy for me to do it, and in English. I've always been nervous about writing and working in a foreign language, even one I have been living with for so many years. But I did it. And then I signed up to take some courses in college. Just for me."

My mother loved her courses and threw herself into them with her usual indomitable discipline. She tackled Hebrew semester after semester. She was determined to master the language "so that I can manage better in Israel." She filled notebook after notebook with her careful, precise Hebrew script.

In an Introduction to Anthropology course, she did a paper on tattoos, piercing, and scarification. She found it fascinating and said that it helped her understand and even appreciate the sometimes bizarre forms of self-expression she saw on the streets of Manhattan and Tel Aviv. Introduction to Psychology proved a double-edged sword, triggering both new insights as well as her rueful conclusion that "I did many things wrong with you and Barry."

And there was also some vindication, long overdue as far as I was concerned: In evaluating my mother's academic performance, one of her college instructors wrote: ". . . Although Helen has expressed anxiety about her skill and ability, she is, in reality, a first-rate student who can manage any program or work in which she wishes to engage," and described her as "industrious, interested, hard-working, intellectually aware, and a participating member of the seminar."

This strong endorsement of my mother's abilities means a lot to me. It's hard for me to hear my mother speak of her unrealized dreams and missed opportunities. When she muses about the mistakes she made, sighs at her frustration at not having completed her education, I wince. I feel a need to contradict her, to console her, to prove her wrong.

My mother is one of the most active, vibrant people I know. To this day she's always race-walking up and down Broadway, doing her own shopping, never having things delivered. Everyone admires her energy, her strength, her vitality. She has been a model of a devoted daughter, wife, and mother. I often wish I could live up to her standards.

She was an involved parent, reading to me and my brother when we were little, helping us with our homework, playing games, listening to us. She hated the fact that our Jewish day school dual-curriculum left very little time for physical activity, and encouraged us to be out and moving as much as possible: to play in the park across the street from our building, to climb the rocks that to us seemed like mountains, to run, to ride our bikes, to go sledding and skating.

She sews beautifully. When I played Vashti, the unfortunate queen, in my fifth-grade Purim play, she sewed my costume out of golden chiffon that still glimmers in my mind's eye. When my kids were little and Purim rolled around, she turned them into adorable clowns and monkeys and lions, preparing their costumes with her usual care and meticulous attention to detail, displaying skill and patience I will never have. I'm not surprised that she couldn't just throw skirts together any old way in some clothing factory in the Bronx. She doesn't like to settle for "good enough."

I loved finding my mother there to greet me when I got home from school. It was my safe harbor at the end of the day. I appreciated the difference: sometimes, rarely, when I'd arrive, she'd be out, shopping or running some errand for us or my grandparents. I'd let myself in, to be greeted by the cold stillness of an empty house with its undisturbed air currents. How different from when I'd come home and the atmosphere was bustling, alive, and warm, because my mother was there, busy with something, and she'd be waiting with a glass of milk, a chocolate-frosted brownie, and her attention.

Now that I know what it's like to juggle so many roles, I can appreciate just how hard it was for her to take care of all of us: sickly parents, survivor husband, and kids, each with our unique demands.

It's said that when you save someone's life, you become responsible for it. I think of her half-dragging, half-carrying her mother, almost paralyzed with fear, across the town square, under the narrowed gaze of a German soldier, when she was only sixteen, the same age as my son. What presence of mind, what courage, to keep going, not to panic, not to stop or let her mother stop. And later, dragging her mother into the central corridor of a pitching ship, plunking the two of them down in a ragtag bed of army-issue blan-

kets and pillows, and defiantly not moving from the spot despite the curses of the crew. And later still, supporting the three of them in a new country. She and her parents owed their lives to each other, which was a gift and a burden.

Then there was my father, a fellow survivor. My mother at least had survived with her nuclear family intact. He was alone. His entire family had been wiped out. All he had left was—ghosts. Memory. Void. She filled that void. She became his mother, his father, his wife, his world. She didn't want to remember, but he never wanted to forget. Sometimes she'd get angry at him for bringing it back, again and again. But in the end she always listened, always absorbed.

And then there were our demands, my brother's and mine. She was raising kids in a foreign system, and in a foreign language, no less. A sacrifice for someone who had never felt comfortable speaking any language but her own.

She also ran afoul of another set of limits: 1950s America, the land of Father Knows Best and Mother Stays Home. Full-time work, requiring full-time babysitting for us, was out: neither parent trusted the world enough for that. Part-time, flextime, these were not options back then.

Was it any wonder that she didn't have much energy or time left for herself? This same little girl who stood up to a nun, took up running in the face of maternal opposition, hid her beloved dog from the Germans—that spark still flickered, but life had dulled it, muted it.

I can barely imagine the effect of sitting and waiting and sitting and waiting—

> *for enemies to decide: how you live. Where you live.*
> *If you live.*
> *for parents to decide: Do you stay or flee?*
> *Finish an education or not?*
> *for bureaucrats to decide: Are you a desirable alien*
> *or not?*

Being cast adrift over and over.
Thrown again and again into the unknown:
> *the vast stormy oceans, the enormous—*
> *and no less stormy—unfamiliarity of America.*
Dependent, again and again,
> *on the mercy and magnanimity of others.*

She eventually did go back to school to get her Graduate Equivalency Diploma, achieving, at long last, that milestone that the war had denied her. And she has continued to study, taking continuing education courses at Hunter College and at New York University.

My mother was caught between her own fears and ambivalence, the zeitgeist of the times, and her enormous responsibilities. Did she take the easy way out? Or the hard way? Was the shorter road the longer one in the end? And if she sometimes wonders if she "wasted her life," as she puts it, what does that say about me? After all, I'm the product into which all that energy, love, frustration, and devotion were poured.

As a child, my mother knew what she wanted to do when she grew up: she wanted to build bridges. She was thinking only in terms of concrete and steel. Those she did not build. But she built different things: a family, a solid harbor for her aging parents and war-scarred husband, a haven for two growing children. And in the end, she did build bridges: between an old world and a new one, between cultures and languages. She is the bridge—arching from darkness to light, from anguish to hope, from the past to the future.

Chapter Twenty-Seven

It's now 1998. Various drafts of this manuscript crowd my file cabinet and fill my computer. I work on it sporadically. Every so often, something inside me catches fire; I'm on to something. I write like mad. At other times, I feel resigned, even defeated. What's the point if I can never truly know how my mother and grandparents felt, crouching helplessly, endlessly, in that cellar, or what motivated Łoziński to hide them?

Where do I go from here?

Flipping through my files, I come across notes I made following my visit, in 1995, to the United States Holocaust Museum in Washington, DC. The designers of the museum wanted to make the enormity of the tragedy a little easier for visitors to grasp by having them identify with at least one person, one name, out of the millions. So, entering the exhibit, you are given a computer-generated identity card bearing the name and brief biography of someone who went through the Holocaust. At various stations, as you proceed chronologically through the war, you can insert "your passport" into a special scanner to find out what had happened to "your person" by that point in the war.

I remembering receiving my passport, opening it, reading the name—

> Helena

—and freezing.

Time passed. Seconds probably, though it felt a lot longer. When my vision cleared, I looked at the passport again.

It was a different Helena. Not my mother. I don't remember anything about this unknown woman except perhaps the most important thing: she survived. She now lives somewhere in the United States.

I felt stunned and shaky. It took some time before I felt ready to enter the exhibit. Eventually I went in and walked through each floor, for four hours.

Nearing the end, I came to the exhibit honoring Righteous Gentiles, those Christians who had risked their lives to save Jews during the war. I couldn't see the exhibit; I was blinded by tears. I touched the wall, saying thank you over and over in my heart. It's so hard to accept that my parents, my grandparents, and so many millions of others, were so hated and shunned. That so few gave a damn about their suffering and dying. These names were a deafening rebuttal to that aloneness, to that desertion by humanity.

Scanning the list, I looked for Łoziński, Emil and Maria. There were several Łozińskis, but not "mine." And they deserved to be there. They saved my grandparents. They saved my mother. They saved me.

After that visit, I asked my mother why she and her parents had never thought of having the Łozińskis officially recognized as Righteous Gentiles. There were several reasons. They had gotten into the habit of continuing to keep his secret, as he had requested. And this was their way to put the whole experience behind them and get on with their lives without looking back.

Now, three years later, sifting through the transcripts of my mother's oral history, I am seized by the idea of having the Łozińskis recognized as Righteous Gentiles. I want their names to be inscribed in the Garden of the Righteous among the Nations at Yad Vashem, the Holocaust Martyrs' and Heroes' Remembrance Authority, Israel's official Holocaust Museum, located in Jerusalem. But it isn't my decision. I approach my mother with the idea. What does she think? Is she willing to go through the procedure?

Yes. Absolutely.

She contacts the Division of the Righteous among the Nations at Yad Vashem to ascertain what documentation is required. I cull the relevant information from the transcripts, organize and edit it.

Preparing the testimony takes several months, what with double-checking details via phone and fax back and forth between me in Jerusalem and her in New York.

Finally the testimony is ready.

August 1998

My parents are visiting us yet again. During some casual conversation, my mother offhandedly mentions that she has scheduled her appointment at Yad Vashem for the upcoming Monday.

I can't believe she went ahead and made it without coordinating with me. After all these hours we spent working together preparing the testimony, it's baffling that she still doesn't realize that I'm a "partner to the business," as she puts it. Is she still trying to shield me from the topic, from "wasting my time?" Doesn't she understand how important this is to me?

I'm angry and frustrated, and start to explain how I feel, and why. She apologizes for not having checked the schedule with me. I'm talking process, she's talking logistics. I catch myself and rein in the irritation before it picks up steam. It's just not her style to delve into these things as I do, I realize. Yes, this is important to her, but it's probably not "Rife with Significance" for her the way it is for me. I tell her to forget it, give her a quick hug, and rearrange my schedule.

We drive to Yad Vashem. My mother sits in the passenger seat to my right, my father sits in the backseat. On her lap, she's holding a bag containing all the documents to be submitted, with extra copies, just in case. Bureaucracy is bureaucracy and we don't want anything to go wrong because of some misplaced (I almost wrote *displaced*!) document.

It's a beautiful summer day. Hot, but that's to be expected. The sky is a blinding bright blue, with not a wisp of cloud. Driving toward Yad Vashem, we pass the entrance to the National Cemetery on Mount Herzl.

I haven't been to the cemetery in many years. I stay away from it, superstitiously, nervously, even as I watch—and cry through—the national commemorations broadcast each year on TV from this spot on Yom Hazikaron, Israel's Memorial Day. Despite the years since my last visit here, I well remember the quiet grandeur, the stillness, the grief and sadness that permeate this place, that permeated me. Under the tall trees, the graves look like beds, each headstone shaped like a small pillow. The names on those stones go back to even before the War of Independence, and up to the present. The very present.

To me, this hallowed ground represents a very chilling, very profound answer to the questions posed by the very place to which we are heading.

Yad Vashem embodies the anguished scream: Can we survive? Will anyone help us?

Mount Herzl is the resounding, unequivocal response: Yes. At all costs, yes.

Both are bathed in blood and drenched in tears.

Yad Vashem is Israel's national Holocaust memorial museum and shrine. It contains a Tent of Remembrance with an eternal flame, an impressive museum depicting everything related to World War II, and particularly the destruction of six million Jews, and a pavilion dedicated to the one-and-a-half million Jewish children who were murdered. Yad Vashem functions as a resource and pedagogical center, providing educational material and conducting seminars, teacher training, and artistic programs related to the Shoah. It is engaged in a massive documentation project to record the names and as much personal data as possible of the victims of the Holocaust. It has a special division devoted to honoring "Righteous Gentiles," those who saved Jews during the war.

Dr. Mordechai Paldiel, head of the Righteous among the Nations Department at Yad Vashem, greets us at the door of his second-floor office and ushers us inside. The thoughtful quiet of the room is bruised by shoes scuffling against the stone tiles, arms and shoulders and bodies bumping softly, self-consciously against one other as we nudge several plastic chairs into position. My father thrusts himself forward and introduces us to Paldiel, although he knows him no better than we do, which is to say, not at all. Maybe he feels more at home here than we do, has more of a sense of ownership as a result of his professional relationship with Yad Vashem; as a graphic artist, he's worked on several of their publicity campaigns in the past and, in fact, is in the midst of preparing one now. Maybe he's just being protective of the women in his life. Maybe this is just him taking over, as he often does in social situations. He has a terrific way with people, and I usually admire him for it. But today I bristle. This is my mother's day, not his, and I don't want him muscling in.

Paldiel takes his seat behind his desk. We sit in front of the desk, my mother on the right, my father on the left, me in the middle, my right leg draped over my left, right big toe beating a fidgety rhythm inside my sandal. I feel like a gawky kid, wedged between my two parents, being introduced by them. (If you ever want to feel young again, go somewhere with your parents.) I wonder what impression we make: another family of refugee-nudniks, with some sort of agenda, some claim to press? *Hey,* I protest silently, *I'm an adult. And don't lump me together with all those summer Zionists parading on and off those buses in front of the Tent of Remembrance in their Crayola-bright baseball caps. I live here, too, same as you.* Do I want him to see me as something special, or as nothing special at all?

Paldiel glances through the folder of neatly typed pages of testimony my mother has handed him.

"The name Łoziński sounds familiar," he says, and types quickly into a nearby computer. Some other Łozińskis appear on the screen, but none of them are "ours."

Paldiel starts asking questions. How did you know this Łoziński? What was his relationship to you? Did he ask for payment in exchange for hiding you? Is there anyone who can corroborate your story? My mother answers his questions quietly, succinctly. Occasionally, however, as she gets more involved in the story, as she gets more excited, she starts to slide into more detail than is necessary and he steers her back on track.

I tense up during her slight digressions, thinking that at any second my father is likely to burst out with something. It's hard for him to stay silent and out of the limelight when it comes to this topic. Everything Holocaust belongs to him. Several times, I hear his sharp intake of breath as he prepares to say something, but each time I give him a tiny nudge with my right toe, dangling close to his leg. The movement is unobtrusive, I hope, hidden by the desk and masked by the slight, nervous noddings of my foot throughout the interview. I hiss, "Not now!" willing him to be quiet, to let my mother speak, to understand that this is *her* time. Each time, he bobs his head, acknowledging what I'm saying, but not accepting it; I can feel him poised, hawklike, waiting for the next suitable blood-bit to be dropped, for him to swoop down and sweep it off, screaming, into the wind. I'm uncomfortable in my self-appointed role as keeper of the gate, censor, guardian, aware of being rude and discourteous, of breaking the commandment to honor my father. But I'm being protective of my mother, of her chance to speak and to set something right in the world. I won't let him interfere.

At one point, Paldiel asks my mother: "Why do you think they saved you?"

She and I have been over this many times before. Now she's giving the same answers/nonanswers she gave me. Who really knows why they did it? Who'll ever know? They were decent people. They didn't know what they were getting into; neither did we. Then they were stuck with us.

My father disengages himself from the snare of my vigilance.

"They were hoping they would convert," he pipes up.

I remember my mother saying that, remember transcribing the words.

"Yes," my mother acknowledges, "and my father even went to the priest."

What? I stare at her, my eyes yanked open like window shades snapped upward, my mouth hanging slack. And the words keep coming, quietly, riding a slight, embarrassed smile:

"Yes, he went to the priest and the priest said, 'You survived as a Jew, thank God for that, and stay what you are—'"

And then my father tosses out: "They even gave her a holy medallion to wear."

My mother, a little abashed, is still smiling, my father is leaning forward, somehow triumphant, and I'm gaping from one to the other, flabbergasted, irritated: I missed the scoop. There is revelation without me.

I ask my mother, "Do you still have it?"

She says, "I don't know where it is."

My father chimes in: "I have it."

She and I swivel at him. "*You* have it?"

"Oh, yes. In my things. At home."

I look at Paldiel. I want to make sure he realizes that a tiny drama is taking place here. Or maybe I just want a sympathetic witness, someone on my side, because I've just found out that I've been shut out. Again. I tell him, "D'you know, I've been working on this story for four years and this is the first time that I've ever heard this?" He smiles—sympathetically? Maybe it's not the first time he's been through this.

The meeting draws to a close with no additional revelations. Paldiel thanks us for coming and outlines the next steps. He'll contact some of the other survivors of Żółkiew for corroboration of my mother's testimony. Then the material will be submitted to a review committee, and in about five or six months the names of Emil and Maria Łoziński should be approved for addition to the list of Righteous Gentiles on the grounds of Yad Vashem.

We thank him and leave his office. I drive down the hillside to the grove set aside as the Garden of the Righteous Gentiles. The names are engraved in Helvetica type onto great stone slabs set under towering pine trees that shade us from the white-hot midday light. Each country has its own stones. Poland has more than any other country

There is room for Emil and Maria Łoziński on the stone marked Poland.

Chapter Twenty-Eight

Back home, I open the computer file containing my mother's transcript. How had I missed this information about the conversion? I activate the "Search" function with the key word: *convert*. The program flips through the transcript and stops at:

"With all this anger about God and your situation, and the books you were reading about saints, did you ever think of converting?"

"Good question. You know, Łoziński wanted us to convert."

"You mean, to save you?"

"No, he wanted us to convert after the war. He said that if we survived, it was only because the Holy Mary was protecting us. They were praying every night to Mary."

"What did your father say? What did you think?"

"I just thought about getting out of there. To be free, to be able to move, to survive."

So that's what happened. Bad interviewing technique. I asked her two questions, she answered the second one, going off in a different direction, and I lost the thread of that story. Maybe I hadn't taken it seriously. Her answer and her offhand tone suggested that she hadn't taken it that seriously either; she had had more important things on her mind.

Now it's time to fill in the blanks. We sit down again.

"While we were still sitting in the cellar," my mother explains, "Łoziński told my father that if we survived, it was only because the Holy Mary was protecting the house, so maybe we should consider converting. He mentioned this a few times, when we'd be sitting upstairs with them in the evenings. My father said he'd think about it. After we came out of the cellar, Łoziński mentioned it again. So my father said to him, 'Okay, I'll go talk to the priest.'"

"Were you thinking of converting?"

"None of us was ready to convert, but we did this because my father promised Łoziński that if we survived, he would talk to the priest."

"Did you know this priest?"

"Yes. This was the Roman Catholic priest that my father knew from before the war. He used to teach religion to the Polish girls in my elementary school, the nuns' school. After the war, he lived in a small house on the street parallel to Lwowska, near the Dominican Church."

"What was his name?"

"I don't remember."

"Did he wear a collar?"

"I don't remember what he wore. He might have worn priest's clothes, or maybe not, because the Russians were back in control and they didn't like priests and nuns much. I think my father made an appointment, and we all went to see him. . . ."

Our footsteps sound so loud, tapping the cobblestones, churning up tiny puffs of dust. We walk down Lwowska Street, pass the Dominican Church, on our way to see the priest.

What would people say if they knew? Agatha and Lutka have come, too. I wonder what they are thinking. Agatha is always with me, my partner in whatever happens. She didn't say anything when I told her what I had decided, just lowered her head for a moment, looked away, then nodded. Lutka is a good daughter, always obedient. She gave a little shrug when I told her that I had made the appointment, but that's all. She didn't seem surprised, nor did she get excited. But then, she's been like that—quiet, contained—for a long time now. She doesn't say much, just presses her lips together. It's as though she's taken the silence of the cellar inside her. She understands that I gave my word to Łoziński to go talk with the priest and I'm going to keep it. What will happen after that, well, we'll see.

How can I even think about converting? Imprisoned all those months in the cellar—just for being a Jew. I was even fasting one day a week and praying—as a Jew. And now, there are so few of us left. The last of the last. When we came out, I was so sure, so afraid, that we'd be the last Jews left alive on the face of the earth. They could put us in an exhibit in the Natural History Museum, like the dinosaurs. All the extinct species. Or maybe in the zoo. The last living remnants. If we convert, there'll be even fewer of us. Even thinking of it, isn't that betrayal? Am I continuing Hitler's work for him? How can I be going to talk to a priest about forsaking my religion and taking on theirs, after everything they did to us in the name of that religion?

On the other hand, look where my religion got me. Months in the dark, being persecuted for no other reason. Maybe I don't need it anymore. Maybe it doesn't really matter what you are, as long as you are a decent person. Maybe it would be better if there were no religion at all. Maybe people would still find reasons to kill each other. But at least they wouldn't be such hypocrites, killing because of some stupid notion that God loves some of his creations better than others, or the even more idiotic conviction that someone actually knows what God thinks and wants.

Still, I gave my word. My poor old friend Łoziński. How he suffered with us. What punishment he endured for doing a good deed. For his sake, I hope there is a heaven; when the time comes, he deserves to go there, to a better place than this. And his wife, too.

I wish I had his faith. He really believes that Mary watched over us, saved us. With them praying to her every morning and every night, who knows? Maybe. (She was a Jewish mother, after all. Maybe she took pity on a few Jews.) I have such doubts. Maybe it's easier for them to believe; they weren't persecuted for their beliefs. Their beliefs were on the winning side.

How strange. The Poles and the Germans were enemies, but they believe in the same God, say the same prayers. This they had in common. And because of this, they hated us. Except that Łoziński and his wife didn't. How did that happen? Why weren't they poisoned, as so many others were? How did they escape that curse, how did they stay true to the spirit of their religion, to its beautiful elements? Which

270

every religion teaches: being good, caring for others, for the weak and miserable. That is a true miracle. I am not much of a believer, but I know for sure that I witnessed a miracle here.

I wonder what the Father will say to us. I remember him well from years ago. He taught religion in Lutka's school. He'd come to the pharmacy; we'd chat. Nothing very personal, but pleasant. A decent man. Very respectful.

I wonder what he'll think of this conversation.

I'm not even sure what to tell him. I have to give him some kind of explanation, some kind of reason, for what we are considering. What can I say? I feel strange telling him the truth, that Łoziński saved us. Even though Łoziński said we should, we must, even. He trusts him completely.

"Tell the Father everything," he said. "He is a man of God. He will understand. He will know what to do."

I don't feel comfortable; there were so many times when Łoziński asked us, begged us not to tell anyone what he did for us that to say anything to anyone now, even a man sworn to secrecy like the priest, feels dangerous, as though I am betraying him. On the other hand, I must admit that there are times when carrying around this secret feels like I have swallowed a pile of stones. A deed such as theirs deserves to be shouted from the rooftops. They should be hoisted onto shoulders and paraded through the town as heroes. They shouldn't have to tiptoe around, to live in fear of their incredible goodness being discovered. At least the priest should know what true Christians they are. If only there had been more like them. . . .

Ah, here we are. I see him peering through the window at us, watching us approach. I feel so strange. . . .

My mother continues her narrative. ". . . So all three of us went to the priest's apartment to meet with him. My father mentioned to him that Łoziński saved us, and that he thinks we should convert. The priest asked, 'Are you converting because you're grateful to Łoziński for saving your life, or because of your convictions?'

"'Well,' my father said, 'I don't feel that strongly, but I am thinking about it because of Łoziński.'

"The priest said, 'If that's the only reason, that's not good enough. Thank God you survived, you survived as a Jew, you are Jewish, stay what you are.'

271

"We went back and told Łoziński what the priest said. He said, 'Well, it's the priest's decision and you have to abide by what he said.'"

"Did you see the priest after that?" I ask.

"I don't think so."

"What about the medallion?" I press, bent on tying up all the loose ends and reclaiming my position as chief chronicler.

"At one point Łozińska gave me a medallion, a Holy Mary, and told me to wear it for protection. So I wore it. I didn't want to hurt her feelings. And I figured it couldn't hurt. You never know. . . ."

I think of all the contradictory messages I absorbed in my life. Be nice to people. Care for them. Take care of them. Do good in the world. Some people are trustworthy. Never trust people. They'll stab you in the back, hurt you, even kill you. The world is a beautiful place, full of culture. The world is a horrible place. The most cultured among us can be killers. Your word is your bond. When you promise something, you must keep it. Nothing is more important than trust. Don't trust. Never trust. The attacks can come at any time. Side by side with trust betrayed is trust fulfilled.

How do I integrate all these contradictory, intertwined threads?

I think of my mother's best friend, Janka, the Christian girl who was "like a sister," who pretended not to know her once the Germans came. I think of Kasia, the Ukrainian maid, who offered to hide my mother in her own home. I think of the Ukrainian pharmacist who didn't denounce my mother and grandparents to the Gestapo. I think of Łoziński and his wife, who risked their lives to save my mother and her parents. And I think of the priest, who gently turned them back to their bruised faith.

What a strange, awful, awesome piece of work is man.

Chapter Twenty-Nine

September 1998

My parents have exciting news. There is interest in publishing my father's memoirs of his survival during the Holocaust.

"I want you to edit it," he says to me, confidently expecting me to tame a raw document consisting of transcriptions based on well over one hundred hours of interviews.

Editing his book means devoting my life to this, essentially full-time (with time off for family and patients and good behavior), for the next half year at least. It means immersing myself in *his* wartime experience, something I always wanted to avoid. And it means stopping work on what I call "my mother's book." Of course, my parents know nothing about any such "book"; to them this is just my project to record and preserve her experiences.

How can I say no?

I put "my mother's book" aside and go to work on my father's.

I take a fine-line red Pilot pen and start marking up his passages. Efficiently, even merrily; I love editing. Soon, the pages begin to look as though they'd been sliced up. There are thin lines of blood all over, like paper cuts slowly opening to the air. Blood begins to seep into my consciousness. I start to *notice*, to *absorb*, what I have been glibly slashing at. The picture shifts back and forth like a mad figure-ground Gestalt exercise: Cut-and-paste to blood-and-guts. I realize: this is not some academic exercise. This is my father's *life*, his pain, his tragedy.

This is just what I had been desperate to avoid. Just as, growing up, I'd never wanted to listen to his stories. I'd always felt overwhelmed by them. Bludgeoned by them.

"You want to hear something?" he'd ask.

"No," I'd say. He'd get offended.

"Okay, so I won't tell you."

A few minutes later, he'd tell me anyway.

He remembers so much: Dates. Streets. Numbers of buildings. Names of the murdered. Names of the murderers. And their faces. An artist, he can still draw them—and does. He's been rehearsing this for over fifty years. The Eleventh Commandment, handed down at Majdanek and Budzyń and Treblinka: "*Gedenk*—Remember."

For years, in self-defense—an angry, helpless, guilty self-defense—I let a lot of it slide past my ears and keep going. I couldn't—or wouldn't—remember the details.

Now, my days, my nights, my life—are Holocaust. *His* Holocaust. Everything I had protected myself from all those years is coming back at me with a vengeance. Reading every word, assimilating every detail, comparing versions, checking facts, watching for inconsistencies—I have never paid attention like this before.

Sometimes, I feel as though I am drowning in blood. I want to flee. But I know I won't. This is my obligation. And a rare opportunity: to give something back. I know you can never repay your parents. You just pass on their love and their legacy to the next generation, and so on. Just as I know I can never make right the wrongs that were done to my father. Or my mother. But I at least can help each of them record those wrongs for posterity, to set their seal on history. For revenge. For solace. For healing. The chance to fulfill that eleventh commandment.

While I edit my father's material, my mother's book waits. Sometimes it's like a racehorse, straining at the bit, just waiting for the chance to be set free. Sometimes it just perches on my shoulder, waiting silently, or whispering, just beyond my ear.

Once in a while, I step back, out of the whirlwind of events, and observe this parallel process of almost-simultaneously writing and editing two books which are related, literally and figuratively. I compare what it's like to write about *him* versus writing about *her*, although even the thought of that is shameful: God help me, now *I'm* being sucked into that game of invidious comparisons played so often by survivors: "You were in a work camp? *I* was in a *death* camp."

The differences in my parents' styles of memory and transmission are sharp.

He is a huge canvas of red and black slashes of paint, all jagged and fierce.

She is a delicate line drawing, brushstrokes, defined but feather-light.

He is the blaze of memory, a pillar of fire and details.

She is dark recesses, stillness, and memory subdued.

He always pursued me with stories, barraged me with information. I'd retreat, turn and flee.

With my mother, *I'm* on the offensive: pulling, pushing, prying, and prodding: "Tell me more. Tell me why." And she protests: "I don't remember, I don't remember. Maybe I didn't pay attention, maybe I forgot, maybe I didn't want to remember."

With both of them, I have to probe, deeper and deeper, though differently, seeking access to the heart of their experience.

"How did it feel?"

"How could you stand it?"

(And could I, if I had to?)

But this digging makes me uneasy. I often have heard my father declare:

"My memory is frightening!"

I'd always experienced this statement as an attack, a challenge thrust outward, sharp as a sword: "My memory is frightening (read: to *you*)! Beware my memory!" Now I realize that the daggers of memory pierce inward as well, that his memory must be at least as terrifying for him. Do I have the right to push him—or my mother—closer to the abyss, just to suit my needs, to try to understand something that will ultimately defy understanding? Am I like those reporters shoving their microphones at a bereaved parent: "Tell us, how *did* you feel when your child was mashed under the truck? Give us a sound bite for the evening news."

On the other hand, what of the commandment: *Remember! Remind!*—bequeathed in fire and pain by those who died? Survivors often declare that one overriding motivation drove them to stay alive in that Hell: the all-consuming drive to tell the world what had happened, so that they and their loved ones would not vanish without a trace, so that their agony would not be in vain. Interesting word: *vain*. It appears in Ecclesiastes where King Solomon writes that all is vanity, *hevel* in Hebrew. *Hevel* also means mist. People need to know that their lives are more than mist floating away, vanishing into nothingness.

It's that urgency, that relentless, restless desperation that propels me forward.

Chapter Thirty

In April 1999, my mother gets the official notification from Yad Vashem:

> We are pleased to announce that Łoziński Emil and Maria [were] awarded the title of "Righteous Among the Nations" for help rendered to Jewish persons during the period of the Holocaust.
>
> Mr. and Mrs. Łoziński are entitled to a medal and a certificate of honor (which will be done as soon as we receive an address), as well as having [their] name added on the Righteous Honor Wall at Yad Vashem.
>
> Signed, Dr. Mordechai Paldiel

My parents are in America at the time, so I drive alone to Yad Vashem, steering the car down the long curving road, between the towering trees. The hum of the motor is the only sound in all that regal silence, and when I park the car near the marker indicating the Garden of the Righteous, the stillness is complete, and deep. Just my footsteps crunching over the fallen pine needles as I make my way to the stone marked Poland. There, under the year 1999, halfway down the column, I find them: Łoziński Emil & Maria.

I take pictures from every angle: close-ups of the names. Wide-angle shots of the entire area.

I put the developed photographs in a small album and send it to my mother in New York. A few days later, after the little package arrives in New York, we speak by phone.

"So—?" I ask.

"I am very satisfied," she says.

Chapter Thirty-One

The work on my father's book is complete. "A Brush with Death: An Artist in the Death Camps" by Morris Wyszogrod is published in 1999. My father came up with the title and also, fittingly, designed the book jacket: a red slash on a black background. The book gets many favorable reviews and my father is invited to speak to religious and civic groups and to audiences of high school and college students. He talks emotionally of the people he meets at these events, describing how they come up to him afterward, telling him how moved they are by what he's just shared with them. He has a growing collection of letters from people who have heard his talks or read his book; he keeps each note, just as he keeps each memory.

Speaking on this subject is difficult, he tells me, each time is like ripping a wound open again, but he must do it.

My mother accompanies him to almost every one of these speaking engagements; my parents are rarely apart, and her support and company are as essential to him as oxygen. She wryly admits that she could do without hearing the stories all over again—we both roll our eyes at that, knowing the territory inside out—but of course she goes with him, a quiet, steadfast presence in the background.

In the background.

And what of this book, which would propel her story—and her—into the foreground?

Given everything I know of my mother's shyness, her reticence, her preference to keep to the shadows, do I have the right to write this, and worse, to even think of having it published? Of course I understand her; like her, I, too, tend to keep my issues private, deep inside the dark recesses of myself. But I'm stubborn, too. I won't give up. Not on something this important.

Despite my qualms, I plow ahead, recording more of her experiences, writing and editing, reviewing and revising. Sometimes I feel a sense of accomplishment at having preserved at least some of her struggle, her spunk, of having kept her voice and spirit alive. At other times, however, I despair: Is this the best I can do? Is this enough?

Did I succeed in transmitting my mother's essence, her vitality? What of her shy smile, the bump on her nose, the hair that once held a curl just by being twirled around a finger and now wafts like soft-spun silver silk? What of the soft veins sculpting her skin in a highway of blue-and-red tracery along her arms, the hands that once stitched clowns and lions and queens into being? Did I capture the spirit of adventure that propelled her across the ice and down snowy slopes, which could not be totally squelched even when squashed into that cellar, that little black hole in the earth? Did I convey her unquenchable zest for life as, laughing with delight, she celebrated her eightieth birthday by burrowing and wriggling through the subterranean caves at Beit Guvrin, the archeological site south of Jerusalem, sifting the dirt for ancient artifacts and fulfilling, at least in part, her long-standing dream of experiencing a dig?

Reading these pages, can anyone besides me hear the lift of laughter when she catches sight of her grandchildren, the soft exhalation of glee as she scoops up a wriggling puppy and gets her face washed by its raspy tongue? Skimming these words, would anyone catch the curl of scorn in her voice or sense the wry incredulity as she shakes her head at her own naïveté, or, as she calls it, her stupidity, looking back from the vantage point of 20/20 hindsight? Or her frustration as she tries to beat back the shadows of forgetfulness and coax something forth from the dark recesses of memory, something that can never be recovered. And the tiny sag in her tone as she realizes that she is the only bearer of these memories still alive, that "there is no one to ask."

And could anyone sense the sag in my soul as I realize that my desperate attempts to get inside that cellar, inside her skin, inside her head are like extending a tentative, tremulous finger toward a glossy iridescent soap bubble, only to have it shatter at the touch, leaving the finger suspended, bereft, in the empty air, foam dripping like spit.

I have to come to terms with this: that all those hours together—talking, listening, taping, transcribing—have moved me a little closer to her experience, but only a little. It's like that math function I dimly remember, the asymptote, where the lines may get close, but will never touch.

Two beings, of the same blood and bone, always linked, as close as could be, and yet always separate.

And yet: all those hours together—talking, listening, taping, transcribing. Laughter and tears and time. Together.

Two beings, of the same blood and bone, always separate, and yet, always linked, as close as could be.

Love.

But—

Will she see it that way?

Will she understand? Will she approve?

I ride a roller coaster of ambivalence and accomplishment, achievement and anxiety. What are my mother's rights? After all, it's her story. What are *my* rights: the daughter, the writer, the *meshuganeh* chronicler?

What's fair—to the dead? To the living?

How do I weigh delicacy and discretion with honesty?

How do I balance tact and treason?

What am I doing?

Hannah, my good friend and fellow child of survivors, urges me to push ahead. Not to be afraid.

"Your mother is going to be so proud," she insists.

I'm not so sure.

281

Chapter Thirty-Two

It's early summer in Jerusalem. The warm air carries the heavy perfumed breath of jasmine through my windows. The pink blossoms on the little tree in the backyard have somehow transformed into small, hard, fuzzy buttons on their way to becoming sweet yellow peaches. Am I ripening, too? Becoming braver? More conscious of time passing? Whatever it is, I have decided: This is done.

I hold the stack of sheets in my palms, the crisp white pages thickly embroidered with black characters, black lines and spaces.

I tap the pile against the tabletop, line it up properly.

The metal rings of the binder slide through the holes like bracelets being slipped onto arms.

I click the binder shut. Its teeth snap into place.

Everything is secure.

"Showtime."

The doorbell rings.

As usual, my mother is carrying—but not wearing—the soft white baseball cap that's supposed to protect her head from the heat and her eyes from the glare the sunglasses can't screen out. (My father is always yelling at her to wear a hat, but she rarely listens. Her head, like mine, is small, and she hates the way hats plaster the fine threads of her hair down against her scalp.)

She pauses in the front hallway to greet the dogs. Lucky, whimpering frantically, is wagging her rear end so hard she looks like a Slinky gone wild. Simba is normally reserved, even aloof, but for my mother he, too, presses close for a cuddle. My mother leans over them, laughing.

"What is it, Lucky? Why are you crying? Simba, stop pushing me! You silly dog, you. Yes. Yes." Each "yes" is punctuated by a stroke, a caress. "Yes, I love you, too. Good doggies. Yes. I am happy to see you, too."

They can't get enough.

When we can separate ourselves from the dogs, I usher her down into my office on the lower level of the house. This is my private domain, where I see my patients, where I hole up when I'm in the thick of writing. I have turned on both the overhead light and the tall black halogen standing lamp in the corner; my mother doesn't like the darkish feel of rooms that perch partially above, partially below ground level.

She sits down on the black couch where my clients sit, switching her sunglasses for her indoor pair, settling herself against the stout, rounded bellies of the three black-and-white back cushions. I jitter around the room, moving a pen from here to there, twiddling the settings on the little brass date-keeper from Niagara Falls, a souvenir my grandparents brought me from one of their rare, brief vacations so many years ago, when I was about eight.

This is the meeting I have been dreading. But I've decided: It's time to tell my mother that all the material we've been working on, everything we've been doing together, and everything I've been doing on my own, is assembled. Complete. Ready to be sent out into the world. If she agrees. If I can convince her.

I've presented my case (my confession?) in the way that's most comfortable, most natural for me: in a letter. Which I've written, and rewritten, again and again. The final version lies on the desktop. Three pages worth. Double-spaced. Fourteen-point type: her eyesight has always been weak, all the more so lately due to a disquieting but thankfully mild case of macular degeneration.

I can't stall any longer. Clutching the pages in my hands, my clammy, sweaty hands, I sit down to my mother's left. I hand her the letter.

I don't dare look at her directly. I'm afraid she can sense the anxiety radiating from me like heat. I sit very still, and concentrate on breathing. Slowly. Breathing in. Breathing out. My mouth is dry. I steal a glance at her.

Her eyes, behind her gold-toned metal-rimmed glasses, are moving down the first page.

What is she thinking?

I don't dare tap my whole foot for fear of shaking the couch and distracting her. All the nervous energy is compressed into tiny movements as my toes twitch imperceptibly, up and down.

She turns the page. I know exactly what she is reading.

> . . . For a long time now, we've been working together on recording your story. You don't always think it's important enough, or dramatic enough, but I do.
>
> At first, the main thing I was interested in was preserving the facts. Then, over time, I began to realize that it wasn't enough for me just to record your story. *I had to understand it.* I still don't know why I've felt so driven to do this. At least part of the reason is that I honor what you and Grandma and Grandpa went through, and because I love you. . . .

I shift my position slightly, as softly as I can, turning my head slightly toward her. I see, or feel, her eyes widen and her eyebrows flick upward. What is she reacting to?

> . . . Our work together has been extremely important to me. . . .

Or:

> . . . You've given me an amazing gift: the chance to know you and your world better. . . .

I keep very still and wait. She's up to the last bit now, where I'd made my pitch:

> . . . Now it's time that I share with you what I've been doing for so long, and get your opinion, and, I hope, your approval. . . .

I remember dithering over "approval" versus "blessing." Was blessing too strong? What if she doesn't give it? What if she curses me, calls me betrayer?

She's finished.

She folds over the last page, cradles the crisp sheets between her palms.

She turns to me.

"Thank you," she says. Her voice catches in her throat. She is crying. I start crying. We hug and hold on tight.

"Thank *me*?" I splutter, over her shoulder. "For what?"

"For this," she says. "For sharing this with me."

"Well, *you* shared everything with *me*," I answer. We are still hugging and sniffling, but we are calming down. We straighten up and move apart.

"I thought you never wanted to get involved with this 'Second Generation' stuff again." She laughs a little, quietly, pulling a tissue from the box beside the couch and wiping her face.

"Yes, well, I obviously can't seem to get away from it," I retort, a bit sheepishly, a bit defiantly, smiling despite myself.

"First you were working on Daddy's memoirs, and suffering with those, now you're doing that with mine. Well, mine don't have all the suffering, the horror stories, that his memoirs do," she continues. "I don't have any horror stories."

I start laughing, shaking my head. There she goes again.

I feel like a kid at show-and-tell—at first hesitant, and then with the tiniest flourish, I proudly hold out my creation: the two-ring binder containing all these pages. This book. My love letter to her. She takes it, an undecipherable look on her face.

Sometime later, she brings it back to me.

"So . . . what do you think?" I ask, a bit breathless.

"It's a nice piece of writing," she says.

She is smiling, her eyes mirrors of tears.

"So it's okay that I send it out?"

"You can send it out."

285

Epilogue

Somewhere up in Heaven, they sit. Four old people. Two couples. Heads gray, or balding. A few blades of hair are held in place over pale pink skin by ripply bobby pins of dull gold or peeling black. The men are in suits, neatly pressed. The women are wearing dark cloth coats, almost identical, fur-trimmed at the collars.

They'd known each other a long time; and it's been a long time since they'd been together. They smile broadly and incline their heads toward one another.

"And how is *Pan?*"

"And *Pani's* health?"

The lilting Polish cadences dance and flit like butterflies. And then:

"So! It is done."

"Yes, we know."

"Are you pleased?"

"It's a strange feeling, no? Our names engraved in honor in Jerusalem. And a certificate of recognition, a medal—" His voice is light, full of wonder.

"But nobody to send them to," his wife breaks in, sighing. "We had no children."

"We know. We remember." The other two nod, gravely.

"You know," the first man continues, "I was always sad that there would be no one to remember us, after we were gone. . . ."

"Our daughter will," responds his friend, "and her children, and all who pass by and see your names there, forever. . . ."

A tiny stitch has been taken up in the great tear of the universe.

The four gently bow their heads in mutual tribute and raise invisible glasses to each other.

"Na zdrowie!"
To Health.
"L'Chaim!"
To Life.

Postscript

That was the way this book was supposed to end. I had it all planned: when it was published, I would throw a party and we would all celebrate, and then I would go on a book tour to promote it—and maybe even succeed in convincing my mother to come with me, visiting communities all over, together. My mother and me.

But it didn't work out that way.

My mother died early on December 18, 2007, after a three-month struggle with idiopathic pulmonary fibrosis. She was eighty-two years old.

Idiopathic simply means that the disease hits without rhyme or reason. She'd never smoked in her life, other than that one puff she'd shared with her childhood friends in pre-ghetto Żółkiew. She'd never suffered any trauma to her lungs that we were aware of; wartime tuberculosis was ruled out by the doctors. But having no known etiology made the disease no less deadly. She died, as did her father before her, of not being able to breathe. An almost unbearable irony for me, who spends her life teaching people to cherish their breathing.

After the final, deadly diagnosis was made, my brother took a leave from his job, home, and family in Massachusetts, I left everything behind in Israel, and we both raced to New York. We brought my mother home from the hospital, and, together with my father, took care of her with the unflagging support of the Home Hospice Program of the Visiting Nurse Service of New York. For a brief, strange, and awesome time, we were reconstituted as our original nuclear family while my mother's life ebbed away.

She was conscious and present to the end. During her first weeks back home, with her consent and at her direction, I went through her drawers and closets, unearthing more documents, photographs, and artifacts, labeling things, taking notes. I found precious things that had survived the war, only God knows how. And that, typically, my mother had not mentioned during all the hours of interviewing and taping and transcribing.

I found my great-grandmother's cookbooks, thin cardboard notebooks filled with recipes written in a delicate script. In one of them, we found the recipe for my mother's favorite poppy seed cake. It was titled, simply, appropriately, *Tort Lutenki* (Lutka's Cake). Racing against time—for her appetite was fading—I rushed to make the cake and fed her tiny pieces of it. She tasted carefully, pronounced it delicious and said that, yes, she thinks this was it. *Her* cake.

I found a linen handkerchief with the hand-embroidered initials L.S. Pinned to it was a small note in my mother's careful print, identifying that this belonged to *My Beloved Grandmother, Laura Schenker.*

Carefully wrapped in soft white tissue paper was a knitted brightly colored cap, with a note slipped inside in my mother's handwriting: *Knitted for me by my Aunt Frycia, 1935.* Amazed that this had survived, I showed it to my mother. She smiled in recognition. "Oh, yes. I think I wore that in the cellar."

My guts twisted.

Opening a square manila envelope, I found a small coloring book, about six inches square, titled *Czarodziejskie Malowanki*, Magical Paintings. I remembered enjoying coloring books like that when I was little: when you "painted" the pages with a damp paintbrush, colors miraculously appeared in all the right places. On the front cover of this little book, in my grandmother's unmistakable handwriting, is the inscription *Mojej najdroższej Lutenki*. My dearest Lutka. *Żółkiew*. It was my mother's.

I found the clipping about the *Spartakiada* under the Russians in 1940, reporting my mother's athletic achievements.

I found mementos from the immediate postwar period: photographs dating from that almost-normal time in Katowice. In one, a group of young people sit, smiling, in the summer sunshine. In another, a grinning blonde named Eulalia Jedrzejowska, nicknamed Wiesia, is about to do a backflip; on the back of that photo, she'd scrawled: *Crazy!* I even found a handful of letters from Wiesia and other friends—Zbyszek and Leszek—that followed my mother to Gabersee.

I found a snapshot of my mother, beaming, on skis, on a snow-covered slope behind the DP camp at Gabersee. And another one of her "class" at the ORT vocational school in Munich; of all the smiling, neatly dressed, carefully coiffed young women, only my mother was not an orphan.

Carefully wrapped in tissue paper were two wallets my mother made in that factory on 125th Street in Manhattan—one red, one brown—the leather still supple and shining.

And, of course, there were boxes and envelopes and albums of all sizes, containing memories through the decades: deckle-edged black-and-white photographs, 35 millimeter slides, color prints. There were report cards from every year of school—mine and my brother's—even my very first experience of music preschool at the 92nd Street Y. And every letter and every postcard ever sent from summer camp and later, from Israel, every card she ever got for every occasion, from her parents, her husband, her children, and from each of her six beloved grandchildren—my children, Yonatan, David, and Yehoshua, and Barry's, Ruthie, Avri, and Adi.

I cataloged and recorded furiously, frantic not to be left with any questions to which, soon enough, there would be no more answers. The more I worked, the more questions I realized I still had: about her adjustment to America in those early years, what it had been like to be a young bride, a young mother. With all my interviewing, I had still not explored enough, could not save enough. Now, with her strength waning steadily, I would never get the chance. I resigned myself to the inevitable barrage of anguish and regret sure to hit later, and concentrated on being as present as possible during the time we had left, and on taking care of her, determined that she not suffer, that this phase be pain-free.

I told her, over and over, how much I loved her. And I thanked her, over and over, for being my mother.

During those weeks, I got the good news that this book would indeed be published. I rushed to tell her, showed her the letter, and braced myself to ask her, one last time, how she felt about it.

With each passing week, she had become progressively thinner and weaker. Her skin, soft as ever, was paper-thin, almost translucent. Even with the ever-present nasal cannula delivering its steady flow of oxygen, she now spoke in short breathless whispers, punctuated by gasps. But her response to my news was firm, and typically straightforward. And just as typically, she was concerned that I get the facts straight, and that justice be served. She hadn't liked the negative feelings I had expressed in some sections of the book, toward Poles and Ukrainians, the way I lumped them all together. She wanted to make it clear that she did not hate all Poles or all Ukrainians. On the contrary, she owed some of them her life. She wanted me to make this clear. I promised that I would. Especially since I had long since come to appreciate—largely through writing this book—that I owed my life to these people as well.

"Anything else?" I asked.

"No," she gave a very tiny toss of the head, conserving energy, but quite definite.

Helena Beata Rosenberg died at home, on Monday, December 18, 2007, the Ninth of Teveth according to the Hebrew calendar. It was just after midnight, a clear and cold night. She had fretted, during her illness, that her dying would take a long time. "I'm not scared of dying," she told me, when I asked her. Because we still talked about everything, openly, as we always had. And she answered all my questions, as she always had. "I'm just worried about your father." (We will always take care of him, always be with him, I promised.) And she didn't want to cause us unnecessary pain and suffering by making us disrupt our lives to care for her. (As if I wouldn't have spent forever taking care of her.) No-nonsense to the end, she just wanted it to be over quickly.

She needn't have worried. Lutka, as my mother was always called, left the world peacefully, only a few short weeks after a final meeting with the medical director of the hospice, Dr. James Avery. She never was one to mince words or evade the truth. Looking him straight in the eye, she asked him how much time she had left.

"It could be as few as two weeks," he said, gently.

Speaking slowly, taking time to catch her breath, she whispered, "That's the—best—news—you could—give me."

Two weeks and three days later, just after midnight, I was sitting on her right, holding her right hand in mine, cradling and stroking her left shoulder with my left hand. To my right sat my father. My brother sat across from me, and Chaim, having flown in only hours before from Israel, in response to my desperate summons, stood on my brother's left, toward the foot of the bed. Together, we watched her last breaths gently and almost imperceptibly slow, get slower, and then stop.

Leaving us to get on with our lives in the shadow of her loss.

Leaving me
       to tell her story.

Tort Lutenki (Lutka's Cake)

5 eggs, separated
Mix yolks with:

> 16 dk* sugar (2/3 cup)
> 15 dk poppy seeds (1 cup), finely ground (originally done with mortar and pestle)
> 1 dk flour (2 rounded tablespoons)
> 1 dk breadcrumbs (2 tablespoons)
> 1 package of vanilla sugar (original recipe called for Oetkera brand)
> 2 ground cloves, crushed
> 5 walnuts, chopped

Beat egg whites until stiff. Fold into above mixture.
Bake in greased tin until springs back to the touch and is golden brown.
Sprinkle with confectioner's sugar, if desired.

*1 dk = dekagram = 10 grams
1 oz. = 28 grams

Acknowledgments

One of the best, and most challenging, parts of writing this section is the chance to thank—officially, and forever—those who have been so much a part of my life, whose friendship and love, in so many different ways, supported me not just through writing this book, but through *living* it. Paraphrasing one of my favorite songs from the movie *Beaches*, you are all the wind beneath my wings.

And one of the worst, and most challenging, parts of writing this is that when all is said and done, the words won't come close to conveying what I feel. They will have to serve as a rough approximation, merely pointing the way to what is, ultimately, inexpressible.

My heroes are my parents Morris and Helen Wyszogrod, and my grandparents Agatha and Joseph Rosenberg, who chose *LIFE!*, living it with determination and grace, passion and perseverance, endless devotion and love.

My brother, Barry Wyshogrod, is my brother-in-arms in every sense of the word. We share a unique bond; he knows the territory as I do. It's impossible to thank him enough for always being there for me with wit, wisdom, patience, and love.

Hannah Levinsky-Koevary was there from the beginning, one of those strangers in a dark-lit room who became my dear friend, a sister, a soul-mate. She selflessly invested herself in this, reading and rereading, always encouraging me, always urging me to keep going, and keep going deeper.

Diane Greenberg, who had every right to wonder what she'd gotten herself into during that first meeting in her living room, and who became my steadfast teacher, mentor, and friend: I thank you from the bottom of my heart.

I am grateful to those friends who were also my readers:

Shira Berliner Bodner, with her infectious zest for life. Her comment that she could hear my mother on these pages has meant the world to me.

Judy Labensohn, for her insightful comments on so many phases of the manuscript, her enthusiasm, and her invaluable guidance.

Daniele Schwartz, whose laughter lights up the room and whose wisdom guides me to find the sources of strength and stillness within.

Laura Sutta, a model of bravery in the face of adversity, of generosity of spirit, and of finding beauty everywhere.

Naomi Tannen, whose friendship and love have been an unfaltering beacon through the years and who awes and inspires me with her quiet courage.

I am grateful for that small group of women who banded together to support each other's passion for creative expression and were among the first to hear excerpts of this work and to cheer me on: Margalit Jakob, Ruth Mason, Tsippi Moss, Sharone Rothenberg, and Bella Savran. A special note of appreciation to Bella, whose aunt, Giza Landau Halpern, was my mother's wonderful childhood friend. If we didn't already share a bond of the heart, that alone would be enough to make us related.

I am grateful to those writers who shared their advice, insight, and encouragement at key points during my journey: Tania Hershman, Jeanne Marie Laskas, Alexander Levy, Chris Lombardi, and Charlotte Sheedy.

I want to acknowledge the love of my wonderful in-laws, Miriam z"l and Abram Zlotogorski.

I thank all those who showered me and my family with affection and support of all kinds (emotional, technical, logistical, artistic, and even culinary) throughout the years: the Bayers—Ellen and Abe z"l, Jenny and Dani Gamulka, Shimmy and Tani, Aaron and Micol; Madeleine Chappell; Lynn and Lee Glassman; the Goldberg-Katcoffs—Donna, Don, Adina and Doron; Suzanne Goldstein; Yasmin Goldschmidt; Adina and Donniel Hartman; Liora Haruni; the Kalmans—Amy and Jonathan, Aaron, David, Alex and Josh, Dorothy and Albert; Carol Kaufman; Adina Kolatch; Mirian, David, Brian and Caroline Landau; Abbe Marcus Rand; Rachel, Amy, and David Pinsen; Sheryl Prenzlau; Diane and Bob Rosenschein; Bob Trachtenberg; Helene and Michael Wolff; Rebeca and Steve Zerobnick. And a special acknowledgment to my terrific cousins, whose lives are part of mine: Blaifeder; Friedfertig; Inbar; Kohlberg; Rogak; Rosenbaum; Rosenblatt; Roth; Schenker; Tadjer; Wyszegrod. What a miracle: an almost-decimated family tree is blossoming and flourishing anew!

I gratefully acknowledge Syracuse University Press for granting permission to include material previously published as a chapter entitled "The Coat" in *Second Generation Voices: Reflections by Children of Holocaust Survivors and Perpetrators* by Alan L. Berger and Naomi Berger, published in 2001 by Syracuse University Press, New York.

I am indebted to Professor Michael Wyschogrod and his beloved wife Edith, z"l, for their role in getting our family story told. I am very grateful to James Peltz for his efforts in publishing this memoir, and for his graciousness, patience, and gentle good humor throughout. And to his terrific team at SUNY Press, particularly Fran Keneston, Ryan Morris, Laura Glenn, and Sue Morreale, who worked so hard and with such dedication to make this possible.

I owe special thanks to Suzanne Balaban, for her indefatigable energy, effervescent optimism, and confidence in me and in this book.

My love and gratitude goes to those beloved friends who have been part of my life from the very beginning, who will be part of me forever: The Kettler family: my "best buddy" Roanna z"l, her mother Geula z"l, her father, Louis (we always called him Jack) z"l, and her brother Ethan. And the Smith family: my good friend Kathy, her mother, Peggy, and her father Jack of blessed memory.

I've left the most important for last. For them, no words will ever be enough. Chaim: you are my rock and my light. Yonatan, David, and Yehoshua: if God and fate bring you one fraction of the joy you've brought me, you will be happy indeed.

May each of you, and may we all,
be blessed with joy, love, serenity, and peace.